THE CHURCH IMPOTENT

THE CHURCH IMPOTENT
The Feminization of Christianity

LEON J. PODLES

SPENCE PUBLISHING COMPANY · DALLAS
1999

Published in the United States by
Spence Publishing Company
111 Cole Street
Dallas, Texas 75207

Library of Congress Cataloging-in-Publication Data

Podles, Leon J., 1946-
     The church impotent : the feminization of Christianity / Leon J. Podles
         p. cm.
     Includes bibliographical references and index.
     ISBN 1-890626-07-4
     1. Masculinity—Religious aspects—Christianity—History.
2. Women in Christianity—History   I. Title.
BT702.P63   1999
270'.081—dc21   98-19150

Printed in the United States of America

To

PAUL VAN K. THOMSON

Minister

Marine Corps Chaplain

Teacher

Writer

Priest

Father

Friend

Contents

A Personal Note

M EN THINK RELIGION, and especially the church, is for
women. Why are women "the more devout sex"?[1] Modern churches are women's clubs with a few male officers.
Or as Brenda E. Basher puts it, "If American religion were imagina-
tively conceptualized as a clothing store, two-thirds of its floor space
would house garments for women; the manager's office would be occupied almost exclusively by men."[2]

Men still run most churches, but in the pews women outnumber
men in all countries of Western civilization, in Europe, in the Americas, in Australia. Nor is the absence of males of recent origin. Cotton Mather puzzled over the absence of men from New England
churches, and medieval preachers claimed women practiced their religion far more than men did. But men do not show this same aversion to all churches and religions. The Orthodox seem to have a
balance, and Islam and Judaism have a predominantly male membership. Something is creating a barrier between Western Christianity
and men, and that something is the subject of this book.

I came to my interest in this subject along a number of paths. I
married late, and the difficulties of adjusting to marriage after a long
bachelorhood made me acutely aware of the differences between men
and women. My wife is an art historian, and in leafing through her

books I became interested in the different portrayals of men and women, how just two lines could suggest the differences between the male and female bodies. We then had twins, a boy and a girl, who not only had very different personalities, but the girl was extremely feminine and the boy extremely masculine. She at age two was already much more verbal than he was. We would ask Tom what he wanted, and Sarah would serve as his spokeswoman: "Tom would like a glass of milk and three cookies." We would ask Tom if that was what he really wanted and he would either nod his head or burst into tears at his inability to articulate his feelings.

A difference between men and women that caused me personal trouble was the lack of interest in religion among men, especially men of pronounced or even normal masculinity. The Catholic priests of my 1950s childhood, many of whom were veterans of World War II, sometimes seemed aware of the difficulty of getting men interested in religion. Football analogies occasionally enlivened sermons. As I was not a football fan, this was explaining the *ignotum per ignotior*. Catholic high school textbooks tried to speak to boys by comparing grace to jet aviation fuel (a metaphor of doubtful theological accuracy) and getting to heaven to winning a race (a comparison solidly founded in scripture).

My adolescent religious awakening occurred at a boys' high school. I read C. S. Lewis and Chesterton and tried to imitate Chesterton's combative style in my writing and conversation. I decided I might have a vocation to the priesthood and went to a pre-seminary house at a men's college. (I was privileged to have a now-rare single-sex education for eight years.) As I discovered, the seminary, unfortunately, was full of homosexuality of various sorts. The policy of the authorities was to ignore the situation, hoping it would go away. Whether it went away, I do not know, but I went away. The regular college students, though they had chosen to go to a religious college, plainly considered the required theology courses a bore and rarely showed up for mass. In fact, the college did not even have a chapel capable of holding more than a small portion of its student body, though its gym was big enough for the crowds drawn to its basketball games.

I occasionally became involved in parish life in the cities in which I lived. I noticed to my discomfort that an unusual percentage, perhaps a quarter, of my male acquaintances were homosexual. On reflection I realized that they were the ones I had met through church or through religious gatherings. They were amusing, but I felt awkward around them, and some of them later died of AIDS. While I do not wish to question the sincerity of their religious commitment, and perhaps it is the wounded who especially know their need for the healing touch of Jesus, it was odd that they seemed to be the type of young men found disproportionately at church. Normal young women were there in abundance; indeed, I must confess that was one reason I spent time in parish activities.

In seeking an explanation for the lack of men in church and the lack of masculinity among some males in church, I read about the differences between men and women. Sociologists remarked in a general way that men were less religious than women, and I realized that my personal experience was only a particular instance of a general situation. This puzzle intrigued me. Why was it that men were so little interested in religion, and that the men who were interested often did not follow the general pattern of masculinity? Why didn't religion seem to interest men much, at least until they reached old age and death loomed? Sociologists have put forward a few theories, which I will discuss, but they did not seem to explain the situation very satisfactorily. The best writer on the general subject of masculinity is David Gilmore, and my great debt to his *Manhood in the Making* will become clear. Nevertheless, he does not treat of the lack of interest in Christianity among modern Western men. Walter Ong, SJ, in *Fighting for Life*, has written in a learned and slightly impenetrable style on the decline of masculinity in modern Catholicism, but seems to have dropped the subject after writing the book. His fellow Jesuit, Patrick Arnold, in *Warriors, Wildmen, and Kings*, has given this question the fullest treatment yet, but his book is marred by pop Jungianism and a very odd attitude to homosexuality.

I had also become interested in the literature of war after coming across Paul Fussell's *The Great War and Modern Memory*. The analysis of tactics and strategy does not interest me, nor does the reporting of battles in which the clichés burst in air, but rather the *experience* of war. Nor is my interest unique. Bookstore customers are mostly women; but they always have a section that might as well be labeled *For Men Only*: books on war.

In reading about war, I realized that here was something that men took with deadly (both literally and metaphorically) earnestness. War, and the vicarious experience of war in literature and reenactments, as well as the analogues and substitutes for war in dangerous sports and avocations, provide the real center of the emotional, and I would even say the spiritual, life of most men in the modern world. The ideology of masculinity has replaced Christianity as the true religion of men. We live in a society with a female religion and a male religion: Christianity, of various sorts, for women and non-masculine men; and masculinity, especially in the forms of competition and violence that culminate in war, for men.

My personal experience is limited to North America, and most sociological work on religion and men has been done in North America and France. Nevertheless, the comparative lack of masculine interest in Christianity is much the same throughout Western Christianity, Catholic and Protestant. South America is notorious. The church is for women; the bars are for men. In 1932, Evelyn Waugh visited a desolate Brazilian town, Boa Vista, where the Benedictines had a mission and had tried in vain to Christianize the inhabitants. Waugh comments that "the Church was, considering the villainy of the place, surprisingly well attended," of course by the women and children, a "weekly blossoming of femininity."[3] The men came to enjoy the women: "They did not come into the Church, for that is contrary to Brazilian etiquette, but they clustered in the porch, sauntering out occasionally to smoke a cigarette."[4]

A friend of mine stayed for several weeks in an Italian town, and he and his wife attended daily mass. He was the only man in the church apart from the priest, and his presence was so unusual that it attracted the attention of the carabinieri, who investigated to see what hanky-panky was going on. After he crossed the Aegean to Greece, he was startled by the difference in the Orthodox churches. If anything, there were more men than women; the men also led the singing and filled the churches with the deep resonance of their voices. The only time Americans will hear anything like this is if they attend a concert by a touring Russian Orthodox choir. There is no church music for *basso profundo* written by Americans.

Historians, theologians, and clergymen have occasionally noticed the lack of men in their own area of study or responsibility, but no one has surveyed the evidence for the lack of men throughout Western Christianity. Scholars try to explain males' relative lack of interest by the peculiar historical or social situation with which the scholars are concerned, but scholars of colonial American history show little awareness of medieval Germany, and sociologists confine their studies to situations they can measure.

The clergy have the most direct, practical interest in the situation, and they have shown a remarkable lack of concern. I suspect that the clergy are not unhappy with the absence of men. Women are easier to deal with than men would be. Even feminists can be satisfied to some extent. Hymns and the Bible are being rewritten to expunge references to men; the few men in the congregation will not protest. Protestant churches ordain women, the seminaries are already half-female, and the Protestant clergy will be a characteristically female occupation, like nursing, within a generation. If priests are unavailable, Rome allows Catholics who are not priests to be appointed administrators of parishes. This permission is intended for mission countries, but American bishops have seized on this provision and appointed nuns and divorced laywomen to head parishes, while staffing their diocesan bureaucracies with priests, or even leaving priests to cool their heels without assignments.

Many Catholic dioceses actively discourage vocations to the priesthood, in a transparent attempt to put pressure on Rome to allow the ordination of women, or at least of married men. The Second Vatican Council revived the permanent diaconate, which enjoyed popularity for several years in the United States, as mature married men were given theological training and then assigned to help in parishes. Nevertheless, these programs have been ended in many dioceses because the deacon is male, and deacons occupy jobs that could be given to women.

Because Christianity is now seen as a part of the sphere of life proper to women rather than to men, it sometimes attracts men whose own masculinity is somewhat doubtful. By this I do not mean homosexuals, although a certain type of homosexual is included. Rather religion is seen as a safe field, a refuge from the challenges of life, and therefore attracts men who are fearful of making the break with the secure world of childhood dominated by women. These are men who have problems following the path of masculine development, a pattern I will examine in detail later in the book. It is a truism among Catholics that priests become priests because of the influence of their mothers, and many priests are emotionally very close to their mothers, more so than to men, even to their fathers.[5] The sentimental sermons on Mother's Day used to be a great set piece, a five-hanky special, in Catholic churches. Even devotion to Mary was affected. Such devotion has a sound theological base, but tended to replace a relationship to Christ or to the Father. The rationale for this was sometimes made explicit. At one Dominican seminary in the 1940s, a professor developed a following, which later matured into a small cult. He explained Catholic devotion to Mary in this way: Men have a more distant relationship with their fathers than with their mothers. They therefore have more trouble relating to a masculine God (the Father or Jesus) than to the reflection of maternal love in Mary. Devotion to Mary, on this view, should be stressed more than devotion to Christ. Despite the extraordinary theological implications of this line of thought, the professor obviously struck a nerve in his seminarian disciples: they were the sort of men who felt more comfortable with the feminine than with the masculine. The situation holds true in most of the Protestant clergy. Mary was not available, but first sentimentality, and now feminism, have filled the void.

This feminization of the clergy explains the lack of reflection on a subject that the clergy should be interested in: Why does half their potential congregation show an active lack of interest in Christianity, an indifference that sometimes considers male attendance at church suspect? Among Catholics, the few writers that have paid much attention to the question are Jesuits. As the early Jesuits were among the most masculine of Catholic religious movements, this is not surprising. Yet the work of Walter Ong and Patrick Arnold has produced no lasting response. Catholic circles are full of committees and conferences on the place of women in the church, and almost none on the absence of men.

Among Protestants some evangelicals are aware of the problem with men and try to reach out to them. I was at a Baptist school to discuss a former teacher with the headmaster. The headmaster observed that the teacher was a decent person, but a bit soft. The headmaster had to teach him how to comport himself in a masculine fashion, to adopt an assertive body language. The teacher had come from a family in which the mother was the dominant religious force; she was the one who had chosen the church and made sure her son went to religious school and college. He was undoubtedly heterosexual, but had trouble breaking away from the feminine milieu and establishing himself as a man. In the 1970s I lived for a year in a household with a number of evangelical and charismatic students at the University of Virginia. They were part of a church, planted by a minister, which later grew into a large Presbyterian church that has some University of Virginia male faculty as members, mostly faculty from the science and engineering schools. Evangelical women perhaps realize the difficulty that men have with church and occasionally step aside to make room for men in the leadership positions in which men feel most comfortable. But a strong stream of evangelicalism, represented by *Christianity Today*, has made as many compromises as it can with feminism and ignores the problem of the lack of men in the church. Dr. James Dobson of Focus on the Family, who has noticed this tendency in *Christianity Today*, is one of the foremost evangelical leaders who is concerned with the role of men in the family and church.

If the evangelicals occasionally show some awareness of the lack of men, the mainline Protestants do not seem to think there is a problem. The Methodist Church is a women's club at prayer. I once attended a Lutheran Ascension Day service that also commemorated Bach's birthday. The celebrants were men; a Catholic friend and I were men; of the three hundred or so Lutheran faithful perhaps three or four were men. Luther, whatever one thinks of his reform, was masculine in his aggressiveness. Bach is one of the most rational of composers in a mathematical-artistic field, muscial composition, that is almost exclusively male. Why would one be astounded if one went to such a service and found three hundred men and only four women? The situation is especially severe in black churches, whether established or storefront. Although the preachers are men, the congregations are overwhelmingly women. The absence of men has especially sad consequences for the black community.

The established churches have long made a parade of their concern for civil rights and for the plight of minorities. But there is one minority whose cause they quietly ignore: black men. The problem of criminality and drug abuse among inner-city black men is a problem of a distortion of masculinity. But the liberal churches have little to say about masculinity except to condemn it as an obstacle to women's liberation. Churches that spend their energy hunting out and obliterating the last vestiges of patriarchy are in no position to help black men attain the status they so desperately need for their own good and the good of black women and children: that of patriarchs, responsible fathers who rule their families in justice and love.

Nor has the absence of men left women untouched. As we shall see, women have been forced into an unnatural mold by a misunderstanding among Christians of the feminine. Much of current feminism is an understandable reaction against a caricature of femininity. The breakdown of the proper relationship of masculinity and femininity, male and female, Adam and Eve, is at the root of many of the church's failures in the modern world. This situation would not surprise the author of Genesis.

In chapter one, *Armies of Women*, I examine the lack of men throughout Western Christianity, beginning with the lack of masculinity among some male Christians. The best evidence comes from France, which has a long tradition of religious sociology, and from England and the United States. The various explanations for the lack of men are covered in chapter two, *Can a Man Be a Christian?*

Most people think not: either men are too bad for Christianity, or Christianity is too effeminate for men.

Masculinity is the key to men's behavior as men. In chapter three, *What is Masculinity?*, I use evidence from anthropology and developmental psychology to clarify the peculiarities of the masculine personality. Initiation into masculinity is a form of religious initiation. The initiated man becomes a hero, about whose adventures Homer sang in the *Odyssey*. Masculinity is essential to the Jewish idea of God and is a primary theme of the Scriptures, as I show in chapter four, *God and Man in Judaism*. Masculinity remains a characteristic of the three persons who are revealed in the New Testament, and the Christian is masculine because he is conformed to the masculine Son. The martyrs and monks were initiated into masculinity, and in *Beowulf* a Christian culture looks back at pagan masculinity, with its glory and self-destructive flaws. I take up these ideas in chapter five, *God and Man in Early Christianity*.

Chapter six, *The Foundations of Feminization*, treats of the conjunction of Bernard of Clairvaux, Scholasticism, and the medieval women's movement that brought about the initial feminization of the Western church. The Church has suffered from being overly feminized, as I show in chapter seven, *Feminized Christianity*. The quality of spirituality has changed. Bridal mysticism makes Christianity individualistic and erotic; feminine tendencies to union without a corrective masculine presence give rise to universalism and quietism. In chapter eight, *Countercurrents*, I look at the forces that have maintained some masculine presence in the church, from the Crusades to Promise Keepers.

Masculinity when it becomes a religion can easily become demonic. Sports may be harmless, but fascism and nihilism are the outcome of a masculinity detached from Christianity. The various forms of masculinity as religion are the subject of chapter nine, *Masculinity as Religion: Transcendence and Nihilism*. In chapter ten, *The Future of Men in the Church*, I look at possibilities for reconnecting men to the church, focusing on the areas of initiation, struggle, and brotherly love.

I WISH TO THANK MY WIFE for her patience in listening to me as I have formed my ideas over the years. Mitchell Muncy, my editor at Spence Publishing, helped me give form to sometimes chaotic ideas and gave this book such structure and organization as it has. The Interlibrary Loan office at Johns Hopkins University tracked down almost every obscure article and book I requested.

THE CHURCH IMPOTENT

Armies of Women

DESPITE THE CONSTANT COMPLAINTS OF FEMINISTS about the patriarchal tendencies of Christianity, men are largely absent from the Christian churches of the modern Western world. Women go to church; men go to football games. Lay men attend church activities because a wife, mother, or girlfriend has pressured them. As Tom Forrest, a priest active in international evangelization, points out, only 25 percent of the participants in Catholic gatherings he has attended are men, and "when men do come, they are often brought along with some resistance by their wives."[1] The strategy of American revivalists in the Second Great Awakening in the 1830s was to approach men through their wives: women were converted first, and then they exerted more or less successful pressure upon fathers, brothers, husbands, and sons to join them in the church. From her reading of conversion accounts written during the revivals of the early nineteenth century, Barbara Epstein concludes that women converted because of spiritual conflicts, but "frequently, it was social pressure, especially from women, rather than the need to resolve internal conflicts that drove men to convert."[2]

Men say they believe in God about as often as women do, but they attend church much less frequently than women, and they engage in private religious activities far less often. British sociologists Michael Argyle and Benjamin Beit-Hallahmi have observed that "the sex ratio [women to men] is consistently greater for saying daily prayers than for church attendance or membership. The latter are again more under the influence of social pressures, while prayers are a private matter and reflect more spontaneous religious concerns. This suggests that the larger sex ratios should be taken more seriously than the smaller one."[3] The lack of commitment by men to the practice of the Christian religion is even more pronounced than the statistics for membership and external practice suggest.

In general, men who have a strong connection with the feminine through a close relationship with a wife, mother, or girlfriend are more likely to be involved in Christian activities than men who do not. If a man goes to church, he goes because a woman has wheedled him into what he would normally consider unmanly behavior. But if he goes voluntarily, he suffers suspicions about his masculinity. John K. White summarizes the popular attitude: "A devastating criticism of Christianity is many men see it as not only irrelevant, but as effeminate. Words and phrases such as 'unmanly,' 'for women and kids,' 'wimps,' and 'they can't make it so they hide behind God' are common."[4] Writing from his experience of charismatic communities, Stephen Clark laments that "Contemporary Christians often lack an ideal of manly character, and they do not value some of the character traits that ought to be prominent in a man . . . . The contemporary picture of Christian character is all too often feminine, and the Victorian notion of femininity at that."[5]

THE RELIGIOUS MALE

The clergy have long had the reputation of not being very masculine. The mainline, liberal Protestant minister in the early twentieth century had a reputation for being soft and working best with women. This reputation provided fuel for fundamentalists, who denounced liberals as "little infidel preacherettes"[6] in sermons with such titles as "She-Men, or How to Become Sissies."[7] But all clergy were open to attack, all had to face the "popular stereotype that men of the cloth were neither male nor female."[8]   The clergy were seen as exempt from masculine trials and agonies; they were part of the safe world of women. As one layman put it, "life is a football game, with the men fighting it out on the gridiron, while the minister is up in the grand-stand, explaining it to the ladies."[9]

In nineteenth-century New England, ministers of the most im-portant churches were "hesitant promulgators of female virtues in an era of militant masculinity."[10]   But the dominant churches of nine-teenth-century New England had long been feminized. Not only was the proportion of women in the churches extremely high, both the milieu and the ministers of the church were far more feminine than masculine. Businessmen disdained the clergy as "people half-way between men and women."[11] Ministers found the most conge-nial environment, not in businesses, political clubs, or saloons, but "in the Sunday school, the parlor, the library, among women and those who flattered and resembled them."[12] Moreover, they were typically recruited from the ranks of weak, sickly boys with indoor tastes who stayed at home with their mothers and came to identify with the feminine world of religion. The popular mind often joined "the idea of ill health with the clerical image."[13] In the vision of Unitarian minister Charles Fenton (1796-1842), playing Sunday school children have replaced stern Pilgrim Fathers and "adult poli-tics have succumbed to infantile piety, *Ecclesia* to a nursery. Mascu-linity is vanquished in the congregation and, even more significantly, in the pulpit."[14]

By the end of the nineteenth century, the effeminacy of the mainline Protestant clergy had become a commonplace of satire. A Catholic novel, *The Last Rosary*, caricatured the minister: "He was a Methodist, a Revivalist, a Baptist, an advocate of women's rights, an earnest worker in the field of missionary labor, provided said field consisted in gliding here and there to nice little evening parties, shaking hands—or, more properly speaking, finger tips—with ladies whose age forbade the custom of whole-hand shaking. . . . Mild tea drinking, a little sherry, claret occasionally, and other helps of spiri-tuous kind, did go some length in elevating whatever there was of manhood in his composition to thoughts of heroic work and conversion of sinners."[15] But Catholics, too, had their problems in nine-teenth-century America, if we may judge by the repeated efforts to get Catholic men to attend to their religious duties.[16]

During the first half of the nineteenth century the English iden-tified weakness and femininity with saintliness. George Arthur, the most Christian figure in Thomas Hughes's *Tom Brown's School Days* has an "overidentification with his mother and sisters."[17] On his sickbed, he looks like "A German picture of an angel . . . transparent and golden and spirit-like."[18] To be Christian, for the mid-Victori-ans, was to lack the exuberant physical masculinity of the normal boy, to be weak, to be helpless, to be a victim. In other words, the religious man was like the Victorian ideal of woman, who was sup-posed to suffer from mysterious complaints, to be unable to engage in vigorous activity, and to find sex distasteful. C. H. Spurgeon com-plained that "There has got abroad a notion, somehow, that if you become a Christian you must sink your manliness and turn milk-sop."[19]

The masculinity of Anglo-Catholics has often been questioned. "[E]ffeminate fanatics" and "womanish men" were some of the milder criticisms of these "not conspicuously virile men."[20] Kings-ley's attack on John Henry Newman in *Water Babies* is grossly unfair; but Kingsley was upset by what he perceived as a lack of masculinity in Newman's celibacy. Bishop Wilburforce of Oxford, in general a supporter of the high church movement, found the Anglo-Catholic seminarians at Cuddeson "too peculiar,"[21] and indeed contemporary historians conjecture that "a homosexual sensibility ha[d] expressed itself within Anglo-Catholicism."[22] The Ritualists, the party among Anglo-Catholics who were more interested in ritual than doctrine, were especially peculiar. They boasted that "we find that multitudes of young people, especially of young men, who have never concerned themselves with the Church or with religion, have been attracted . . . by the Church's reformed and animated services."[23] In *Brideshead Revisited* Evelyn Waugh has Cousin Jasper warn Charles Ryder: "Beware of the Anglo-Catholics—they're all sodomites with un-pleasant accents."[24] The vicar in Pat Barker's *The Ghost Road* "was one of those Anglo-Catholic young men who waft about in a positive miasma of stale incense and seminal fluid."[25] The whole atmosphere of Anglo-Catholicism, its preciosity, its fussiness, its concern for laces and cassocks and candles, struck the average Victorian (and later observers) as unmanly.

Hugh McLeod notes that the homosexual subculture of late Victorian England "quite consciously combined homosexuality (or 'Uranianism' as it was often termed) with Roman Catholic or, more often, Anglo-Catholic religion."[26] Roman Catholicism attracted converts such as Oscar Wilde, Aubrey Beardsley, and Lionel Johnson.[27] James R. Moore, discussing Cardinal Manning's paean to the Catholic Revival and the memoirs of a young convert to Catholicism, St. George Jackson Mivart, dryly notes that "His [Mivart's] aesthetic preferences—architectural, theatrical, sartorial—his perceptions of older men, and the single-sex camaraderie of his education will not go unnoticed by twentieth-century readers. These suggest rather different explanations than Manning offered for the penetration of the Catholic Church in England."[28] Moore cannot resist the innuendo of "penetration" to suggest that interest in religion is equivalent to passive homosexuality.

Anglo-Catholics among the clergy of the Church of England continue to attract attention for their weak masculinity. In the mid-1990s several hundred Anglo-Catholic clergy wanted to leave the Church of England for Rome, largely because of the Anglican decision to ordain women and all that it implies for the Anglican claims to catholicity and to the possession of valid orders. The Roman Catholic Church in England has a shortage of priests, but has been hesitant to accept these converts as clerics. Liberal English Roman Catholics warn the hierarchy of the "misogyny" of these Anglo-Catholics, many of whom are single—misogyny a polite euphemism for homosexuality. As Paul Johnson writes, "We have certainly learned in recent years what some Anglican clerics have known all along, that the Church is riddled with deviant sexuality. Some time ago, one or two Anglican theological colleges were dominated by sodomites, and the consequences are still with us."[29] William Oddie, who was ordained as an Anglican, admits that Johnson gives a "slightly tactless but nevertheless accurate description of reality."[30]

The situation is similar in Episcopal and Roman Catholic churches in the United States.

The clergy of the Anglo-Saxon world are not the only ones to suffer doubts about their masculinity. In Spain, for instance, the main exception to the male detachment from religion has been its priests. These men have usually been shielded from the harsh tests that other Spanish men have to undergo to prove their manhood and do not have "the sensitivity wrung out of them and the hardness instilled in them that normally happens in the course of attaining manhood in the village. They are better able to preserve affection for Mary, and in seminary they feel no need to be ashamed of sentimentality."[31] The men of the village tell "endless stories about the priests' ambiguous sexual position" and make "jokes referring to priests' emasculation."[32]

Studies have tended to confirm the popular stereotype of the unmanly cleric. The more masculine the man, the less likely he is to be interested in religion; the more feminine the man, the more likely he is to be interested in religion. Patricia Sexton recognized, as far back as the 1960s, the hostility to masculinity in American society, noting that the highest masculinity scores in one study were found among bright underachievers, boys who were intelligent but had little use for the feminized milieu of schools. She also notes that a "striking characteristic of low scholarship boys was their low level of interest in religion."[33]

Lewis M. Terman and Catherine Cox Miles used, in their study, a Masculinity-Femininity test that characterized answers to a questionnaire as indicative of masculinity and femininity if men tended to answer a question one way and women another.[34] In other words, the test was descriptive and did not engage arguments about what is essentially masculine or feminine. Young men, athletic men, and uneducated men tended to be more consistently masculine than old men, sedentary men, and educated men. Men who were interested in religion were less masculine than the average man: "Interest in religion or art is a mark of definitely greater femininity than lack of interest in these matters."[35] Men who showed little interest in religion had more masculine scores: "Most masculine of all are still the men who have little or no interest in religion."[36] Very masculine men showed little interest in religion, very feminine men great interest.[37] Women who had highly feminine scores were also "specially religious,"[38] while women who had more masculine scores were neutral or adverse to religion. The difference was clearly not physical sex, but attitude, or gender, as the term is now used.

Terman and Miles gathered data from three groups: Catholic seminarians, Protestant seminarians, and Protestant ministers. As one might expect, men attracted to the religious life differed strikingly in their masculinity from the general male population: "The Catholic student priests score at a point far less masculine than any other male group of their age; in their early twenties they are more feminine than the general male population at middle life. The Protestant theological students in their middle twenties are, however, more feminine than they and exceed in femininity the sixty-year-old man of equal education. The adult ministerial group is barely more masculine than the Protestant theological students and less so than the student priests. They exceed in femininity the college men of the seventh decade."[39] Terman and Miles concluded that "some dominant factors must be present in all three groups to make them, without regard to age, conspicuously and almost equally lacking in mental masculinity."[40] Interestingly enough, the similarities between the Protestant and Catholic groups and the Catholic group's slightly higher scores ruled out celibacy as a major factor in a lack of masculinity. Nor does the lack of masculinity have any necessary connection with sexual deviance.[41]

Western Religious Observance

Every sociologist, and indeed every observer, who has looked at the question has found that women are more religious than men.[42] While they realize "religiosity may be measured in a number of ways," they also have confirmed the observations of pastors and others that "on most measures, women appear more religious than men."[43] James H. Fichter asks "Are males really less religious than females? Most of the studies made on the question seem to indicate that they are, and this appears to be true for all the Christian churches, denominations, and sects in Western civilization"[44] Argyle and Beit-Hallahmi claim "it is obvious that women are more religious than men on every criterion."[45] Argyle generalizes: "Women are more religious than men on all criteria, particularly for private prayer, also for membership, attendance, and attitude."[46] C. Daniel Bassoon and W. Larry Ventis note that "there is considerable evidence that women are more likely to be interested and involved in religion than men."[47] Gail Malmgreen points out the disparity between the gender of the clergy and the gender of the faithful: "In modern Western cultures, religion has been a predominantly female sphere. In nearly every sect and denomination of Christianity, though men monopolized the positions of authority, women had the superior numbers."[48] Kenneth Guentert concurs: "The Roman Catholic Church has a rather rigid division of labor. The men have the priesthood. The women have everything else."[49] For David de Vaus and Ian McAllister the difference is not simply one of numbers: "A consistent finding in studies of religion is that on a wide range of measures females tend to be more religious than males."[50] George Gallup Jr. and Jim Castelli see the external differences as expressing different internal attitudes: "Women continue to place a higher value on religious involvement and to be more active in religious activities than do men."[51] Barry A. Kosmin and Seymour P. Lachman conclude that popular stereotypes are correct: "The lay and professional literature has consistently shown what ministers and parishioners have observed: that women are more likely than men to join religious organizations and participate actively. Christianity is especially associated with female spirituality. Adolescent girls exhibit stronger belief in the inerrancy of the Bible, and higher rates of participation in religious services."[52]

Patterns of religious observance differ both among and within nations, as might be expected, although there are no exceptions to the feminization of Western Christianity. American and French sociological research has developed the most extensive evidence for Christian feminization, but research in other countries, while scantier, has not revealed any divergence from this pattern. Northern countries may show a higher level of religious practice among men than southern countries; but it would be hard to show a lower level of practice, for Latin male is notoriously resistant to participation in the life of the church. Nor is the feminization of Christianity a recent development: it goes back to pre-industrial times.

Twentieth-Century America

The "rapid feminization of the mainline religious community"[53] in America has been going on for some time. The most exact figures for the United States come from the 1936 Census, the last governmental tally of religious affiliation: in Eastern Orthodoxy the ratio of women to men is .75-.99 to one; Roman Catholics, 1.09 to one; Lutherans, 1.04-1.23 to one; Mennonites, 1.14-1.16 to one; Friends, 1.25 to one; Presbyterians, 1.34 to one; Episcopalians, 1.37 to one; Unitarians, 1.40 to one; Methodists, 1.33-1.47 to one; Baptists, 1.35 to one; Assembly of God, 1.71 to one; Pentecostalists, 1.71-2.09 to one; Christian Scientists, 3.19 to one.[54] Because the respondents to the census identified themselves by denomination, the census probably overstates the proportion of men in the liturgical churches because they practice infant baptism: a current non-believer who was baptized as a Catholic, for instance, will tend to identify himself as a Catholic. The charismatic churches have a higher proportion of women, but all churches except the Eastern Orthodox had a majority of women in their membership.

Not only do women join churches more than men do, they are more active and loyal. Of Americans in the mid-1990s, George Barna writes that "women are twice as likely to attend a church service during any given week. Women are also 50 percent more likely than men to say they are 'religious' and to state that they are 'absolutely committed' to the Christian faith."[55] These gender differences seem to be increasing rapidly. Lyle E. Schaler, an authority on church growth, observes that "In 1952 the adult attenders on Sunday morning in the typical Methodist, Presbyterian, Episcopal, Lutheran, Disciples, or Congregational worship service were approximately 53 percent female and 47 percent male, almost exactly the same as the distribution of the adult population. By 1986 . . . these ratios were closer to 60 percent female and 40 percent male with many congregations reporting a 67-37 or 65-35 ratio."[56] In 1992, 43 percent of men attended church, in 1996 only 28 percent.[57] Patrick Arnold, a Jesuit of liberal theological leanings, claims that at churches he has visited "it is not at all unusual to find a female-to-male ratio of 2:1 or 3:1. I have seen ratios in parish churches as high as 7:1." Furthermore, he notes, "some liberal Presbyterian or Methodist congregations are practically bereft of men." Kenneth Woodward reports that Protestant pastors "say that women usually outnumber the men three to one."[58] The Notre Dame Study of Catholic Parish Life showed that in the 1990s women continue to participate in church life far more than men do:

- More than 85 percent of those involved in ministry to the poor, sick and grieving are women, and social justice and peace efforts draw heavily on women.

- More than 80 percent of CCD teachers and sponsors of the catechumenate are women.

- More than 80 percent of the members of prayer groups are women.

- More than 75 percent of those who lead or take part in adult Bible study or religious discussions are women.

- Almost 60 percent of those involved in youth and recreational ministries are women.

- 52 percent of parish council members are female.

- 58 percent of those identified as the most influential leaders in the thirty-six-parish survey were women.[59]

Women are more active in all aspects of church life, both in public and social activities, such as peace and justice committees, and in spiritual activities, such as prayer and Bible study.

The situation was much the same in the 1950s. In 1955 Ed Wilcock complained that "the average Catholic man considers religion a thing for women and children."[60] Joseph H. Fichter, a Jesuit sociologist, admitted that "among Catholics women appear to pray more often and probably better than males. They say the rosary, attend Mass, novenas and evening devotions more frequently. In any parish more females than males go to confession and Communion. There are at least three times as many nuns in the United States as there are priests and brothers put together."[61] In all activities that demonstrate personal devotion and commitment, women outnumbered men by a vast margin: "Of every one hundred persons who go to confession, only thirty-six are males; of those who attend evening services, thirty are males; and, of those who attend special Lenten services, twenty-four are males."[62] Although parish activities have changed in the post-Vatican ii era, as prayer groups replace novenas, women are still more active. Felt banners may have taken the place of embroidered altar cushions, but female hands still make them.

Moreover, men and women differ not simply in the frequency of their participation in church activities, but in the attitudes that inspire their participation. Attitudes are, of course, harder to quantify than participation. Nevertheless, the techniques of American political poll-taking have been applied to religious bodies by George Gallup Jr., a committed Episcopal layman with a long-standing interest in religion in American society. While the questions asked in the Gallup poll were somewhat vague, the replies confirmed the general pattern of difference between men and women in all matters of religion.[63] Men and women not only act differently, they feel differently when it comes to religion.

After reviewing poll data, George Barna observed that women tend

- strongly to assert that the Bible is totally accurate in all it teaches;

- strongly to affirm the importance of religious faith in their life;

- strongly to disagree that Christ sinned while he was on earth;

- to choose an orthodox, biblical description of their God;

- to meet the criteria for born-again Christians;

- to read their horoscope in a given month[!];

- strongly to agree that the Bible can be taken literally;

- to believe that if a person does not consciously accept Christ as their Savior, he will be condemned to hell;

- to contend that the Bible teaches that "money is the root of all evil."[64]

This difference of feelings about religious matters is evidence of deep differences in fundamental approaches to religion and basic attitudes of faith. The Search Institute of Minneapolis studied five mainline Protestant denominations and the Southern Baptist Convention to determine the quality of faith among church members. Male church members had a far higher percentage of "undeveloped faith," which the Institute defined as a lack of both the vertical dimension, a close personal relationship with God, and the horizontal dimension, loving service of others. Large numbers of men and women in the mainline churches have a weak, undeveloped faith.[65]

"Integrated faith" combines both vertical and horizontal dimensions, and the proportion of women to men who hold an integrated faith is three to two or two to one in the mainline denominations, the Southern Baptists being an exception. The only dimension in which men score consistently higher than women is in horizontal faith, the loving service of others without a close relationship to God.[66] Southern Baptists are more religious than members of mainline denominations: almost half of Southern Baptists have an integrated faith that combines a personal relationship to God and loving service of others. Southern Baptists also have more success in fostering the faith of their male members.

Edward H. Thompson Jr. summarizes the received wisdom: "Among women, religion appears to be more salient to everyday activities, personal faith is stronger, commitment to orthodox beliefs is greater, and involvement in religious ritual and worship is more common than among men."[67] In African-American denominations the preponderance of women is extreme: "Throughout all varieties of black religious activity, women represent from 75 to 90 percent of the participants."[68] Surprisingly, "men are more underrepresented in rural than in urban churches."[69]

But female predominance in religion was noticed long before it was documented by contemporary sociologists and census takers. In *The Bible Status of Women*, published in 1926, after the Men and Church Forward movement had worked to bring men back to the church, Anna Lee Starr observed that "the Interchurch Movement's Survey showed that in the Protestant church in America the ratio of women to men was fifty-nine to forty-one. Almost three-fifths of the membership are women."[70] Of the two million Sunday school teachers, "it is claimed that sixty-seven percent"[71] are women. David Macleod confirms this figure and hints at its significance: "Most [Sunday school] teachers were women—73 percent in the 1920 Indiana survey—and by a form of guilt by association, . . . male teachers were suspect."[72]

The departure of boys from Sunday school after age twelve was likewise noticed and lamented: "Sunday schools lost 60 to 80 percent of their boys between ages twelve and eighteen."[73] Although girls left too, they did not leave in such numbers. The ratio of males to females in Sunday schools around 1920 declined from eighty-four per hundred at age six to forty-eight per hundred at age eighteen.[74] Nor did the boys ever return. Among the millions in the young people's societies, "the proportion of females to males is two to one. It is safe to say that four-fifths of the superintendents of Junior work are women."[75] Young men especially were absent: "Only some seven percent of the young men of the country are in the churches."[76]

Their criticism of the mainline churches notwithstanding, fundamentalist churches of this period did not escape the general feminization. As hard as they fought against it, they found that their congregations were predominantly female: "In 1910 a newspaper account of a talk by William Bell Bentley on 'The Church and Men' noted that three-fourths of his audience was female, despite the sending of 2,000 invitations to the men of Minneapolis."[77]

At the turn of the century, the New York Baptist minister Cortland Myers asked, "Where are the men?"[78] Myers had noticed that "in New York City not more than three percent of the male population are members of Protestant churches" and that the percentage for Catholics was little better.[79] The lack of membership was made worse by the lack of participation in services by male church members: "Of the membership of the churches nearly three-fourths are women. Of the attendants in most places of worship nine-tenths are women. In one great church I counted two hundred women and ten men."[80] A 1902 *New York Times* survey of church attendance in Manhattan showed that "69 percent of Manhattan worshippers were women."[81]

Shortly before Myers described the situation in New York City, Howard Allen Bridgman in New England had observed that "the mainstay of the modern church is its consecrated women,"[82] and therefore "the world gets the idea that the church of God is, to a very great extent, an army of women."[83] The world had the correct impression: "three fourths of the Sabbath congregations and nine tenths of the mid-week assembly"[84] were women. The YMCA discovered "that only one young man in twenty in this country is a church member, and that seventy-five out of every hundred never attend church."[85]

So it was that the men of the century 1830-1930, who saw the United States transformed from an agrarian republic into an industrial and commercial nation, distanced themselves from Christianity. Evelyn A. Kirkley writes of the Freethinking movement in the 1880s that "men constituted 70 to 80 percent of this movement. . . . To Freethinkers, that 70 to 80 percent of church members were women while the same percentage of atheists were men clearly demonstrated men's superior reasoning and intellectual capabilities."[86]

Nineteenth-Century America

Yet industrialization alone cannot have been the sole cause of male retreat from Christianity because the situation was the same at the beginning of the nineteenth century. Frances Trollope, mother of the novelist Anthony Trollope, lived in Cincinnati for two years in the late 1820s. She found trans-Appalachian America barbaric, and cast her acute eye, and exercised her sharp tongue, on the religious customs of the new country. She was appalled by the revivalistic atmosphere that pervaded Protestantism, and she also declared "I never saw, or read, of any country where religion had so strong a hold upon the women, or a slighter hold upon the men."[87]

Trollope was correct in her observation. Even in the nineteenth century the church was a largely female institution. Throughout the nineteenth century, women outnumbered men in the churches by about two to one, which seems to have been the ratio even in the Second Great Awakening. In 1833, the Universalist Sebastian Streeter claimed that "Christian churches are composed of a great disproportion of females."[88] In 1859, another minister, William Gage, said of the Unitarians, "the church is almost without male members."[89] Opponents of revivalism claimed that it "appealed to the weak-minded portion of the community, and while proponents of revival rejected this conclusion, they did not dispute assertions about the sex ratio."[90] Throughout the nineteenth century, and seemingly more so at the end than at the beginning, the church was for women. "The nineteenth century minister moved in a world of women. He preached mainly to women; he administered what sacraments he performed largely for women; he worked not only for them but with them, in mission and charity work of all kinds."[91] When the founder of Wellesley College, Henry Fowler Durant, left the bar to become a minister and "forswore the conflict of the court to work for the Lord, he increasingly entered the realm of women."[92] Orestes Brownson complained about the "female religion" that Protestantism had become.[93] Post–Civil War observers in the evangelical South lamented that "the altars of our churches are pitiably devoid of young men," "there has scarce been a religious young man here in years," and there are but few married men who attend services at any of our churches."[94] The women both dominated the membership rolls and the activities of the southern churches.[95]

This was true not only of liberal Unitarians. Revivalists such as the famous Charles Grandison Finney who preached in the Second Great Awakening found a feminized church in the 1830s: "Women composed the great majority of members in all churches. They dominated revivals and praying circles, pressing husbands, fathers, and sons towards conversion and facilitating every move of the evangelist."[96]   In her study of revivals in Oneida, New York, in the 1810s, Mary P. Ryan mentions "the conspicuous absence of men in the churches of Oneida County."[97]   In one Presbyterian church, "prior to 1814, 70 percent of those admitted to full communion in the society were females."[98]   Nevertheless, during revivals the proportion of male converts increased.[99]

Colonial and Revolutionary America

Perhaps the American Revolution caused a marked decline in interest in religion among men because "republicanism meant the freedom *not to defer* to traditional hierarchical authority, whether in the form of king, community scion, or church."[100]   But interest in religion had been weak among men from almost the very beginnings of the English settlements.

In his study of Congregationalism, Richard D. Shields states that 59 percent of all new members from 1730 to 1769 were women.[101] The figures for southern churches were the same. In 1792, "southern women outnumbered southern men in the churches (65 to 35) though men outnumbered women in the general population (51.5 to 48.5)."[102] During the First Great Awakening, which began in 1797, women continued to dominate church life: "Ministers wrote that converts were usually young, most often between the ages of fifteen and twenty-five, either single or married but without children, and predominantly female."[103]

Such revivals invariably began with women. They "were initiated by the conversion of a young woman or of a group of young women, and often the efforts of such women were opposed by men,"[104] especially young men, who, "according to the accounts of ministers, often ridiculed converts, refused to attend church meetings, and conspired to break up revivals in progress."[105] Family men, fathers and husbands, wanted to have nothing to do with these revivals, and though they "tried to prevent their wives or daughters from attending church," they "were eventually brought into the church themselves by these women."[106] Such pressure sometimes worked, but did not win the long-term affection of men for the church. Female zeal later found outlets in such crusades as the temperance movement, in which female church members allied with ministers to conquer male vices, to the continued annoyance of men, who chafed under the reins of the alliance of women and the clergy.

Some New England churches have registers of members extending back to their foundations in the seventeenth century. These registers are lists of adults who joined the church, and therefore provide evidence for a public commitment to religion. From the very beginning women constituted the majority of members. At the beginning of the European settlement of North America, the Puritans noticed that their churches, voluntary associations of the saved, were predominantly women. Cotton Mather was the first English American to notice and comment that there were more women then men in Christian congregations: "I have seen it without going a Mile from home, That in a Church of Three or Four Hundred Communicants, there are but a few more that One Hundred Men, all the Rest are Women, of whom Charity will Think no Evil."[107] Even this ratio is misleading, because there were more men than women in colonial society.[108] Studies of parish records confirm Mather's impression: "One group—the women of the community—was especially active religiously and came more and more to predominate numerically in the church."[109] As it is in the twentieth century in America, so it was in the seventeenth: "Women proved superior in almost every external measure of religious life."[110] The pattern that was established then has continued to the present, through all changes in government and through the change from an agrarian to an industrial, urban economy.

Modern England

The Britain from which the American colonists came has long shown a similar lack of male interest in religion. Of the late twentieth-century church, Grace Davie asks, "why do women so often predominate in the pews?"[111] Men may be, for a while, the majority of the clergy, but the laity are predominantly female. Of a typical rural churchgoer, it could be said "*she* would probably be age 45 and belong to one of the higher social classes"; the corresponding non-church-goer, would be "a young man . . . of the lower social classes."[112] Moreover, the difference has been growing: "The imbalance between the sexes . . . is becoming more rather than less marked in contemporary society."[113] The differences in the 1979 and 1989 censuses reveal this pattern: "In 1979 the proportion of male churchgoers was 45 percent, in 1989 in England it had dropped to 42 percent, nearer to the 1982 Welsh figure of 38 percent and the 1984 Scottish figure of 37 percent."[114] The difference can be traced back as far as there are statistics for church involvement—not only a difference in outward observance, but in belief: "The nature . . . of women's beliefs is different from that of their male counterparts."[115] Far more women than men subscribe to basic Christian beliefs[116] and the image of the God in whom they believe differs: "Women, if they are asked to describe the God in whom they believe, concentrate rather more on the God of love, comfort and forgiveness than on the God of power, planning and control. Men, it seems, do the reverse."[117] A 1989 poll in Great Britain revealed numerous differences between men and women, not only in religious practice, but in beliefs, though men and women identified themselves as members of denominations about equally.[118] Nevertheless, women's greater religiosity appears somewhat free-floating. It makes them more orthodox Christians, but it also makes them more open to alternative religions. The same poll shows that 44 percent of women believe in astrology, an irrationality in which only 30 percent of men indulge.[119]

A 1951 study of churches in York showed "57 percent more women in nonconformist churches, 48 percent more in the Church of England and   23 percent more in the Roman Catholic churches."[120] For more personal religious activities, which are less susceptible to social pressure, the difference is even greater. Studies in the 1940s showed that for weekly attendance at church the ratio of women to men was 1.5 to one and for quarterly attendance, 1.25 to one.[121] Among English adults in 1955, the ratio of women who prayed daily to men who prayed daily was 1.87 to one.[122] About the same number of men and women claimed to believe that God exists, but men were less orthodox than women in the specifics of their beliefs. The ratio of women believers in a personal God to male believers was 1.5 to one, the ratio of women who believe that Jesus was the Son of God to men who believe that doctrine was 1.54 to one.[123]

In the 1920s in working-class London, as in Spain, going to church was for women, and men helped keep their masculine reputation intact by staying away from church: "Male bravado precluded anything as effeminate as going to church."[124] The statistics from a church census in London at the beginning of the twentieth century moved the Reverend J. E. Watts of Ditchfield to remark that there was all too much truth in "the assertion that the Church is only for women and children." In London proper, during the morning services, there were 133,322 men and 180,513 women present, for the evening services, 133,305 men and 232,486 women. The same pattern was found in Greater London.[125]

Within the Church of England attendance by men varied according to the ideological posture of the parish. The Anglo-Catholics were the most feminized.[126] The enemies of the high church movement claimed that the Tractarian cleric "rules with despotic sway over ever so many young ladies, not a few old ones, some sentimental young gentlemen, and one or two old men in their dotage."[127] The Anglo-Catholics were sensitive to "the scoffing censure that our churches are filled and our Altars crowded with women."[128] But the same censure could, as we have seen, be applied at all churches in London: "In the Borough of Westminster, for example, in the morning congregations at two ritualist strongholds, St. Barnabas, Pimlico, and St. Thomas, Regent Street, women made up 75 percent and 71 percent, respectively, of the adults present, compared with 66 percent of the adults in all Church of England congregations in the borough."[129] The difference in the percentage of women was slight, but it was noticed, as was the presence of "sentimental young men."

In the mid-nineteenth century the evangelical clergyman John Angell James had remarked that "a very large proportion of the members of all Christian churches are females, and young females

too."[130] The predominance of women in the Church of England has
apparently been of long standing. In the sixteenth century Richard
Hooker had remarked that women in particular were "propense and
inclinable to holiness."[131] Presumably English men, in Hooker's experience, were not.

Germanic and Latin Countries

Catholic Latin countries have even fewer males in church than do
churches in northern Europe, although whether this is because
French, Spanish, and Italian men are less "propense and inclinable to
holiness" than Irishmen or Germans is open to question, for German
men are not especially religious. In the Federal Republic, the
churches are "women's companies."[132] In Latin countries the situation is simply worse. The Jesuit James Fichter states that "South
American males, and also those of France and of Italy are notoriously poor church participants."[133] South America has for a long
time had a culture in which men stayed away from church.[134] How
far back this male lack of interest goes is not clear, but at least since
the wars of independence from Spain (and probably earlier) men
have left the church to women. Catholic priests who have worked in
Latin America have been disturbed by the lack of men, low even by
North American standards: "Few Latin American men are seen in
church . . . the index of religious practice for men is very, very low."[135]
In Latin America there is "a long standing tradition among the
Spanish clergy that women are more religious; priests seem to write
off men as rather hopeless, and concentrate on women, particularly
on the younger women, 'the *virgenes*' who are to be the 'guardians of
purity' and the 'preservers of the faith.'"[136] Latin American men may
consider themselves Catholics, and may be willing to support the
church, but they leave the outward manifestations of their religion
to women and priests.

Spanish men also leave the church largely to women, which suggests that the Hispanic attitude toward religion antedates the Spanish colonization of the Americas in the sixteenth century. In a
Spanish village, even a conservative and Catholic one, religion is an

affair for women and priests. For example, in 1896 in a small city in Spain, Belmonte de los Caballeros, the parish records show that 443 Catholics had made their Easter duty, and 232 had failed to do so (151 men and 81 women did not fulfill this elementary obligation).[137] In the 1960s average mass attendance in this city was 55 percent, "39 percent among the men and some 71 percent among the women."[138] Stanley Brandes writes that his experience in the town of Monteros confirms the impression that men are less religious: "Within all segments of society, men are the religious sceptics, women the religious supporters."[139] The wife is not the head of the family, but she "assumes control of all affairs pertaining to the spiritual well-being of the household: the masses for the dead, the children's prayers, the husband's annual communion, and the negotiations with the important divine figures."[140] "The woman is expected to be more religious than the man and to fulfill her religious duties more punctiliously. The wife/mother has to elicit blessings for her children and husband by her prayers. She puts pictures and images of her favorite saints in places of honor, and at times she may force the husband not to overlook his religious obligations. If a child is ill she, never the father, will light small lamps or candles before the image of the Virgin or will recite the Rosary or commission a holy hour."[141] For a man to be outstandingly religious is considered shameful. A man is humiliated, *pasar verguenza*, if he is in debt, or "if he is seen in church holding a rosary, or sitting in the front benches in church."[142] A man can be a Catholic without disgrace, but to be outwardly religious is incompatible with masculinity. This attitude, as we have seen, also affects the Spanish layman's attitude to the only group of men who are more religious even than the women, that is, the priests.

In France, as Ruth Graham observes, somewhat ambiguously, in her essay on the relationship of women and clergy in the French Enlightenment, "At the beginning of the eighteenth century, men dominated religious life in France; at the end of the century, women were by far the greater number of the faithful."[143] Men may have been in leadership positions at the beginning of the century, and the French revolution, like the American one, may have even further alienated men from the church, but probably women were the more numerous and more devout members of French congregations throughout the eighteenth century, although the proportion of women in congregations may have varied. Although the convulsionaries of St. Medard may not have been representative, still, as Graham notes, in 1731-32 the reports were that three-fourths of the convulsionaries were women.[144]

In modern France as well the church is the domain of women. In the 1980s, 84 percent of catechists were women.[145] This is the situation after France had recovered from its bout of extreme anti-clericalism in the nineteenth century. The difference between men and women had grown less in the mid-twentieth century, in part because more men were going to church, and in part because fewer women were going to church.[146] Church surveys in the 1930s point to a predominance of women. In the parish of St. Pierre in Arras 20 to 30 men, 70 to 80 women attended mass; [147] in the communes of Sillé-le-Guillaume and Pontvallain, 1,300 men and 2,300 women made their Easter duty (confessed and received communion).[148] St. Claude, a center of practicing Catholicism, had about 100,000 in its rural parishes. Of the men, 32 percent made their Easter duty (*pascalisant*) and 24 percent attended mass (*messés*); of the women 60 percent made their Easter duty and 44 percent attended mass. Even in parts of France not subjected to severe secularization, the disparity between the sexes is great. As the sociologist le Bras says, "One will notice the great number of those making their Easter duty and the difference between the sexes."[149] In Pithiviers, more famous for its pastry than its piety and "destitute of religious ardor," at Easter there were 370 men and 1,125 women in church; at Sunday mass, 192 men and 1,064 women.[150] More French men than women never went to church. Of those men and women who were believers, women were more regular churchgoers than men.

The situation was even worse in the nineteenth century when anti-clericalism was in full swing. In 1858 the rector of Montpellier lamented that "religious duties are almost completely neglected by the men or practiced only for appearance sake. Generally only women observe their duties."[151] He said this because only 15 percent of the men made their Easter duty. In 1863, 16 percent of the men and 57 percent of the women of Marseilles made their Easter duty; in Toulon 8 to 10 percent were practicing. In 1877, in the western part of the diocese of Orléans, only 4.7 percent of the men made their Easter communion, although 26 percent of the women did.[152]

The Catholic Church in France has maintained its presence in society through the influence of women.[153] This strategy has even affected the teaching of doctrine. Though the Church had always condemned contraception, in France even peasants practiced coitus interruptus to limit the division of their inheritance. Acting on the advice of Alphonse de Ligouri, confessors decided that women were not guilty if their husbands practiced this form of contraception. This decision was based on a fear that rigorism would alienate women and the Church would lose all influence in French society. In 1842 the Trappist (and doctor) Debryne argued against a rigorist position on the use of contraception: "One should give serious attention to this; that one should not alienate women through an imprudent rigor; the matter is one of immense importance. The coming generation is in the hands of women, the future belongs to her. . . . If the woman gets away from us [the *us* seems to be his priest-readers] with her everything will disappear and vanish into the abyss of atheism—faith, morality, and our whole civilization."[154]

This clerical focus on women irritated men. In 1845 Jules Michelet complained that Frenchwomen were under the thumbs of the clergy, who realized that "the direction, the government of women, is the vital point of ecclesiastical power, which they will defend to the death."[155] The Jesuits, according to Michelet, had "a great attempt to fasten on the man through the woman and on the woman through the child."[156] An 1876 diocesan report in Orléans complained that attendance among women was declining "but above all because of the bad influence of their husbands."[157] These husbands followed the orders of "Sociétés secrètes" ("secret societies," no doubt Freemasons) that "it was necessary to forbid all communication with the priest."[158] Nevertheless, many French men approved of religion for women as a guarantor of marital fidelity and encouraged women to go to church.[159]

Wherever Western Christianity has spread, the church is feminized. Rosemary Reuther observes: "In Germany, France, Norway, and Ireland women are 60 to 65 percent of the active churchgoers. In Korea, India, and the Philippines, women are 65 to 70 percent of the active churchgoers."[160] This pattern seems to hold true in Western and Central Europe. The political upheavals in Eastern Europe, first Naziism and then Communism, have disorganized church life to an extreme and have prevented any studies of patterns of church attendance. Czechs and Slovaks to whom I have spoken indicate that in those countries the pattern is Western: more women than men attend church, and religion is felt to be somehow feminine. Poles, on the other hand, indicate that Poland seems to follow the Eastern pattern: men and women attend church equally, and there is no sense that religion is somehow proper to women. Factory workers in Solidarity were not embarrassed to display their piety publicly. The fusion of religion and national feeling is connected with this high male participation in church life, but it is unclear whether it is a cause or a consequence.

The exceptions to the general pattern of feminization of religious life are worth noting: the Eastern Orthodox (perhaps), the Jews (definitely) and non-Christian religions. In America, in comparison even to the Jews, "Muslims, adherents of Eastern religions, agnostics and religious 'Nones' have even more unbalanced sex ratios: almost two males for every female in each group. In contrast to the sex ratio among black Christians, only 36 percent of black Muslim and 40 percent of black religious 'Nones' are women."[161] The pattern is found in England as well. In contrast to the feminized congregations among all major Christian denominations documented by the census taken early this century, the ratio of men to women in synagogues was over three to one.[162] There is something about Christianity, especially Western Christianity, that drives a wedge between the church and men who want to be masculine.

2

Can a Man Be a Christian?

W HY ARE THE PEWS of Christian churches filled with women? Mary Maples Dunn despairs of explaining "gender differentiation" in Christianity: "How and why this gender differentiation develops in respect to religion is imperfectly understood; we are not certain that it is inherent in Christianity itself; we do not know why it becomes part of a social-religious order, what function it might have in that society, nor what conditions produce the dichotomy."[1] Despite her profession of ignorance, Dunn attributes male flight from churches to social features peculiar to seventeenth-century New England—the incipient separation of church and state, for instance. But such features do not explain similar paucities of men in England, France, and Latin America.

Various theories may explain why male participation sinks to particularly low levels at certain times. Historians look at the forces at work in a certain period and find the source of lower male participation. Without a doubt, circumstances may reinforce the barrier between men and the church. Yet, as Tony Walter observes, though "These theories may explain why a particular church at a particular time appeals to women, there is as yet no generally accepted theory of why women in general seem to be more religious than men."[2] Explanations that rely on accidents of time and place explain too little.

27

Philosophers and theologians seek for deeper explanations in the nature of religion or of man. Yet they often seem unaware that the lack of male religious observance, though widespread in Western Christianity, is not universal either in Christianity or religion in general. Their explanations go too far. If men are by nature non-religious, why do Islam and Judaism have predominantly male memberships and why have they for centuries evoked intense commitment from men? If Christianity in itself is obnoxious to men in some peculiar way, why was there little comment on the lack of men during its first millennium, and why do Orthodox churches seem to differ from Western ones in the proportion of male membership? What is it about the nature of men and of Western Christianity that has created such a tension in their relationship in the last millenium?

POLITICAL AND ECONOMIC CHANGES

Female interest in religion, according to one school, is a result of a sexual division of labor that emerged in modern European society. The revolutionary thinkers of the Enlightenment regarded the established churches of Europe with suspicion. The churches were departments of state, and therefore, whether they were Anglican, Catholic, Lutheran, or Calvinist, buttressed the established order. Though the first disestablishment of churches was brought about by peaceful means after the American Revolution, disestablishment was bloodier in Europe. The revolutionaries of the continental Enlightenment tended to atheism rather than stoicism and attacked the French church root and branch. Wherever Napoleon's armies conquered, the church lost its estates and wealth. The age of a secular laity had replaced the alliance of throne and altar in the *ancien regime*.

Before the industrial revolution, men and women labored together on farms or household workshops, but the industrial revolution separated work from the home. Initially, women and children worked in factories because they would accept low pay. When men replaced them as the principal workers in factories, these men separated their families as much as possible from the squalor and dangers of the industrial city, and suburbia was born. Women specialized in taking care of the house and children, separated themselves from the competitive, workaday world, and gave the home a sacred and sentimental aura. As religion had no place in politics or business, men relegated it to the home and to the woman's sphere of responsibility. Walter Rauschenbusch, at the beginning of the twentieth century, claimed the failure to preach the Social Gospel as the reason "that our churches are overwhelmingly feminine."[3] Women are domestic and religious, men are public and therefore irreligious: "Men's life faces the outward world, and his instincts and interests lie that way. Hence, men crowd where public questions get downright discussion. Our individualistic religion has helped to feminize our churches."[4]

A related explanation for women's greater interest in religion is that religion somehow compensates for their inferior social position. Men want women to be religious so that women will not rebel against oppression, and indeed will accept oppression as a blessing: "Religion was a means of enculturating women to their domestic maternal role, to acceptance of powerlessness and dependency on men."[5] This version of Marxist theory holds that religion is the opiate, not only of the masses, but especially of women. Simone de Beauvoir ascribes the existence of religion to the oppression of women: "There is a justification, a supreme compensation, which society is ever wont to bestow upon woman: that is, religion. There must be a religion for women as there must be one for the common people and for exactly the same reasons. When a sex or a class is condemned to immanence, it is necessary to offer it the mirage of some sort of transcendence."[6] Denied the attainment of true transcendence of their biological selves, a transcendence attainable only through careers in public life, women seek false transcendence in the illusions of religion.

A variation of this theory is that religion (inadvertently no doubt) has given oppressed women a sphere of influence and an outlet for their frustrated talents. Though women have been confined to the private sphere of home and family—*Kinder, Kirche, Küche*—in their own sphere they can have a great deal of autonomy. Just as in the Middle Ages, women, excluded from the governance of the church by clericalism, had turned to visions to establish a charismatic authority for themselves, now women, excluded from government, commerce, and education, turned to the church, which allowed them to exercise their abilities and to gain some power and respect.

The clergy, ignored by men, turned their attention to women. Francis Trollope observed this phenomenon in America, but her observations can be generalized. Men's crudity of manners led them to neglect women and prefer coarse male company. The only exception to this male neglect of women was the clergy: "It is from the clergy only that the women of America receive that sort of attention which is so dearly valued by every female heart throughout the world."[7] Trollope was both fascinated and horrified by the emotionalism of the American religion of the revival and the campground. She ascribed part of the interest in revivals to the lack of other amusements.[8] Young women were reduced to hysteria in the revivals, and ministers "whispered comfortings, and from time to time [bestowed] a mystic caress. More than once I saw a young neck encircled by a reverend arm."[9] Americans tended to let the emotional excitement of their religion lead to more carnal excitement. English enthusiasts too, according to Msgr. Ronald Knox, reverted to an orgiastic religion.[10] A few "smart young clerks" attended the evening prayer meetings that Trollope observed, perhaps with this in mind.[11] Among American young men it is a matter of folklore that a revival is an excellent place to pick up a young woman; but apparently not even the prospect of sexually excited women was enough to get men interested in church.

THE WEAKNESS OF WOMEN

Cotton Mather described the Christian fidelity of Puritan women as their response to the danger of death in childbirth: "The *Curse* in the Difficulties both of *Subjection* and of *Child bearing*, which the *Female Sex* is doom'd unto, has been turned into a *Blessing*."[12] On this view, it is the desire to seek shelter from the weakness of their bodies that leads women to Christianity. Another suspicion (and it is probably the widestspread) is that women are more emotional than men and that religion (the hidden assumption) is a matter of emotion. In the eighteenth century, Bishop Gregoire pointed to the supposed greater emotionalism of women: "Men are directed to conviction by reason; women to persuasion by sentiment."[13]

Freud thought that women were more religious than men because they were more feminine, as he understood femininity. In his theory of masculinity and femininity,[14] masculinity is the reality principle, "correspondence with the real, external world."[15] The masculine, scientific mind is tough: it is able to face such unpleasant realities as the absence of a benevolent Providence that guides human affairs. Femininity, according to Freud, is the principle of wish-fulfillment, and their femininity causes women to view reality as ultimately promising a fulfillment of our infantile desires for love and safety. Freud wanted all adults, including women, to adopt the reality principle, to become masculine, and to give up the fantasy world of wish-fulfillment that Christianity embodies. Freud's "guiding contrast is between wish fulfillment provided by the illusion of a father-God's loving existence and scientifically based resignation to reason and necessity, a resignation which stems from renunciation of childhood wishes."[16] If women would accept the reality principle, they would become tough-minded and give up the childish indulgence of religion.

By the nineteenth century, the home, mother, and God were joined in a Victorian Trinity, and heaven was the restoration of the family circle beyond the grave: Women, confined to the home, already lived half in heaven. Because Christianity reverses natural values, and thinks better of seeming failure and weakness—the cross—than of superficial worldly success, women's exclusion from public life redounded to their benefit. The London preacher James Fordyce attributed women's greater religiosity to their more sheltered lives, protected from temptation and with leisure for piety: "Nothing can be more plain, than that Providence has placed you most commonly in circumstances peculiarly advantageous for the exercises of devotion, and for the preservation of that virtue, without

which every profession of godliness must be regarded as an imprudent pretense. The situation of men lays them open to a variety of
temptations, that lay out of your road. The bustle of life, in which
they are generally engaged, leaves them but little leisure for holy
offices."[17] But the Reverend Fordyce is only saying that women are
more religious because religion is a feminine activity, a matter of exalted sentiment, removed from activity and strife.

Throughout the nineteenth century the temperance movement
aimed to protect women from the vicious pleasures of men. Ministers and women worked together against men, especially young men:
"It was often as a covert crusade to salvage not the alcoholic but the
woman at his mercy. The drunkard, usually a male, destroys by his
debauches himself and his saintly wife, mother, daughter, or sister
who loves him and would draw him from the saloon to the
fireside."[18] Women took over the leadership of family prayers; men
were obviously unsuitable.[19]

THE GOODNESS OF WOMEN

Msgr. James Alberione's *Woman: Her Influence and Zeal* embodies the
attitudes to gender that have dominated Western Christianity and
provided the seeds of the feminism that now dominates the church.
This book, directed to priests, lays down the principle "that woman
is more naturally inclined to the practice of holiness"[20] than the male
is. In this he echoes Pius XI, who calls woman "the devout sex."[21]
Why are women more religious than men? Alberione has the answer: "She is more understanding in things of the heart, she is more
spiritual than man. More humble, more tender, and consequently,
more religious than man, she is more inclined to prayer, to charity,
and to hope. More than man, woman feels the need for pure love;
her love, less egoistic, is unselfish and prone to sacrifice."[22] Religion
is, in Alberione's estimation, primarily an affair of the heart. Hence,
to be religious, one has to be feminine.

A feminist novelist has a character say "to bring about true
Christian civilization . . . the men must become more like women,
and the women more like angels."[23] A clergyman in 1854 asserted

that "the womanly element predominated" in Jesus,[24] and Henry Ward Beecher said that a mother's love is "a revelation of the love of God."[25] Another Unitarian, in 1858, claimed that Christianity involved a rejection of masculinity; it had "proclaimed the Gospel of the 'Ever Feminine'" and also preached "the utter nothingness of masculine self-sufficiency."[26] Goethe's "Ewig-weibliche" had become the locus of divine activity in the world. Women had to be the saviors of men, drawing the errant male sinner back to home and heaven. Protestants recovered a sympathy with Catholic devotion to Mary ("Our tainted nature's solitary boast"), who tended to displace Jesus in Catholic popular devotion. One priest, it is alleged, after preaching a sermon on the greatness of Mary, concluded that it was no wonder her son turned out so well.[27]

Sarah J. Hale went so far as to claim that women are not as fallen as men: "He is naturally selfish in his affections; and *selfishness* is the sin of depravity. But woman was not thus cast down."[28] Women preserve an unselfish affection and love which men have lost. They are therefore God's chosen instruments. For Hale, "the Christian and the feminine are one."[29] Men are wicked, women are good, and that is why "more than three-fourths of the professed followers of Christ are women."[30] Christians are followers of a male, but one who had no earthly father, and got his human nature entirely from a woman. Therefore, Jesus's "human soul, derived from a woman, trained by a woman, was most truly womanly in its characteristics."[31] His closest disciples were either women or like women, such as "the faithful, gentle, loving, *womanlike* John"[32] (for so the image of the Son of Thunder has become in the Church).

Allen Bridgman believed that an overvaluation of the feminine and an undervaluation of the masculine were at the root of the feminization of religion. His contemporaries were "impressed chiefly with the angelic side of the daughters of men and with the earthward tendencies of his brethren."[33] He admits the possible truth of this characterization, but reminds Christians that their religion is addressed to sinners, not the just.

In a medieval manuscript, in what is perhaps a rhetorical exercise in *sic et non*, we find claims that "Woman is to be preferred to man, to wit in material: Adam made from clay and Eve from the side of Adam; in place: Adam made outside paradise and Eve w'in; in conception: a woman conceived God which a man did not do; in apparition: Christ appeared to a woman after the Resurrection, to wit the Magdalene; in exaltation: a woman is exalted above the choirs of angels, to wit the Blessed Mary."[34] Humbert of Romans, (d. 1277) the Master-General of the Dominicans echoed this attitude:

> Note that God gave women many prerogatives, not only over other living things, but even over man himself, and this (i) by nature; (ii) by grace; and (iii) by glory.
>
> (i) In the world of nature she excelled man by her origin, for man He made of the vile earth, but woman He made in Paradise. Man he formed of the slime, but woman of man's rib. She was not made of a lower limb of man—as for example of his foot—lest man should esteem her his servant, but from his midmost part, that he should hold her to be his fellow, as Adam himself said: "The woman whom Thou gavest me as my helpmate."
>
> (ii) In the world of grace she excelled man. . . . We do not read of any man trying to prevent the Passion of Our Lord, but we do read of a woman who tried—namely, Pilate's wife, who sought to dissuade her husband from so great a crime. . . . Again at His Resurrection, it was to a woman that He first appeared—namely, to Mary Magdalene.
>
> (iii) In the world of glory, for the king in that country is no mere man but a mere woman is its queen; nor is anyone who is merely man as powerful there as a mere woman. Thus is woman's nature in Our Lady ranked. It is not a mere man who is set above the angels and all the rest of the heavenly country in worth, and dignity, and power; and this should lead woman to love God and hate evil.[35]

St. Bernadine even declared that "It is a great grace to be a woman: More women are saved than men."[36] Protestants, despite their rejection of the Catholic veneration of Mary, inherited this attitude to women. Jonathan Edwards reminded his congregation that "this sex has the peculiar honor in the affair of the redemption of the second."[37]

FEMININE RECEPTIVITY

The virtue that made women good and loving was, above all, obedience. Because women are weak, helpless, and trained to obedience, they more easily become Christians, who are likewise weak, helpless, and trained to obedience. Gertrud von le Fort speculates that "perhaps the realization that man's weakness is his real and only strength, his surrender to God's holy will his only true victory he can achieve, perhaps such an awareness is more connate to feminine that to masculine nature."[38] In the Christian paradox, woman's feminine passivity is more valuable than masculine activity: "The receptive, passive attitude of the feminine principle appears as the decisive, the positive element in the Christian order of grace."[39] This receptivity is bridal. Christians must be brides of Christ, and men do not like this role, which could hardly be a greater denial of their masculinity.

This approach to the meaning of gender in religion continues to be popular in many Christian circles, especially those influenced by C. S. Lewis and Hans Urs von Balthasar.[40] Manfred Hauke states that "in relation to God, the soul is receptive, feminine."[41] F. X. Arnold describes "the special inclination which woman has for religion" as "the truly feminine, the will to surrender, the readiness to be receptive."[42] The essential element in a religious attitude is a "passive receptivity," because "in this readiness for self-sacrifice and in this cooperation of the creature, all that is truly religious in humanity is revealed."[43] Of Mary, George T. Montague says "She is response and instrument."[44]

MASCULINITY IS UNCHRISTIAN

Nietzsche saw a contradiction between the Christian and the masculine. Christianity is a denial of life, and "life itself is essentially appropriation, injury, overpowering of what is alien and weaker; suppression, hardness, imposition of one's own forms, incorporation, and at least, at its mildest, exploitation."[45] Christianity is a religion for slaves, weaklings, the effeminate, "a sacrifice of all freedom, all pride, all self-confidence of the spirit; at the same time, enslavement and self mockery, self mutilation."[46] Christianity denies the will to power, so it cannot be masculine. A man must therefore choose between being masculine and Christian; he cannot be both.

Tony Walter comes to the same conclusion as Nietzsche. Walter blames "the macho ethic" that "hinders men from worshipping God."[47] Men have a strong drive toward separation, autonomy, and independence. Walter sees this drive as making men enemies of the Gospel: "Taking up the cross, denying himself, and abasing himself before God is hardly the fulfillment of his masculinity!"[48] Therefore masculinity is evil: "The macho ethic of pride in independence thus appears as a Satanic device for keeping men from faith in Christ, while the feminine ethic appears as a schoolmistress to bring women to faith in Christ."[49] Men must change, not the Church: "It is secular male culture that needs to be challenged and changed, not female church culture."[50] Only if men become like women can they become Christian.

THOSE WHO LOOK to social forces to explain the comparatively weak religious commitment of men fail in their explanations because the phenomenon appears always to antedate the historical period under consideration. Evidence exists that even in the high Middle Ages women were already more devotedly religious than men.

Nietzsche and those who take a more theoretical approach, seeing an eternal animosity between masculinity and Christianity (or even religion in general), cannot account for Judaism and Islam, or for the first millenium of Christianity, the age of the Church Fathers, in which there is no evidence of a substantial disparity in religious practice between men and women. Something has happened in Western Christianity that has caused it to react unfavorably to masculinity. But what is masculinity? Is it the macho ethic of Walter's caricature, or is it violent self-will, as in Nietzsche's estimation? What is it that men seek to become? To answer that question I shall turn in the next chapter to anthropology and developmental psychology, as well as to the literature of masculinity, the epic.

3

What Is Masculinity?

MALENESS AND MASCULINITY ARE NOT THE SAME THING. We commonly recognize a distinction between facts of biology and masculine identity. Simply being an adult male is not enough; one must in addition *be a man*, which means more than simply having a male body. Being a man in the fullest sense is a matter of the will, a choice to live in a certain way. A male can be praised for acting like a man, or blamed for not being manly.

Psychology and anthropology support the popular distinction between sex and gender. *Sex* is what the body is, that is, male or female. *Gender* is everything that is not limited to the body; it is a complex of behavior, mental qualities, and personality characteristics—everything we mean when we say that someone is masculine, a real man, a *Mensch*, or (more rarely), feminine, a real woman, a lady. Gender sometimes refers specifically to sexual behavior; that is, *masculinity* can mean the male desire for heterosexual intercourse, but I do not mean it in that restricted sense. Gender means, in a distinction that is becoming widely accepted, the wide range of qualities and behavior (including the sexual) that make up the realities we call masculine and feminine. Maleness is a physical quality, masculinity a cultural and spiritual one, although one that is connected with the physical realities of being male. Nevertheless, a male must be initiated into the mysteries of masculinity before he can become a man in the fullest sense of the word, and it is this initiation that is the theme of much of world literature, from Homer to Hemingway.

BIOLOGY

The first thing to note is that the female is the norm from which the male must be differentiated. The basic pattern of the human body is roughly female, as one would expect in a mammalian species, and male characteristics develop from that pattern only under certain circumstances. "The female," says J. M. Tanner, "is the 'basic sex' into which embryos develop if not stimulated to do otherwise."[1] Even the primary sex characteristics of males are produced by the action of androgens on a fetus with female genitals. The presence of nipples on the male body is a constant reminder that the male is a variation on the basic female type.

Moreover, the male is expendable. His physical role in reproduction is over in a few moments, and for almost all species that is the end of his involvement. The cultural role that human society has developed for males, that of the expendable sex, is rooted in his biological status, his lesser role in reproduction. The male can die and the species still reproduce. But if the mother dies before the child is capable of taking care of itself, the child will die and with it the hope for the propagation of the species.

While the male body itself explains male behavior to some extent, it does not determine it, but rather gives males a predisposition to act in certain ways. Nevertheless, some qualities emerge so early in childhood it is hard to know whether they are based in biology or are the first stages of masculine psychological development. Eleanor Maccoby and Carol Jacklin have concluded that four differences appear so early in childhood that they could be described as innate. First, "girls have greater verbal abilities"; that is, girls are more fluent than boys and are also better at understanding difficult reading material and at creative writing. Second, "boys excel in visual-spatial tasks" and increase their lead over girls as their testosterone levels increase during adolescence. Third, "boys excel in mathematical ability," a difference in which boys also increase their lead during adolescence. Fourth, and most obvious, "males are more aggressive," even from infancy.[2] The reaction of testosterone and adrenaline gives a pleasurable high, encouraging men to seek danger. Men have greater upper body strength and a higher ratio of muscle to body fat that enables them to face danger and survive.

Yet there is some evidence that even these qualities are not exactly innate. Male children deprived of a father in early childhood will not develop some of these qualities. A study of Harvard students identified a group whose fathers had been in the military and were away during their infancy. These male students were high achievers, but were highly verbal and had academic profiles of high-achieving female students. At the other end of the social spectrum, in the inner city, boys whose fathers were absent also showed little of the masculine tendency to excel in math. Hence, these qualities are not a given, but they are potentialities that will develop in favorable circumstances. They provide the raw material for masculine behavior, but they do not in themselves constitute masculinity. Males who mature in a biologically normal fashion may still fail to be men. What must be added to male biology is masculinity, which is not a physical, but a cultural and spiritual quality.[3]

The male body is differentiated from the female by a complex process which can go wrong at many points and which is the basis of the later psychological differentiation that parallels and reinforces it. Like the physical differentiation on which it is based, the psychological differentiation of the male from the female, that is, masculinization, is a fragile and complex process. The boy must achieve masculinity by rejecting the female and differentiating himself from the feminine to which he reverts unless he constantly exerts himself—a reversion which will destroy him as a man. The power of the female identity, which males try to escape, is the basis of the fundamental "bisexuality" that Freud and others have observed in human nature. Bisexuality is a vague word, since it implies that male and female are present in the same way, but femaleness is a condition from which the male is already differentiated biologically. A male that does not undergo the later psychological differentiation is not a female, but a failed man.

DEVELOPMENTAL PSYCHOLOGY

According to developmental psychologists, personality traits are set down, at least in outline, during infancy. What we experience in the first months and years of life gives us categories of thought of which we are often scarcely aware, but by which we tend to organize and classify later experiences. The relationship to the mother is crucial. Boys and girls have different developmental patterns because a girl is the same sex as the parent to whom she is closest, her mother, while the boy is a different sex from the mother and may never even know his father. A girl, though she must develop her own identity, can model it after her mother's, while the boy must, in a sense, reject his mother, or he will never become masculine.

At first an infant, male or female, exists in an oceanic consciousness, in which the mother and child merge into one, blissful, erotic identity.[4] Gradually the child realizes the mother is a distinct person, and a boy realizes further that his mother is in some way alien to him. This gives males and females distinct personality patterns: "From the retention of preoedipal attachment to their mother," Nancy Chodorow claims, "growing girls come to define and experience themselves as continuous with others; their experience of self contains more flexible or permeable ego boundaries. Boys come to define themselves as more separate and distinct, with a greater sense of rigid ego boundaries and differentiation. The basic feminine sense of self is connected to the world, the basic masculine sense of self is separate."[5] This process occurs first of all because the boy learns that the mother's body is undeniably different from his: "The very body parts that confirm his male identity are ones she does not have."[6] If a boy fails to achieve this differentiation, he will have problems with his identity as a male.[7] Becoming a man begins with a break with the mother, but continues throughout life with a rejection of the feminine.[8]

But even if he achieves differentiation, a boy must complete his masculine identity by identifying with a male, especially his father, whom he sees is loved by his mother. He must give up his desire to *be* his mother, and learn to *love* her, or at least to love another woman. But to love any woman as an adult the boy must first reject his mother—or more accurately, being mothered—because her femininity is a trap that will lure him back into an infantile narcissism. Hence, he dreads the feminine as a perpetual threat to his masculinity.[9] Likewise, he must give up a desire to love the male erotically, as his mother does, and instead learn to be a full male, that is, a father.

Even if all goes well with this complex process of disidentification from the female and counter-identification with the male, the boy will still have problems, although they will be ones that are intrinsic to being a male. The consciousness of the primal union with his mother and the break he has had to endure creates a wound in the masculine personality.[10] There is always a nagging feeling of alienation, that the primal experience of loving, blissful, narcissistic unity cannot be trusted. This fundamental psychological experience already leads the boy to misogyny, a mistrust of women, and insensitivity, an inability to place trust in another and to commit himself to that other.

But a boy derives a benefit from this psychic wound, or at least is made to benefit society by his attempts to deal with the wound. Since a girl maintains a far closer identification with her mother (and therefore with others in general) she learns to tolerate or accommodate frustration so as not to break this unity. On the other hand, "the male infant discovers that you can reject a source of frustration, and simultaneously, find a stance independent of it."[11] A boy finds an endless source of psychic energy in the space between himself and his mother, as well as an opportunity for a strong sense of agency, of acting on the world to change it, rather than simply accepting it.

Masculinity and femininity are characterized, respectively, by separation and communion, as David Bakan describes: "Agency manifests itself in the formation of separations; communion in the lack of separation."[12] Bakan explains that agency manifests itself "in isolation, alienation, and aloneness . . . in the urge to master . . . in the repression of thought, feeling, and impulse . . . ," and that communion manifests itself in "contact, openness, and union . . . in noncontractual cooperation . . . in the lack and removal of repression."[13] The process of the formation of agency parallels the formation of masculine identity: "The very split of agency from communion, which is a separation, arises from the agency feature itself; and it represses the communion from which it has separated itself."[14] Separation implies death, and in the Freudian view is based on "the separation of the ego from the world" which produces "aggression."[15] Satan, according to Bakan, is the image of "agency unmitigated by communion."[16] Both by their maleness and by their masculinity, men, far more than women, are oriented to death, as all statistics of mortality show, and men are often tempted to the final separation of nihilism, which is satanic. Even their different sexual responses reinforce the difference between men and women. Since "the aim of agency is the *reduction of tension*, whereas the aim of communion is *union*,"[17] men seek to reduce tension (the *petite mort* of orgasm is a parallel and foretaste of the final death of the body), while women seek communion, which is initially fulfilled in pregnancy, but stretches forth to a communion with all beings that reaches beyond death.

Hudson and Jacot find evidence of this wound of alienation in the male tendency to invest passion in abstractions rather than things, because abstractions cannot betray. Men also let this experience of separation influence the way they think. The masculine mind likes "arguments cast in terms of dualities and dialectical oppositions . . . that depend on the maintenance of conceptual boundaries and segregations . . . that depend on a deep preoccupation with similarities and differences . . . that are reductive."[18] This pattern of thought characterizes the Western philosophical and scientific tradition, which is sometimes more pronouncedly masculine that at other times, but always bears the imprint of the masculine minds which formed it. As Walter Ong notes, "we find adversatives in the all but ubiquitous Mother Earth and Father Sky, the Chinese *li* and *ch'i*, yin and yang, Empedoclean attraction and repulsion, the Platonic dialectic, matter and form, Abelard's *sic et non*, essence and existence,

Hegelian dialectic, and countless other binary modes of analysis."[19] The computer, with its binary switches, is but the latest incarnation of male thought patterns.

ANTHROPOLOGY

David Gilmore, an anthropologist from Yale, analyzes the phenomenon of masculinity in *Manhood in the Making: Cultural Concepts of Masculinity*.[20] Gilmore discovered that almost all human societies have an ideology of masculinity, a set of beliefs the purpose of which is to convince boys to undertake the dangerous work in society. Manhood, on this view, is not inborn, but a great and difficult achievement, "a matter of storm and stress, of challenges and trials."[21] The infantile and the feminine are always threatening to drag a man back, to keep him from achieving masculinity. Males have a "need for constant vigilance against their unacceptable yearning to return to the merging in the symbiosis" of mother and child.[22] Paradoxically, men cultivate misogyny for the sake of women: A man must give up the state of boyhood, in which he is protected by women, fed by women, and cared for by women, so that he may become a protector and provider for women and children. In other words, he must give up being mothered before he can become a father. He must reject the feminine in himself, cultivating a distance from the world of women, so that he can one day return to it, not as a recipient, but as a giver.

To be masculine, a man must be willing to fight and inflict pain, but also to suffer and endure pain. He seeks out dangers and tests of his courage and wears the scars of his adventures proudly. He does this not for his own sake, but for the community's, to protect it from its enemies, both human and natural. Masculine self-affirmation is, paradoxically, a kind of self-abnegation. A man must always be ready to give up his life: "The accepting of this very expendability... often constitutes the measure of manhood, a circumstance that may help explain the constant emphasis on risk-taking as evidence of manliness."[23] A woman faces danger in childbirth, a risk that she cannot (in pre-contraceptive societies) escape. A man has to accept danger freely and willingly, or else he is not masculine, nor yet is he feminine, since his sex preserves him from the burdens of childbirth. A woman bleeds in menstruation and childbirth; a man bleeds in war, or in the rituals of circumcision and of subincision, or in the hazardous occupations he undertakes so that women may raise their children in safety. It is only through suffering and violence that men can achieve what women achieve by their almost-compulsory experience of childbirth: "Men nurture their society by shedding their blood, their sweat, and their semen, by bringing home food for both child and mother, and by dying if necessary in faraway places to provide a safe haven for their people." [24]

Male social dominance must be seen in this context. A man seeks power and wealth and success not for himself, but for others. He is honored for his willingness to serve and to die, his "selfless generosity, even to the point of sacrifice"[25] and is therefore given charge of the community. Masculinity is an honor, but often a deadly one. As Michael Levin points out, "If sex roles are to be regarded as the outcome of bargaining in which men received dominance in exchange for the risk of violent death, it is hardly clear that they got the better deal."[26] Walter Farrell, in *The Myth of Male Power*,[27] and Herb Goldberg, in *The Hazards of Being Male*,[28] have documented that men have more physical and mental diseases, commit more crimes, go to jail more often, and finally die earlier than women: "every critical statistic in the area of longevity, disease, suicide, crime, accidents, childhood emotional disorders, alcoholism, and drug addiction shows a disproportionately higher male rate."[29] Men willingly take far more than their share of the risks in society; of the twenty most dangerous civilian occupations, all but one are almost entirely male.[30] The history of human suffering makes it hard to say whether men or women have suffered more.[31]

Both men and women still think of men as privileged, but the ideology of masculinity is not a rational construct. Masculinity is paradoxical: It is the privilege of dying that others may live, which is, in the highest philosophical and religious sense, a privilege. Yet it is surprising how many men, especially those not philosophically or religiously inclined, are willing to follow this path of self-sacrifice, and regard it as a privilege. Although masculine self-sacrifice has been abused, it is not something which society can do without. Masculinity has always been full of dangerous paradoxes that stem from the very root of masculine identity: the separation of the male from the feminine from which he sprang. As Goldberg explains, "If he is in touch with and expressive of his feminine component he may be subject to great feelings of anxiety and humiliation. If he successfully manages to repress, disown, and deny this critical part of himself he will have to live as an incomplete person, alienated from an important part of himself and consequently susceptible to emotional and interpersonal rigidity and numerous psychological and psychophysiological problems that result from this repression."[32]

A Theory of Masculinity

The masculine is a pattern of initial union, separation, and reunion, while the feminine is a maintenance of unity. This pattern is found on the biological level, and even more on the psychological, anthropological, and cultural levels. Femininity is not merely receptivity or passivity, as some have thought. Activity and receptivity are both proper to the masculine and the feminine in distinctive ways. The maintenance of unity typical of the feminine may not be as obviously a state of activity as the pattern of separation and reunification typical of the masculine, but the integration of personality, social unity, and love require effort.

Nevertheless, the most striking feature of masculinity is its separation from the feminine, and it is this part of the developmental pattern that is usually thought of as uniquely masculine. As Richard A. Hawley says, "Masculinity is best understood as a trajectory . . . a journey or a quest."[33] It is always a journey away from something, especially the feminine: "The male trajectory begins with the first gesture of separation from the mother. This need to differentiate sets the boy on a life-long path of, literally, proving himself."[34] Yet this is only part of masculinity. Having achieved his first goal of separation, a man must then achieve a reunion and reconnection with the feminine, although one which is marked by his departure from it. The first union is sterile, and must be broken, so that this second, fruitful union may take place. This second union is achieved only through a man's suffering the pain of separation and in his confrontation with death.

Masculinity is not a state or quality, but a pattern of union and separation. It is never fully possessed, but always to be lived. It has its biological basis in the differentiation of maleness from the basic female pattern of the body. The inescapable fact that man is born of woman gives every male a taste of a painful separation, "the drama of his infant experiences as he begins to conceive of his identity in relation to the mother from whose body he issues and who is now sustaining his life. He cannot identify entirely because he is different from her, not just a separate being, but a different kind of being." The painful differentiation of his body from the female pattern and the even more painful separation from the mother prepare a boy for a life of separations, which may, if all goes well, end in reunions. As Shakespeare wrote, "Journeys end in lovers' meeting/Every wise man's son doth know."

The ideology of masculinity is founded on biology and psychology, but goes beyond them in its cultural manifestations. Simple societies can have an initiatory ritual that recognizes boys as men after they have proved themselves able and willing to confront the dangers of life. More complex societies, on the other hand, give boys no such rites of passage, and they must face every test afresh, not knowing whether they have yet proved themselves men.

Initiation

Initiation is not simply a beginning; life has many beginnings, but not every one of them is an initiation in the anthropological sense. Initiation entails a sharp break, and has a threefold structure: a departure from a previous way of life, a "liminal" period in which the one being initiated is suspended between two worlds, and the entry into a new way of life. If an initiation is profound, it can also be an experience of death and rebirth. Such a deep initiation gives the initiate insight into the mysteries of life and death and is always, in the broad sense, a religious experience, although there are specifically religious initiations. The two basic types of initiation, the initiation of the child into adulthood and the initiation of the believer into the mysteries of a religion, have a common structure and use the same language. The initiate must leave behind one world, be transformed, and enter a new world in which he has a new status, perhaps even a new life; a boy is reborn as a man, and a believer as a new creature.

Initiation is usually marked by ceremony. Arnold van Gennep identified, in primitive societies, "ceremonial patterns which accompany a passage from one situation to another or from one cosmic or social world to another."[35] These "rites of separation, transition rites, and rites of incorporation" often have a distinct beginning, middle, and end.[36] Their fullness is found at the most important points in a person's life, but they can be present even in seemingly trivial events. Writing before World War I, van Gennep reminded his readers that although "a person in these days may pass freely from one civilized region to another,"[37] in previous times crossing a frontier was accompanied by various formalities, not only legal, but even religious.

Tribal societies have a simple structure and often a single initiatory event for boys. Such societies usually have a simple economy and face a limited number of dangers. To be a man in these societies, therefore, is a simpler, although still difficult, process. Though anthropologists find it more convenient to examine well-defined ceremonies, the meaning and essence of these rites may inhere in events that are not recognizable as ceremonies. Many societies, such as the ancient Germanic and Mediterranean, did not have a single puberty rite: A boy had to go through many tests to prove himself a man. Such initiations have parallels in more developed societies, including our own. The general absence of ceremony in our own culture has meant that a boy who seeks initiation finds it outside of ceremonies, in seemingly secular events that take on a religious significance for the one who achieves his initiation through them. Any sort of transition can become sufficiently important, depending on social circumstances, to be surrounded by the full panoply of the rites of passage.

The first stage, that of departure, is marked by a rite of separation, which removes the individual from a common life and sets him apart from the rest of humanity. This separation can be accomplished by physical movement—sending a young man off into the wilderness; by changes in the body—painting or mutilation or scarification; by a symbolic death—a descent into the earth or water; or by a feast of some kind. All these rites serve to mark the end of one stage of life that must be rejected if the boy is to grow. The more important the transition, the more violent and thorough the separation. Each transition may have its own rite of separation, so a life may be marked by many such rites, separations from childhood, from bachelorhood, from civilian life, from homeland, from life itself.

After being separated from the previous way of life, the individual enters a transitional stage in which he is neither the person he was before, nor the person he will become after being incorporated into the new way of life for which he is destined. This is the liminal stage, from the Latin *limes*, a threshold. The liminal stage is one of chaos, in which the individual hovers between two worlds—between childhood and adulthood, between boy and man, between the profane and the sacred: "The coincidence of opposite processes and notions in a single representation characterizes the peculiar unity of the liminal: that which is neither this nor that, and yet is both."[38] From this undifferentiated state of chaos a new identity is born.

The initiation is completed by rites of incorporation, in which the person enters a new way of life, a new world, and assumes a new identity. He is now an initiate, and has new knowledge, new powers, new abilities, and new wisdom. He may receive a new name, or new clothes, to embody his new status. He has been reborn, to a greater or lesser degree, as a new person. Thus, all males who mature into men experience some initiation into masculinity. The process of masculine development demands that a boy experience something that he would not attain on his own simply by following his boyish desires for security or his adolescent instincts and appetites.

Puberty rituals are mainly an enactment of the psychological separation that the boy must achieve from his mother. The three stages that van Gennep identified, separation, transition, and incorporation are visible in these ceremonies. Among the Australian Kurnai, the pattern of separation is vivid: "The intention of all that is done at this ceremony is to make a momentous change in the boy's life; the past is to be cut off from him by a gulf that he can never repass. His connection with his mother as her child is broken off, and he becomes henceforth attached to the men."[39] The initiate is often considered dead.[40] He is often whipped and mutilated to remove him from ordinary society, and van Gennep understands the Jewish rite of circumcision in this context.[41] The Jewish boy is set apart from Gentiles and women by a mutilation that is also a separation of the flesh from the body. Only after this separation can he join the community of Israel.

The period of separation is distinctively masculine, but in the male initiation ritual the boy sometimes becomes female during the liminal, transitional phase, in which chaos returns, normal order and practice are deliberately violated, and the boy is totally separated from the protective world of the mother.[42] The boy sometimes takes on a temporarily feminine identity, like Achilles among the maids. Sometimes the boy is simply dressed as a girl; sometimes the resemblance is carved into his body by circumcision or subincision. The boy must bleed genitally, as a woman does, before he can become a man. In the New Guinea tribe studied by Gilbert Herdt, boys have to be passive homosexual partners for older men as a necessary stage of becoming a man, even though adult homosexuality is considered peculiar, and the boys themselves feel that their role is somehow feminine.[43]

Mircea Eliade interprets this transformation as a desire to recover unity before a fully differentiated male identity is established: "The novice has a better chance of attaining to a particular mode of being . . . if he first symbolically becomes a totality. For mythical thought, a particular mode of being is necessarily preceded by a total mode of being. The androgyne is considered superior to the two sexes just because it incarnates totality and hence perfection."[44] Bruno Bettelheim theorizes that boys have an envy of the femininity of their mother; they especially feel that men, too, should be able to have babies.[45] They therefore try to imitate menstruation, or wear feminine clothes, or act in a feminine manner in certain situations in which chaos returns, as at Halloween.

Nevertheless, this transformation into a woman is not based on simple envy of women's fertility. As Bettelheim notes, both "anthropologists and psychoanalysts agree that pain in initiation is the price adolescents must pay for the prerogatives of the adult world."[46] The boy must become like a woman, who experiences bleeding and pain because of the necessities of menstruation, conception, and childbirth. A male escapes these pains, but he will never become a full human being until he, too, learns to suffer and bleed that others may live. In transitional rites, a male is wounded so that he can achieve sympathy and compassion for his people and be trained to suffer and die for them. What a woman receives from her experience of her physical female nature, a man must receive from his culture, because he will not receive it by simply living out the logic of his male body. In other words, through initiation ceremonies, men try to achieve what women possess by nature. In her survey of the literature on initiation, Monika Vizedom notes "among the instances recorded for the societies covered, there is a great deal more emulation of women by men that vice versa."[47] A man who has not bled and suffered, a man without scars, is no man at all.[48]

The boy is finally incorporated into the world of men. The periods of separation and liminality have prepared him for a new life: "The passivity of neophytes to their instructors, their malleability, which is increased by submission to ordeal, their reduction to a uniform condition, are signs of the process whereby they are ground down to be fashioned anew and endowed with additional powers to cope with their new station in life."[49] The boy is taught the religion of his group, that is, those things that the group regards as sacred and ultimate. Religion, in the modern sense, is an essential element, perhaps the heart, of masculine initiation. Rosalind Miles describes this dynamic: "To be a male is the opposite of being mother. To be a man, the boy must break away from her, and the further he travels, the greater will be the success of his journey."[50] He is born again, but this time of man, not of woman. This birth, like the first one, is bloody and violent: "To make the break, however, the boy has to be constantly encouraged, threatened, thrust forward at every turn and side, and never, never permitted to fall back."[51] Boys who undergo this transformation have a life-long bond with all others who have so suffered. Miles describes the bonding that results from masculine initiation: "No boy, of course, could ever forget an experience like this. . . . The only others able to share his experience will be those who have undergone it with him, pain for pain, blood for blood: that group will then be bonded closer than husband and wife, closer than siblings, closer than mother and child. As the boy is violently disassociated from mother, home, and family, so he is associated, with equal violence, with the group of other boys who will henceforward be from rebirth or death his blood brothers."[52] This blood brotherhood is very close to the comradeship that men feel in war. For some reason violence is necessary for men to attain ultimate self-transcendence through love.

These rites and the facts of human psychology upon which they are based are the foundation for similar patterns of initiation in the higher religions. The idea of death to an old nature and rebirth to a new one is common to masculine experience.[53] Eliade notes that "all the rites of rebirth or resurrection, and the symbols that they imply, indicate that the novice has attained to another mode of existence, inaccessible to those who have not undergone the initiatory ordeals, who have not tasted death."[54] To be born only once is to be trapped in the secular world. Only by being born again can one enter the sacred world, and to be born again one must first die. To the Brahmins of India, the "twice born" is the one who has knowledge of the sacred. He "belongs to his caste by birth and incorporated into it by childhood rites, [and] later undergoes initiating ceremonies enacting death in a previous world and birth in a new one, and giving him the power to devote himself to the magico-religious activity that is to be his occupational specialty."[55] Death and rebirth were also the key themes of the most deeply felt religions of the Mediterranean basin, the mystery religions.

Mystery Religions and Initiation

The popular and official mythologies of the ancient world did not really satisfy the individual's quest for religious initiation, especially the individual man's. Instead, he sought initiation in the mystery religions. All the mysteries promised the believer a death and a rebirth.

The Eleusinian mysteries of the ancient Greek world have been reconstructed by Harold Willoughby from indirect evidence.[56] They consisted of a sacred drama, sacred instruction, and the exhibition of sacred objects. The drama was based upon the myth of Demeter, the goddess of the harvest, and her daughter Persephone: While gathering flowers at Eleusis, Persephone was abducted by Pluto, the god of the underworld, with the permission of Zeus, king of the gods. Demeter came to Eleusis and, disguising herself as an old woman, searched for her daughter. She was offered hospitality by the king, her identity was discovered, and she was worshipped by the populace. In return, she taught them her mysteries. She refused to let grain grow on the earth until Zeus ordered Pluto to return Persephone. Pluto relented, but Persephone had eaten some pomegranate seeds in the underworld, and had to return to her husband for three months of each year, during which Demeter would permit nothing to grow.

The Eleusinian mysteries seem to have been a reenactment of Demeter's search for Persephone on the very spot it was supposed to have occurred. After extensive preparation, the initiates gathered at night and by torchlight accompanied Demeter in her search until she was reunited with Persephone. The sacred instruction was given, and the sacred objects shown. The initiates felt that they had witnessed a death and a rebirth which somehow promised them a blessed immortality. The seriousness with which the initiates took the mysteries can be judged by the fact that, of the hundreds of thousands of initiates over a millennium, none revealed the secret.

Most of the mystery religions attracted both men and women, although there seems to be some scholarly disagreement about the degree of feminine participation. The Eleusinian, which were the most famous and probably the most influential of the mysteries, were open to women, probably because these mysteries stemmed from agricultural rituals. The key element in all the mysteries was, for men, initiation, that is, death and rebirth. The presence of women initiates did not necessarily cause men to regard the mysteries as feminine, because the pattern of the mysteries was so intensely masculine.

The most masculine of the mysteries was the Mithraic, almost a pure religion of masculinity, a religion of soldiers who spread it throughout the Roman Empire. Women were not initiated, as far as can be determined.[57] Mithras was a young male god who eternally battled the forces of evil. Again, the secrets of his mystery were well kept, but many surviving sculptures show his killing of the bull, from whose blood grain and flowers first sprouted on the earth. Franz Cumont's reconstruction of this mystery may be too heavily influenced by Christianity,[58] but the mysteries in general have an obvious affinity to Christianity. Earlier this century, modernists such as Alfred Loisy, author of *Les Mystères païen et le mystère chrétien*, thought they had found the source of Christianity in Mithraism. At present, scholars tend to think that the mysteries of Mithras resembled Christianity closely because Mithraism borrowed from Christianity.[59] It is very likely that there is a generic resemblance and that the borrowings went both ways. The Church Fathers noticed the close resemblance and thought it was a diabolical ploy to lead the faithful astray. But the main reason that Mithraism resembled Christianity is that both were religions of masculinity, especially of the man as Savior. And the purpose of the ideology of masculinity is to teach men to save others, even at the cost of sacrificing themselves.

The ceremonies of the Easter vigil, and indeed of the whole Triduum, the three days that recount the passion, death, and resurrection of Christ, have a strong atmosphere of the mysteries, not only in their essential rites (although these are common in their general structure to all religions of death and rebirth), but in their accessory rituals. Early Christians saw Christianity as the fulfillment of the mystery and Christ as the true Hierophant, the one who reveals

the sacred and initiates those who come to him. The message is
clear: Christianity is the true mystery, the true initiation. It reveals
true manhood, the real and ultimate contest against evil, and the triumph and victory of which the Sol Invictus, Mithras, was but a
shadow. The church of the first millennium emphasized the mys-
tery-aspect of Christianity, and its message was comprehensible to
men, who forever seek to achieve an initiation that finally and in
reality makes them a new man.[60]

MASCULINE INITIATION AND LITERATURE

Attempting to write about masculinity and initiation in literature is
very much like undertaking a history of world literature. What it is
to be a man and the problems a man faces in trying to be masculine
are the themes of much of the writing of the world.[61] Heroic literature is concerned in a special way with the masculine, because the
pattern of masculine development is manifest in a dramatic way in
the literary figure of the hero, a model for men in his culture. In the
life of the hero, men see what it is to become a man, what type of
experiences they may expect, what achievements they must attain,
what qualities they must have, for the life of the hero follows the
development of masculinity that anthropologists and psychologists
have observed, including the initiations that a male must undergo to
become a man.[62] The hero leaves normal life to confront death and
returns to ordinary life to assume social responsibilities.

This pattern is cross-cultural: it is found in Andean folk-tales,[63]
in Babylonian epics, in Greek epics, in Anglo-Saxon poetry.[64] Since
the challenges each society faces are different, the hero's adventures
are different, but the purpose for those adventures is always the same.
In complex societies, such as the Greece of the Homeric age, a man
must undergo repeated initiations.

Homer

Themes of initiation dominate the *Odyssey*. The departure from the
normal, civilized world of childhood is often achieved by a journey

into dangerous lands. Odysseus's trials are initiatory: he must establish his identity as a man and as a hero not once, but by facing trials again and again. In doing so, he confronts man-eaters, who attack identity in a direct way by assimilating other bodies to their own. Homer describes how the cyclops Polyphemos kills Odysseus's men:

> *Then he cut them up limb by limb and got supper ready,*
> *and like a lion reared in the hills, without leaving anything,*
> *ate them, flesh and the marrowy bones alike.* (IX.291-293)[65]

The cyclops almost makes Odysseus a No Body indeed. In his pride at having escaped this threat to his physical identity, Odysseus cannot resist taunting the Cyclops by flaunting his name:

> *Cyclops, if any mortal man ever asks you who it was*
> *that inflicted upon your eye this shameful blinding,*
> *tell him that you were blinded by Odysseus, sacker of cities,*
> *Laertes is his father, and he makes his home in Ithaca.* (IX.502-505)

Odysseus's identity is so important to him that he brings disaster on himself by telling the cyclops his real name. The cyclops prays to Poseidon, his father, who destroys Odysseus's ship, ensuring that Odysseus returns home alone and only after great sorrow and delay.

In Scylla and Charybdis, Odysseus confronts two types of loss of identity. Scylla is the devouring monster; she seizes his men and "Right in her doorway she [eats] them up" (XII.256). Charybdis represents a slightly different threat, and a more dangerous one:

> *shining Charybdis sucks down the black water,*
> *For three times a day she flows it up, and three times she sucks it*
> *terribly down; may you not be there when she sucks down the water*
> *or not even the Earthshaker could rescue you out of that evil.*
>
> (XII.104-107)

Charybdis represents a type of engulfment that the sea in particular threatens. Homer sees the sea as even more dangerous than man-eating monsters, for it "is primal violence ever encroaching upon the gains of civilization."[66] For Odysseus, to drown would be ignominious, "an unheroic death altogether abhorrent to the Greeks, with no survivors to testify to the place of his going and with no tomb to mark his final resting."[67]

Odysseus is constantly tempted to retreat from the struggle to establish male identity into the safety of the feminine. David Gilmore notes that "the knight has mastered the most primitive of the demands of the pleasure principle—the temptation to drown in the arms of an omnipotent woman, to withdraw into a puerile cocoon of pleasure and safety. And in the *Odyssey*, the scene of the great decision is one in which water imagery abounds: murky grottos, dim pools, misty waterfalls."[68] The chief threat to Odysseus's manhood is Calypso:

> Calypso is oblivion. Her name suggests cover and concealment, or engulfing; she lives "in the midst of the sea"—the middle of nowhere, as Hermes almost remarks—and the whole struggle of the fifth book, indeed of the whole poem, is not to be engulfed by that sea. When the third great wave of Book v breaks over Odysseus' head, Homer's words are: *ton de mega kyma kalypsen*—"and the great wave engulfed him." If this wave had drowned him, it would have been a "vile death," surely, as Odysseus remarks at the beginning of the storm. Much better, he says, to have died where "the spears flew thickest" at Troy; then he would have had "recognition," *kleos*.[69]

The hero represents Everyman (at least every freeborn warrior), because all men in cultures of manhood, especially in warrior cultures, face the problem of establishing a male identity. By the example of heroes, men are constantly encouraged to resist "indolence, self-doubt, squeamishness, hesitancy, the impulse to withdraw or surrender, the 'sleepiness' of quietude (symbolized in Greek legend in death by drowning—a universal metaphor for returning to the womb)."[70] Threats of engulfment of the hero dominate the *Odyssey*, but he triumphs over them, returns home, and reestablishes his position in Ithacan society. Having escaped being eaten, Odysseus makes the suitors who have been devouring his substance eat death:

> *Now is the time for their dinner to be served the Achaians*

in the daylight, then follow with other entertainment,
  the dances and the lyre; for these things come at the end of feasting.
                                                          (XXI.428-430)

The hero by his deeds can hold off the forces of engulfment and preserve his identity as a man, remaining a model for those who also wish to become men.

The Hero

The hero is the one who is fully initiated into the mystery of masculinity. He leaves the ordinary world, and is separated from the feminine—the mother, the protection of society—and journeys out into an alien world of chaos to confront danger, monsters, and ultimately death itself. Having died, in some sense, the hero is reborn and attains a wisdom that comes only from suffering. He then can be reincorporated into the normal world that includes the feminine and become the king.

The hero embodies on an almost super-human scale what every male must endure. The hero at birth is "different from other men,"[71] just as males are different from women, set apart from the basic female pattern of the body, and just as boys realize they are different from their mothers and have a different destiny. The hero is not only different, he is too much for the institutions of ordinary life: "His endowments of strength, initiative and courage are too great to be contained easily."[72] The problems of both developing and controlling masculinity are familiar to all societies that cultivate an ideology of masculinity.

The hero leaves the familiar world to confront danger, whether it is human, monstrous, or divine. The boy must leave the safe, protective world of his mother to confront the dangers of life, to seek his fortune in a hostile world, to journey afar to meet the strange and alien, or to protect his people in the ultimate test of masculinity: war. A warrior must be able both to give and to receive pain, as Odysseus's name shows. The root of the name *Odysseus* is the verb *odyssathia*, which means "to cause pain (*odyne*), and to be willing to do so." [73]

The hero faces death; indeed he descends into death, and only after this descent and his rebirth can he become the king, because "the primary source of a king's power is his knowledge, which is based on experience of a particular kind, that is, the confrontation with, and survival of, death."[74] For the hero this is not simply surviving his enemies; he "enters the jaws of death, and the jaws close."[75]

The figure of the hero is closely allied to that of the warrior, and both have a dangerous element that is implicit in masculinity. The *furor heroicus* transforms him into something non-human. Achilles is scarcely human in battle: he may be a god or he may be a monster, but he is not just a man. Images of fire surround him, because in the heat of battle he becomes a primordial force, divine, destroying.[76] The Irish hero CuChulain becomes, "horrible, many-shaped and unrecognizable."[77] Like Grendel, Beowulf is *gebolgen*, swollen larger than life[78] and is monstrous, *aglaeca*[79]; indeed Grendel is almost a monstrous double of Beowulf.[80] These are not just literary devices. The transformations of man in war are known in every culture. In New Guinea, Gilbert Lewis was told of "men who went into a trance" in war; they were "dangerous, unreliable, deaf to calls or appeals."[81] The ordinary man, even apart from battle, is often dangerous to his society, because the forces set loose by the ideology of masculinity may destroy the society. Aggression may rage unchecked, and may provoke attack from foreign powers too strong to resist, or provoke internal wars that destroy the commonwealth. David Gilmore is too sanguine in his description of the ideology of masculinity: the chroniclers of civil wars, from those that destroyed the Roman Republic to those that brought down the Icelandic Commonwealth in the thirteenth century (not to mention more recent horrors), have testified to the destructiveness of aggression, even when it exists within the "normal" range that is deliberately cultivated in a society.

Despite all its problems and tendencies to self-destruction, masculinity is essential to the survival of any society that faces challenges. Men must be warned against the dangerous attractions of the safe, feminine world, so that they will accept the task of being masculine. Males must be trained to struggle, suffer, and die so that the life of the community can go on. This self-sacrifice is a form of self-transcendence that has captured the imagination of almost all cultures. The gods at their noblest reflect something of the glory of the hero. Monotheistic religions emerged from societies that had ideologies of masculinity, and this ideology served as a means of explaining what God was and what he wanted men to be. The Jews lived in a corner of the world, the Middle East, that has for millennia been the scene of conflict. They had to develop an ideology of masculinity to survive, and that ideology can be found in what Christians call the Old Testament. It is to this text, as an anthropological and literary source, that I shall now turn.

4

God and Man in Judaism: Fathers and the Father-God

MASCULINITY IS A CENTRAL CONCERN of the Old Testament. God is masculine, and the response he calls for entails special responsibilities for men. The position of the male is a problem and receives attention in the Old Testament for the same reason that it is a primary concern of pagan literature: masculinity is a difficult achievement. Even when achieved, masculinity contains tensions that may destroy the very social peace that men are called to protect. Though masculinity is always threatened by femininity, men cannot simply abandon all contact with women; they must have a fruitful union with women. Yet that union itself is a chronic source of problems for men.

Creation and procreation were intimately linked in the Hebrew mind, and flaws in the locus of procreation, the relationship of man and woman, had dire consequences for the relationship of mankind and God. From the very beginning, trouble arose for Israel from the relationship of man and woman, and that trouble disrupted the harmony between the creator and the creature. The writers of the historical and sapiential books traced the course of this disharmony in the history of the Jewish people, warning men to avoid the pitfalls that had caused the nation to stumble in the past.

The Masculinity of God and Man

Judaism was not concerned with things in themselves, but with the knowledge of things in their actions. *By their fruits you shall know them* was the operative principle for a Jew; being was manifested in action, and existence apart from its action could not be known, or at least was of little interest. This applied to both God and man. What is man? What is God? To answer those questions, Jews looked at the characteristic actions of each.

Various translators of Scripture and revisers of liturgies have tried to excise references to God as masculine or balance them with feminine references. But these translators confuse maleness and masculinity, a crucial distinction of which the Scriptures are well aware. Maleness is a bodily given, but God does not have a body; maleness is sexual, but Yahweh is not a sexual being. As Gerhard van Rad says, "any thought of sex in him, or of his acting in creation by means of sex, was completely alien to Israel."[1]

There is indeed a distinctively male god prominent in the Hebrew Scriptures: his name is Ba'al. He was the principle of male fertility, and in his name the sacred male prostitutes were put into the pagan temples. The name Ba'al, "Lord," seems to have had connotations of sexual mastery, and sexuality is absolutely excluded from Yahweh and his worship. Sexuality is good, but it is a created reality, not a divine one: "The distinction between the sexes is a *creation* by God since there is no such distinction on the divine level; the polarity of the sexes belongs to the created order and not to God."[2] God did not create by means of sexuality, but by his Word.[3]

God is always masculine in the Scriptures[4] for two main reasons, or rather one that is known in the other. He transcends creation: it is not part of him, nor did it come out of him—he spoke, and it was. God is, therefore, utterly *separate* from creation; that is, he is holy. The holy is a masculine category. To be holy is to be separated, set apart from common or profane use. The English *holy* comes from a root meaning pure, sound, or uncontaminated, but this moral connotation is not the precise meaning of the original word. As Rudolph Otto points out, the holy is the wholly other, the numinous, the being which transcends all categories, the *mysterium tremendens et fascinans* that provokes awe, fear, and wonder.[5] The Hebrew *kaddosh* means separated, and the Pharisee was so called because he kept himself apart from all that was unclean and therefore took his name from the Aramaic *perisha*, "separated." Though God transcends his creation, he loves it and is involved with it. A transcendent God is a masculine God, a feminine or bisexual God is an immanent God, one who is part of creation or the creation is part of him-her. Such an immanent deity is not holy (separate), and does not demand holiness, that is, separation from the standards of the natural world. A god who was one with creation would not be Yahweh.

The Hebrews came to know the nature of God through his actions. And the God who acts, acts by separating: "It is the biblical God who inaugurates separation at the beginning of creation. He creates a division which is also a mark of his presence."[6] Separation, as we have seen, is a leitmotif of the masculine, its identifying characteristic. Both maleness and masculinity are created by separation. If God's actions establish unity, they do so first by creating a division, and therefore God is masculine in his actions and in his nature. Even scriptural references to God that seem to be feminine emphasize the final unity at which God aims, a unity that follows masculine actions of separation. A reunion with the feminine is the sign of a completed masculinity, although in the Old Testament the nature of this union is not as fully articulated as it becomes in the Trinitarian spirituality of the New Testament.

God does not leave the universe an undifferentiated chaos; he as creator separates light from darkness, the waters above the earth from the waters below the earth. He creates the sun and moon and stars to separate time into discrete intervals. He creates mankind male and female, and creates Eve by separating her from Adam. For this reason, "a man leaves his mother and father, and the two become one flesh" the narrator explains. In marriage man imitates God by following the pattern first of separation and then union. The separation is for the sake of the union, but the action of separation dominates in the man. The man in this famous passage, not the woman, is the one who leaves his family. Whether Jewish families were indeed matrilocal is not known; there is little evidence for it in the Scriptures. But Scripture does not describe a sociological reality (which partner leaves the family to join the family of the other partner), but a characteristic action of the man, separation, which reflects the divine pattern of action. Leo Strauss summarizes the theme of separation at the beginning of Genesis: "Creation is the making of separated things, of things or groups of things that are separated from each other, which are distinguished from each other, which are distinguishable, which are discernible."[7] The "sequence of creation in the first chapter of the Bible can be stated as follows: from the principle of separation, light; via something which separates, heaven; to something which is separated, earth and sea; to things which are productive of separated things, trees, for example; then things which can separate themselves from their places, heavenly bodies; then things which can separate themselves from their courses, brutes; and finally a being which can separate itself from its way, the right way."[8] The separation of the creature from God contains within it the potentiality for another type of separation, the rebellion against God: that which is not God can reject God.

To describe God as feminine or as an equal mixture of masculine and feminine undermines his identity in Israelite monotheism. It was the pagan world that fused the gods and nature. Israel, especially under the tutelage of the prophets, insisted they were separate. Every time Israel spoke of God as *he* (and Hebrew verbs express gender), Israel was reminded that God was the totally other, the Holy One. The feminine, on the other hand, is a principle of union or communion.

Only a masculine God can love his creature with the type of love that Yahweh shows. This God loves freely; he is under no necessity to love. He chooses Israel freely, he elects this one people from all the peoples of the world and separates them from the nations so that he can show his love for them. And his law obliges them to be a separate people: "I am the Lord your God, who separated you from the peoples. You shall therefore make a distinction between the clean beast and the unclean. . . . You shall be holy to me, for I the Lord am holy, and have separated you from the peoples, and you should be mine" (Lev. 20:25-26). God's love is undeserved; it is sheer grace. An immanent God is not free, nor is it capable of love for the other, since finally there is no other: all is God. A masculine God is both fully transcendent and fully immanent *through love*. Such an immanence through love is possible only to a being who is transcendent and separate from creation, that is, masculine. The object of God's love is feminine, the Virgin Daughter Zion and the Church, although this femininity reflects, as we shall see, something in God himself.

MAN, WOMAN, AND PATRIARCHY

Israel developed its anthropology not as a speculative exercise but in its attempts to understand its history and its relationship to the world. This understanding of human nature was based on reflection on how man acts in history, and in particular on how Israelite man had acted. Israelite history is reflected in protology, the story of origins. The writers of Genesis had a great interest in the relationship of man and woman at the beginning because the relationship of man and woman has been important throughout the history of the Jewish people. They looked back from the time of the Exile at the history of Israel, and traced the roots of the punishment of the Exile to a flaw in the relationship of man and woman. This flaw was projected back to the very beginning of history. The disobedience of Eve and Adam in the garden was repeated by the women and men of Israel at key moments in their history: the Exile from the Garden was a result of the same failures that led to the Exile from the Promised Land.

In Genesis we see that man and woman are both important in the divine plan. Woman is not an afterthought: she is made from the man, and expresses something in him, although he remains different from her. What is the nature of unfallen man? He works, even in Eden. He is a co-creator with God, and the opinions of some platonizing Church Fathers notwithstanding, man and woman were obviously meant to procreate. But even the relationship of unfallen man and woman has the potential for problems. The distinction of man and woman is good, as everything created by God is, but provides an opportunity for the serpent to foment rebellion. In this respect, the distinction of the sexes is like the distinction between God and man: separation can become a source of rebellion and sin. Perhaps because she is the last element in creation to be separated, Eve is more susceptible to the serpent than Adam. In the moment they rebel, Adam and Eve know the distinction between good and evil and recognize their nakedness before God and the world. What experiences of Jewish history lead the author to articulate this proto-type of the dynamic between man and woman?

The main books of the Old Testament took their canonical form in the midst of the Exile, either just before or just after Israel had experienced a forced separation from the Promised Land. Israel's confidence in God underwent a trial because of its near extinction as a nation. Was God faithful? God had promised to be with Israel; why had he deserted his people and let them be made captive? The Babylonian captivity must, the Israelites reasoned, be the result of some grievous failing on the part of the people, who had not kept their part of the covenant. What was the failure and what were the roots of that failure? Could Israel avoid such sin in the future, and never again go into exile?

In Nehemiah the repatriated exiles have been contaminated with paganism because they have married pagan women "of Ashdod, Ammon, and Moab" (Neh. 13:23) who import the worship of idols into Israel. Idolatry, failure to worship Yahweh as God, replacing him with other gods, was the sin for which Israel was punished in the first place. Men failed to keep themselves free from such sin and were punished with exile. And they failed because they were led astray by their wives. Uxoriousness was a vice that could lead to calamity. Pagan wives led their Israelite husbands astray, and the husbands, besotted by love for their wives, were weak, refusing to discipline their families. Even Solomon was led astray: "Did not Solomon king of Israel sin on account of such women? Among the many nations there was no king like him, and he was beloved by his God, and God made him king over all Israel; nevertheless foreign women made even him to sin" (Neh. 13:26).

Eve listened to the tempter and was deceived; Adam let himself by ruled by Eve instead of rebuking her for her disobedience. He should have listened to God, but instead obeyed his wife. This pattern, according to the various Old Testament authors, was repeated several times in Israel's history. Solomon's sexual prowess and interest in women led to the introduction of paganism and idolatry, and finally to the punishment of the Exile. The historical books clearly connect David's sin with Bathsheba and Absalom's rebellion, Solomon's marriage to foreign wives, his draining of the wealth of the kingdom in an erotic display of luxury, the consequent dissatisfaction and division of the Kingdom, and the extinction of the northern and southern kingdoms. Susanne Heine summarizes: "The queens of Israel brought with them the religious cults with which they were familiar, so that Yahweh, the God of Israel, became one among many gods and indeed goddesses. The prophetic history writing sees this apostasy to the alien idols as the occasion for punitive judgment by Yahweh, which finally leads to the destruction of the kingdom and the dispersion of the people."[9] Both men and women sinned and apostatized, but their roles in the apostasy differed.

The authors of the Old Testament recognize the dynamics of masculinity, but they do not see the primary danger as the tendency of men to nihilism once they have broken free of the maternal world. Rather, the chief danger is the failure of men to maintain their relationship to God because of a disordered love for women, a love that leads men to follow the directions of women rather than the laws of God. A man needs a woman to make him a patriarch, as Adam needed Eve, but the closeness of communion with the wife, bone of his bone, flesh of his flesh, exposes him to the danger of feminization, to the loss of the separation that makes him a man, a separation necessary for the free obedience that man owes God as his creator. Patriarchy, therefore, is a danger to masculinity. Though a great achievement of the Israelites, patriarchy, like all male achievements, contained tensions that threatened to destroy it.

Patriarchy is not simply an affirmation of masculinity; it is not "a synonym for male dominance or for a system in which male traits are valued over female ones."[10] Still less is it simply a synonym for exploitation and domination, though that is the current feminist usage. Patriarchy is a system in which fathers care for their families and find their emotional centers in their offspring. In ancient Israel, "the image of father was not primarily one of authority and power, but one of adoptive love, covenant bonding, tenderness, and compassion."[11] Patriarchy, we can easily forget, was and is a great achievement in the face of the male tendency to promiscuity and alienation from children and the women who bear them. As John W. Miller shows in *Biblical Faith and Fathering: Why We Call God "Father,"* patriarchy was not a universal ideal in the cultures surrounding Israel. Miller asserts that biblical patriarchy, far from a curse, is one of the greatest achievements of any religion.

Miller bases his conclusions on his analysis of human nature, on the emphasis on fatherhood in the Bible, and most of all on the processes of psychological development and maturation in the child. First of all, there is the indisputable fact that "fathers, biologically speaking, are marginal to the reproductive process."[12] If fathers are to play a role in the family, "culture must intervene on behalf of fathers if they are to be equally (and as significantly) involved."[13] The culture that has done this with the greatest consistency and success is that of the Jewish. The Jews of antiquity did not exist in a world dominated by patriarchal myths. Certainly the religions of the pagans were not patriarchal. Miller notes that in Near Eastern myths the father-god's "marginality, cruelty, incompetence, or powerlessness, more often than not, poses dilemmas to which mother, son or daughter deities must respond by defending themselves or by taking action to uphold the universe in their stead."[14] Only in the Hebrew Scriptures do we find an all-powerful and all-good Father-God.

The patriarchs reflected the fatherhood of God, although very imperfectly. The God of the Hebrews was not like the irresponsible masculine gods of the surrounding pagan cultures,[15] because he did not abandon the children he begot, but cared for them. The patriarchs followed the example of God, or the idea of God was influenced by the experience of patriarchy. Their culture taught Jewish men that they should not be simply male animals, aggressive, assertive, and violent, but fathers, whose aggressiveness would be transformed by responsibility and who would manifest a gentleness and a concern for children, an expression of a completed masculinity that has reunited with the feminine world of the family, while still maintaining the separation necessary to exercise authority. Because the family is at the very heart of the Jewish way of life, sexual ethics is a central concern of the Hebrew Scriptures. The principal rituals of the Jews, circumcision, the redemption of the firstborn son, and the Passover meal, all express the importance of fathers in the culture. The wisdom literature repeatedly admonishes fathers to be the teachers of their children. Indeed, this paternal teaching role gave rise to the corpus of Scripture itself. Feminists are correct in their characterization of the Old Testament as inescapably patriarchal. The Hebrew Scriptures were written by fathers to teach men to imitate the Father in heaven.

ABRAHAM AND MOSES

In the work of forming Israel, God acts in a masculine way. He first separates Abraham from his ancestral homeland. God's first words to him are "Go from your country and your kindred and your father's house" (Gen. 12:1). God makes a covenant with Abraham that involves cutting animals in two and separating the halves of the carcass (Gen. 15:13); symbols of the divine presence pass between these pieces (Gen. 15:17). The sign of the covenant will be circumcision (Gen. 17:11), the separation of a piece of flesh from the body.

Abraham is a war leader, and protects those close to him, rescuing Lot from the kings who raided Sodom (Gen. 14:16). But his relationships with women cause him trouble. He fears for his safety in Egypt—the beauty of his wife might tempt the Egyptians to kill him and take her—and he pretends they are brother and sister. As a consequence, "the woman was taken into Pharaoh's house" (Gen. 12:15). Pharaoh's standards are higher than Abraham's, and when he realizes that the evils he suffers have come upon him because he has taken another man's wife, he sends Abraham and Sarah away. Abraham later tries to deceive Abimelech in the same way (Gen. 20:2).

God promises Abraham that his descendents shall be as number-less as the stars (Gen. 15:5), but Abraham heeds Sarah rather than the Lord. She complains that "the Lord has prevented me from bearing children," and she instructs him to "go into my maid; it may be that I shall obtain children from her." (Gen. 16:2). When Abraham obeys Sarah and begets a child by the slave Hagar, trouble starts immedi-ately. When Hagar conceived, "she looked with contempt on her mistress" (Gen. 16:4). Ironically, Sarah blames Abraham: "May the wrong done to me be on you! I gave my maid to your embrace, and when she saw she had conceived she looked on me with contempt. May the Lord judge between you and me!"(Gen. 16:5). Abraham again gives in to Sarah: "Your maid is in your power; do to her as you please." It pleases Sarah to maltreat Hagar, who flees, and has to be rescued by an angel of the Lord.

The sacrifice of Isaac, the heir and carrier of God's promise, is at the heart of Abraham's mysterious relationship to God.[16] Abraham, because he was a patriarch, fell prey to uxoriousness. He had to re-deem himself and demonstrate his obedience by his willingness to sacrifice the child whom he loved with a mother's tenderness. Abraham's sacrifice makes explicit in an extreme form what all fa-thers must be willing to do: encourage (if not force) their sons to separate from the safe world of the mother and assume the sacrificial male role. Without the achievement of sacrificial masculinity, the son remains stuck in the profane world. In his sacrifice, he is re-moved from the profane world and enters the sacred world, like the sacrificial animals that were slain and burned to remove them from this world into the divine world. The ultimate significance of this sacrifice becomes clear only in the Crucifixion. The Father is willing to separate the Son from himself, so that the Son may taste death for all.

In Exodus, God continues to act in a masculine way, making a distinction between Israel and Egypt in the plagues. What harms the Egyptians does no harm to his own people. The hail does not kill the Israelite's cattle, the darkness does not envelop the land of Goshen, and most of all, only the first born of the Egyptians die. When the angel of death sees the blood of the sacrificed lamb on the doorpost, he also makes a distinction between Egyptian and Jew. The Red Sea parts for Israel, but clogs the wheels of Pharaoh's army and drowns his host. Moses sees that God treats Israel in a unique way, and tells God that "we are distinct, I and thy people, from all other people that are upon the face of the earth" (Exod. 33:16). This distinction must be preserved at all costs, and God instructs Moses to command the Israelites to drive out the pagan nations from the Promised Land, "lest . . . you take of their daughters for your sons, and their daughters play the harlot after their gods and make your sons play the harlot after their gods" (Exod. 34:16).

In Moses we see the role of protector exercised though mediation and substitution. When Israel sins, Moses repeatedly pleads with God to spare them and establishes the institutions of the sacrifices and the scapegoat. The sacrificers, the priests, are male, but the sacrifices too, if they are for the sins of the high priest or leaders of the community, must also be male, as must be the lamb of the Passover. The scapegoat bears the sins of the people and is driven into the wilderness.

DAVID

David is the ideal of Israelite manhood, a man after God's own heart. He is a man of spirit, of *thymos*, and fits Plato's portrait of the spirited man. His nature is passionate, impetuous, and affectionate, in his dealings with both God and man, not to mention woman. David loves Jonathan, for instance, with a love surpassing that of woman. The Hebrew Scriptures recognize a male eros, a real desire for union that is distinct from homosexual desire (which the Scriptures condemn). This is the eros of comradeship in suffering, especially in war. This love is physical because the Hebrews know of no purely spiritual action of the human being, who is both body and soul. Jonathan and David embrace, and even exchange clothes. Their friendship is so close as to cause talk, and allegations of homosexuality may be implied in Saul's insults ("You have chosen the son of Jesse to your shame, and to the shame of your mother's nakedness" [1

Sam. 20:30]). Saul does not say this because he believes it has occurred, but because it is the worse possible thing he can say about
David.

David is passionate and physical even in his relationship to God.
The Psalms are full of cries that his soul and body yearn for the Lord.
David displays his exuberant masculinity in his dance before the ark,
when it is brought into Jerusalem. Micael implies in her remarks
that, in his "leaping and dancing" (2 Sam. 6:16), David inadvertently
exposed himself: "How the king of Israel honored himself today, un-
covering himself today before the eyes of his servants' maids, as one
of the vulgar fellows shamelessly uncovers himself!" (1 Sam. 6:20).
David rebukes her, and the narrator shows that God concurs with
David's rebuke by remarking that Micael was childless after her de-
spising of David's virility: "And Micael the daughter of Saul had no
child to the day of her death" (1 Sam. 6:23).

David's life follows the pattern of masculinity, and indeed that is
why David is a type of the Messiah and why so many of the Psalms
can be understood as spoken by the Messiah.[17] David must leave his
ordinary life because of Saul's anger and becomes a scapegoat wandering in the wilderness, an outlaw who confronts death at every
turn: "How many are my foes!" (Ps. 3:1). Even God forgets him:
"How long wilt thou hide thy face from me? (Ps. 13:1), "My God, my
God, why hast thou forsaken me?" (Ps. 22:1) Pursued by Saul, David
constantly faces death: "The cords of Sheol entangled me, the snares
of death confronted me" (Ps. 18:5). But David is delivered from
death as if by a resurrection: "O Lord, thou hast brought up my soul
from Sheol, restored me to life from among those gone down to the
Pit" (Ps. 30:3). David attains the wisdom of compassion, and is able
to become the king, the father of his people.

David's personality is attractive because he is erotic and
affectionate, although these good qualities lead him astray. David
was the model king and model of Israelite manhood; but who is the
true man, who plays the masculine role more fully in the matter of
Bathsheba, David or Uriah, the Hittite, the non-Jew?: "In the spring
of the year, the time when kings go forth to battle" (2 Sam. 11:1),

David sent his army off to war, but he stayed at home lounging on a rooftop, from which he saw Bathsheba performing her Mikvah, the ceremonial bath at the end of menstruation just before ovulation, when a woman is at the peak of her fertility and most likely to conceive. The Law enjoined continence during menstruation, and then had the wife cleanse herself so that she would be most attractive to her husband just at the time she was most likely to conceive. David desires her, and as masterful kings will, has her. When she becomes pregnant, he tries to get Uriah to sleep with her so the child will be mistaken for Uriah's. Uriah is off fighting, and comes back to his king as commanded. But after the feast he does not return home. When David asks why, Uriah replies that he will not take his ease at home while his men are suffering in the field: "Shall I then go to my house, to eat and to drink, and to lie with my wife?" (2 Sam. 11:11). Uriah, a pagan, is nobler than David and feels the demands of comradeship, while David stays in ease and safety. Although celibacy did not receive its full due until Christian times, it is not true that celibacy, at least temporary celibacy, was condemned by Judaism. Abstention from sexual relations was required in certain ritual contexts and was also a demand of warfare. In practical terms, an army in the field had to be celibate; but in Uriah's remarks we can also see an appreciation of the value of comradeship, which has demands that override those of marriage. David's sexual desires, on the other hand, lead him astray and bring civil war upon Israel.

David passes on his strong sexual desires to his children, and endless trouble results. David's children are all too like their father. Amnon desires his half-sister Tamar and rapes her. He then refuses to marry her and drives her away. Yet David does not punish Amnon because of his affection for him. Absalom bides his time, as David bided his time with Joab and Zeruiah, and at last kills his half-brother to avenge his sister. Again, David lets himself be ruled by his affections, permits Absalom to return from exile, and then allows him to plot against the kingdom. Even before the decisive battle, David's heart is still with Absalom, and he gives orders to spare the boy. After the victory and Absalom's death, David can only mourn until Joab warns him that his grief is costing him his kingdom.

THE PARADOXES OF MASCULINITY

The writers of the Old Testament were aware of the paradoxes of masculinity. The male had to undergo a lonely journey away from home, into the desert and into death, so that he could find God. The detachment from ordinary family life was dangerous. A man had to be firmly attached to a family and had to expend all his energies in protecting and providing for his wife and children. Yet this emotional closeness created a danger that he would listen to his wife and children and neglect duties to God. Not tyranny, but uxoriousness, is the chief danger of patriarchy. As a father he had to love his children, but he had to be willing to sacrifice them. A father's role is to separate his children from the safe maternal world and send them off to face the dangers of life. As an Israelite, a father had the additional burden that he may have had to sacrifice his love for his children to his greater duty to God. Then, as now, it was not easy to be a man.

5

God and Man in Early Christianity: Sons in the Son

C HRISTIANITY WAS THE FULFILLMENT OF JUDAISM. The masculinity and the patriarchy that Judaism cultivated were
fulfilled in the revelation of a tri-personal God who was
both Father and Son. All human beings, male and female, were invited to share in the inner life of God, to receive the Spirit and to be
conformed to the Son. The early Church knew that the vocation of
the Christian was essentially masculine. Later, the white martyrdom
of the monk replaced the red martyrdom of the early Church. Femininity also received a new appraisal, as the godhead itself was shown
to be a communion of persons. The unity and communion of all
men, and indeed of all creation, is accomplished by the divine Spirit
himself. Only a few warning signs in the early Church, especially in
the West, gave any indication that masculinity would one day find
itself at odds with Christianity.

MASCULINITY IN THE NEW TESTAMENT

The God and Father of Jesus Christ is the same God as the God of
Abraham, Isaac, and Jacob. Although gnosticism has enjoyed a rebirth in the attempts to oppose an androgynous Jesus to the patriarchal Jehovah, such an interpretation must be ruled out at the start.

From the very beginning, Christianity distinguished itself from Gnosticism: the God of the Old Testament is not the devil of the New Testament. The Jesus who walked the roads of Galilee is the same person as the risen Lord and Christ. His male body is risen from the dead; the masculinity of the Son reveals the Father.

The revelation of the trinitarian life of God maintains the masculinity of each divine person in relation to creation. That is, in relation to creation, each person is creator, redeemer, and sanctifier. In relationship to creation, therefore, each person is masculine, as Yahweh was in the Hebrew Scriptures. Only God's self-revelation in the Scriptures gives us access to an understanding of his inner life, and the Scriptures constantly characterize the intra-Trinitarian relationship of God as masculine. The generation of the Son by the Father has the created analogue of parenthood. Although the mother is more obviously a parent than the father, the First Person nonetheless is called Father by the only one who truly knows him, Jesus. The First Person is Father, indeed Father specifies what he is, because he eternally begets the Son. Paul rejects the idea that the Father is a religious projection of patriarchal social structures. The reverse is true. The Father is, in terms reminiscent of Platonic archetypes, the model, and created fatherhood is the image: "Blessed be the Father of our Lord Jesus Christ, from whom all fatherhood on earth takes its name." Human masculinity, whose purpose is the protection and provision of the community, finds its fulfillment in the one who is Lord because he is sacrifice and savior. In their conformity to the Son, all Christians, male and female, become sons of God, and are therefore called to be masculine. In his relationship to the creation, the Third Person is also consistently characterized as masculine, and in the new creation he is the Spirit of sonship, as he is within the Trinity. Yet his intra-trinitarian function of uniting the Father and Son explains the Spirit's association with femininity as reflected in the Church's unity. Mary stands as a sign of that unity.

The Masculinity of the Father and the Son

Thomas Aquinas touches on the question of why the First Person is called *Father* rather than simply a gender-free *Begetter*. Rather than focusing on the paternal authority of the Father, Aquinas seems to imply that begetting, the proper action of a father, is a single act, while the role of the mother is a process.[1] The Father is eternally not the Son, the Son is eternally not the Father. There was never a time when the Son was not; therefore there was never a time when the Son was part of the Father. This eternal and real distinction of the persons creates, as it were, a space in the Trinity. The Son became incarnate because creation is analogous to begetting. The incarnate Son, Jesus Christ, is an icon of the Father, his perfect image. The image does not consist in a corporeal resemblance, since God does not have a body, but rather in the resemblance of their modes of action. The Son does only what he sees the Father doing; he does nothing of himself, but imitates his Father in all things. Jesus is therefore the perfect Son, differing in no way from his Father, although not the same as his Father. The Son, having become incarnate, can take the sinful creation and return it to the Father. Sin is an emptiness and a separation from God; since there is already a separation within God, the separation of sin can be inserted into the already existent separation of the Father and the Son, a space which is filled with the Holy Spirit. In the return of the creation to the Father, when God will become all in all, the emptiness of sin is replaced by fullness, the pleroma.

Since the characteristic actions of God in the Old Testament involve separation, we should expect to see the same mode of action in Jesus. Jesus enjoys a unique freedom, for unlike all other human beings, he freely chose to enter life, as he freely chose to leave it. He was born not of the will of man, but of God; that is, he was virginally conceived. Born of a woman, from childhood he knew he must leave her to follow his Father. When he is lost in the temple, and Mary expresses her distress, he answers that he must be about his Father's business. At the beginning of his public life, he leaves his family, insisting that those who do the will of his Father are his brother and sister and mother.

Jesus, too, works by separating. He introduces a new principle of separation: no longer observance of the Law, but faith in him. Thus,

Jesus exercises the divine prerogative of election. He chooses the twelve from all those he knows and teaches them, although they do not understand his mission until after Pentecost. By his own account, Jesus comes not to bring peace, but a sword. His presence provokes conflict, even when he is an infant: Herod destroys all the male children of Bethlehem in an attempt to destroy the rival king. Jesus does nothing to avert a growing conflict with the Jewish authorities and the Pharisees and Sadducees and often speaks harshly to them: "Brood of vipers, fit for hell." They accuse him of being possessed by demons, and of being a Samaritan, an apostate who mixes Judaism and paganism.

It is a misunderstanding to see Jesus and the God he manifests as masculine simply because they are powerful and authoritative. While God and Jesus have the right to exercise naked authority and demand obedience from creatures, they do not. In the Old Testament, God is shown as a lover and husband, stung by the infidelities of Israel. The prophet Hosea takes a whore as a wife, symbolically enacting the relationship of Yahweh and Israel. God's heart is somehow wounded by the failure of Israel to respond to his love. In the New Testament, Jesus has no wife because his spouse is the Church, redeemed humanity.[2] His authority over the Church is like that of a husband over his wife. Paul assumes the sacrificial nature of masculinity in the passage (Eph. 5:21-31) that has so troubled feminists. He commands husbands to love their wives, as Christ loved the Church, *laying down his life for her*. The husband has an obligation to imitate the divine Bridegroom, who sacrifices his life for his Spouse. The divine Bridegroom fulfills and perfects the created reality of masculinity, which is characterized by self-sacrifice unto death for the sake of others.[3] The wife's obedience to her husband has the same basis as the Church's obedience to her Savior. The Church obeys Christ, not from slavish fear or a sense of duty, but from overwhelming gratitude for what he has done for her. The Bridegroom has given his utmost for his Bride, and she in turn obeys him and seeks, from a grateful love that knows no bounds, to imitate his boundless self-giving. As Karl Barth correctly observes, the husband who is only human cannot be his wife's savior in this full sense.[4] But what Barth does not see is that the husband, by reason of his masculinity, is also called to be a savior in the realm of created realities. He is to be ready to sacrifice his life, whether in work or in death in battle, for his wife. Her obedience to him is not that of a slave, but that of a grateful equal. Yet she has no corresponding obligation to sacrifice herself for him: Her sacrifice is for her children. She obeys her husband because she knows that he always has her best interests at heart, that he is willing, without drama, as part of the normal course of life, to die for her at any moment.

Of course, human sinfulness obscures this pattern, but in general it is present to a surprising degree. As we have seen, men fill the dangerous occupations of American society and have fought in numerous wars to protect their families. As Gilmore explains the essence of masculinity, "men nurture their societies by shedding their blood, their sweat, and their semen, by bringing home food for both child and mother, by producing children, and by dying if necessary in faraway places to provide a safe haven for their people."[5] As savior, Jesus both follows the pattern of masculinity and surpasses it by fulfilling it.

Feminists have been troubled by Jesus's choice of men as his closest friends, especially in light of his disregard for the Jewish restrictions on contact with women. He spoke to the Samaritan woman, who was triply despised, being a woman, a Samaritan, and a sinner. He praised the faith of the woman with the flow of blood who touched him in the belief he would make her well. She was ritually unclean, and made him unclean by touching him, but he likewise disregarded the laws of uncleanness. He spoke intimately with Mary, sister of the famously busy Martha. Nevertheless, he chose men as his closest companions, the twelve, for two reasons. First, they were to be sent as he was sent by the Father and would meet similar fates. To be called to be an apostle, "one sent," was to be called to be a martyr, as Jesus made clear to Peter. His injunction (John 21:15-19) to feed his lambs (and the authority that flows from it) was closely joined to the prophecy that Peter would be martyred. The apostolic office, and the presbyterial office that flows from it, is closely allied to martyrdom. The man who offers the sacrifice on the altar in an unbloody manner must also be ready to sacrifice his life in a bloody fashion. Indeed, early bishops were usually martyrs. Jesus wished to spare women that burden and show men the true nature of the sacrificial vocation of masculinity.

But within the inner life of Jesus there is a second reason that he chose male companions, fishermen with hot tempers, zealots ready to fight with the Roman army. While his universal motives in his passion and death are stressed by theologians, his immediate human motives are not well explored. There is a medieval poem that portrays a dialogue between Jesus on the cross and Mary, in which he tells her that he dies to save her from everlasting death and hell. Hence, his love for those he knew in his earthly life was also a motive for his obedience to his Father, to save all humanity, and especially those he loved, from death. The apostles are the comrades of Jesus; they were the small group for whom he was prepared to die. When Peter tries to dissuade him from the passion, Jesus turns and looks at his disciples before rebuking Peter. The evangelists recount this glance because it is the fate of the disciples, their own spiritual doom, from which Jesus must rescue them, that was a principal human motivation for his decision to die as savior.

Jesus's death overshadows the Last Supper. Before his death, he wished to leave his closest friends with a memorial of him. During the words of institution of the Eucharist, his glance first falls on the twelve—*for you*—before it goes out to all humanity, the many. His human love for his disciples, a love that finds its closest analogue in military comradeship, was the immediate motivation for the Eucharist and passion. In the Eucharist, if Jesus had simply wished to give his body to them, a single consecration of the bread would have sufficed. It is in this way that women give their bodies to their children. But instead, Jesus consecrated the bread and wine separately, suggesting that they would soon be separated in his sacrifice. The body is specified as the body "given for you," the blood as the blood "poured out for you."

Jesus nurtures his disciples by his death, in the fashion in which Gilmore describes men nurturing, achieving what women attain through pregnancy, childbirth, and lactation.[6] Therefore, incipiently in Scripture and in a full-blown way in medieval devotion, Jesus was described as Mother. He achieves in a masculine way what women achieve in their feminine way. The Church Fathers saw the Church as born from the side of Jesus, as Eve was born from the side of Adam. Later devotions presented the nurturing that Jesus provided in the Eucharist as the equivalent of nursing. Jesus, because he is a man, can achieve the self-giving that women achieve in pregnancy, childbirth, and lactation only in a masculine fashion, that is, through a bloody death.

This dimension of Jesus's work of redemption has led to claims that he is androgynous, embodying both masculine and feminine characteristics. But nurturing is not opposed to masculinity. One can confront pain in two ways: by desensitizing oneself to it, or by courageously accepting the fullness of pain. Although many men understandably seek to limit their pain by desensitizing themselves, their attitude is a distortion of masculinity, not an intrinsic part of it. Jesus was willing to accept pain without any attempt to desensitize himself. He chose the twelve, knowing that one was to betray him, and felt the pain of the betrayal—*Do you betray the Son of Man with a kiss?* He loved the people to whom he had been sent, weeping over the Jerusalem that rejected him, because he knew that this rejection would call down God's wrath on the city and lead to a destruction and exile more final than that of the Babylonian captivity. He blessed the children and felt deep anguish at Lazarus's death. Even as he was led to his death, he told the women of Jerusalem who wept for him to weep instead for themselves and their children. On the cross, he refused the drug that was traditionally offered to criminals to dull their pain. He wanted to taste the pain of human life and death to the full; he chose freely to taste it, in an exercise of the highest courage.

His tenderness and compassion were not a grafting of feminine characteristics onto a masculine personality, but rather a profound expression of masculinity. Masculinity entails initiation; initiation involves pain—the greater the pain, the more profound the initiation. Jesus called his passion his baptism, which initiated him into the mystery of suffering. This is one aspect of Christ's life that theologians have always had trouble grasping. Christ's passion is often seen more or less as play-acting; that is, he acted out something but did not really achieve anything that he could not have achieved otherwise. In one sense, this seems true: how can anything be added to God? But Scripture explicitly says that son though he was, he learned obedience through suffering. He was never disobedient, for his sonship consisted in his perfect obedience. Thus, he learned the price of obedience, what it cost man to repent and to obey, through experiencing the suffering that obedience brings.

Jesus's suffering involved not only physical pain, but a sense of guilt, of abandonment by God, and a descent into hell. The Holy Saturday theology of Hans Urs von Balthasar attempts to convey the meaning of this experience. The descent into hell is a familiar motif, even in pagan literature, because it is a part of the initiation into suffering and death that all heroes, and indeed all men who wish to be truly men, must undergo. Only by defeating Satan and death can Jesus receive the name that is above every other name, kyrios, *Lord*, and be honored as king of the universe, absolute sovereign and judge, who has the right to separate the sheep from the goats, to make the ultimate distinctions of salvation and damnation for all beings, human and angelic.

In the Gospels, the ultimate conflict is not between Jesus and certain Jewish leaders, or between Jesus and an ambitious Roman governor. These men are but unwitting tools of spiritual powers: *Father, forgive them for they know not what they do.* The real enemy is Satan, who is behind all the machinations of Jesus's mortal enemies. Jesus came to confront and defeat the strong one, the prince of this world. At the beginning of his public ministry, he fasted like a shaman and confronted the spiritual force of evil, a real being who tried to turn him from his mission.

The Gospels were written with an apologetic motive, to try to show the Roman world that Jesus was not a revolutionary and was crucified unjustly. Therefore the Jews, for whom the Romans felt no special affection, were the enemies given most prominence. But the Apocalypse, written to comfort persecuted Christians by revealing to them the spiritual battle that was going on invisibly behind the events of history, identified the true conflict between the Word of God and his enemy, the dragon. The Lamb of God, who stands forever in heaven bearing the marks of his wounds, is scarred from his celestial conflict like a man who has gone through initiation. Jesus then, in his earthly mission, in his role as Son in the Trinity, and in his hidden role as lord of the universe, follows the pattern of the masculine personality.

The Masculinity of the Spirit

The Holy Spirit is often associated with the feminine in the work of redemption.[7] He comes upon Mary so that she conceives. When she visits her cousin Elizabeth, the Word is dwelling in her womb. But the Word also dwells in Mary's words, and at the sound of her voice the baby in Elizabeth's womb leaps for joy and is filled with the Holy Spirit. In the Apocalypse the Spirit and the Bride both say "Come." Mary, like Eve, is more sensitive than men (Zacharias and Adam) to the Spirit, but Mary listens to the Holy Spirit rather than the evil one. Yet is this association with the feminine enough to justify Maximilian Kolbe's description of the "quasi-hypostatic union" of Mary and the Spirit,[8] or of Leonardo Boff's claim that Mary "is to be hypostatically united to the Third Person of the Blessed Trinity"?[9] The Spirit is God, and as such bears a relationship to creation which can only be described as masculine. Nevertheless, there is a valid reason that he is associated with the feminine. But we must be clear about the Spirit's masculinity. He is masculine for three reasons: he separates (a characteristic masculine action), he works with power, and most importantly, he is the spirit of sonship.

The Spirit is a spirit of holiness. To be holy means to be set apart. Therefore, like the spirit of Yahweh, the Spirit is at work in the process of election, of setting apart. The Spirit sets apart Mary from the normal course of human life, telling her that she had been chosen to bear the Messiah outside the course of nature. The Spirit descends upon Jesus at his baptism, separating him from the life of a carpenter that he had led. The first action of the Spirit is to lead Jesus out into the wilderness, to separate him from society and bring him into confrontation with Satan. The Spirit anoints Jesus as the Messiah, and leads him to play his role as sacrifice. Jesus is set apart from humanity by his enemies, the unwitting agents of God, as a criminal, but paradoxically this separation is the greatest holiness. Having fulfilled his mission on earth, Jesus sends the Holy Spirit upon the earth, who descends on the disciples, separating them and marking them out from the rest of Israel. The Spirit is at work in the early Church, bringing it into confrontation with the Jews and the pagans.

Power is such an attribute of the Spirit that it is almost, like joy, a synonym for him. Energy is an aspect of the holy; it is the wrath of God, but it is also "vitality, passion, emotional temper, will, force, movement, excitement, activity, impetus."[10] The Spirit, *pneuma*, is like the spirit, *thymos*. Christ baptizes with the Holy Spirit and with fire; fieriness and power are characteristic of the spiritedness of youthful masculinity. A young man expresses his spirit through his combativeness, his desire for fame and glory through displays of his power and excellence, especially in contests and combats.[11] The Spirit is jealous, one must be careful not to offend him, but he also gives true glory. Stephen, filled with the Holy Spirit, becomes combative, and denounces his audience, who stone him. Yet, echoing Jesus, Stephen with his last breath forgives his murderers.

The Spirit is not simply a spirit of holiness and power, but a spirit of love and a spirit of sonship. He is the love of the Father for the Son, and the Son for the Father. The Son goes forth from the Father in the Spirit, and returns to the Father in the Spirit. Thomas Weinandy, in his presentation of the doctrine of the Trinity, states that "the Holy Spirit, in proceeding from the Father as the one in whom the Father begets the Son, conforms the Father to be Father for the Son and the Son to be Son for (of) the Father."[12] Weinandy reached his conclusion from the premise that the economic Trinity, the Trinity as revealed in the history of salvation, accurately reflects the internal, immanent Trinity and indeed is the only path we have to knowledge of the immanent Trinity. "Therefore," Weinandy argues, "as the Spirit conformed Jesus to be the faithful Son on earth, so the Spirit conforms him as the Son, within the Trinity, so as to be eternally pleasing to the Father."[13] As the Holy Spirit acts in Jesus, so the Spirit of Jesus acts on his disciples: "The Holy Spirit, the Spirit of sonship, transforms us into the glorious image of God that is Christ fashioning us into sons of God."[14] Though the Spirit is also associated with femininity, his proper activity, the paternal/filial love that makes the Father a father and the Son a son, is masculine.

The Femininity of the Church

Although Christians, both men and women, are sons of God, and follow a masculine way of life, one of struggle, of descent into death, and of resurrection, the Church itself is nonetheless always feminine, the Bride and Mother. The meaning of the ascription of feminine titles to the Church has been obscured by the faulty apprehension of the meanings of masculinity and femininity. A more accurate conception of femininity reveals the reason for the femininity of the Church, the association of the Spirit with femininity, and the roots of femininity in God.

Most Christian writers, following Aristotle, see masculinity as activity and femininity as receptivity. Mary's role in salvation and the Church's role have usually been presented in these terms: Mary is receptive to the message of the Spirit, and receives the Word first in her heart and then in her womb, becoming the Theotokos, the mother of God. She is the mother of all believers, because she is the first to believe, and in a sense all other belief stems from her assent to the Incarnation. The church should imitate her, listening to the Word and responding to it. A Christian should be feminine and Marian, seeking only to hear the Word and respond to it. God is masculine, believers are feminine (and usually women); only those in the church who represent God's activity and authority can act in a masculine fashion, and they are usually men, the clergy.

But receptivity is not the center of femininity. Integration and communion are at the heart of femininity, as separation and differentiation are at the heart of masculinity. Women and men have the same openness to the outward world and to the invisible world. Women may be more perceptive than men, but the key to their feminine role is not precisely their responsiveness. Rather, it is their tendency to integrate rather than separate. The feminine is not responsiveness, but relationship and communion.

Mary hears the Word that comes forth in divine freedom, at the sole initiative of the Father, and indeed responds to it, but the important thing is that her response puts her into a relationship with God. The Church is made up of those who have been chosen by God in his freedom and who enter into relationship with each other because they have first entered into a relationship with God. Mary's response to the Word is not passivity. She does not remain in quiet contemplation, but acts, and acts to renew and revivify a relationship with her kinswoman Elizabeth. She celebrates in her song, the *Magnificat*, God's action in forming a people, the posterity of Abraham.

The Church stems from this first relationship. Catholics therefore honor Mary as the Mother of the Church, and Mary is the mother of the Church because she is the mother of God, with whom she has entered into intimate relationship through the Incarnation. In images of Pentecost, when the Church is visibly born of the action of the Holy Spirit of Jesus, Mary is put in the center of the action of the Spirit. Thus, the Church is a spouse because the Word enters and indwells it through his spirit, making her a mother because he makes her fruitful in giving birth to many sons of God.

The Spirit is the principle of unity in the Church because he is the principle of unity in the Trinity. As Manfred Hauke says, "The movement of the Father's love brings forth the Son as its perfect image, and the reciprocal love between Father and Son attains such fullness that it becomes itself a person, the Holy Spirit, the person in two persons, in whom archetype and image are interfused with one another. The divine 'circular movement' is closed in and through personal love."[15] As Hauke points out, "relationality" is more feminine than masculine, and therefore the Holy Spirit is associated with the feminine.[16]

The Church is feminine because it is a communion, and a reflection of the divine communion of the three persons of the Trinity. The Holy Spirit is the soul of the Church, and the Church is not simply an assembly, an *ecclesia*, but even more profoundly a *communio*, a created reflection of the *communio* of the Three Persons. David L. Schindler encapsulates *communio* ecclesiology: "[T]he church has its proper reality as sharer in the divine trinitarian communio."[17] Femininity connotes union, and the three persons are eternally united without being confused. The Trinity is the feminine aspect of God. It is the unity that exists in and through the divine persons, not apart from them. The Trinity is not a separate person, and cannot be addressed as *She*, even though the Latin liturgy calls upon the *sancta Trinitas, unus Deus*. *Trinitas* is feminine in Latin and in many Indo-European languages. On Trinity Sunday in Russia, Christians are called to forgive their enemies and to be reunited in love with all, for the Trinity is a mystery of love and union, and therefore of the feminine.

Thus, God is feminine in that he is a communion, but he cannot be addressed as feminine since we speak to him as a person, and his tripersonal nature is masculine. The Church is a personification rather than a person; in Scripture she is new Israel, the new daughter of Sion, the bride of Yahweh and of the Lamb, the Body of Christ which he cherishes. But the individuals who make up the Church are masculine because they are called to be imitators of the Son in his masculine action of sacrifice and expiation. Women can participate in this spiritual masculinity, but men could be expected to have a greater natural understanding of the pattern. Masculinity itself is part of the proto-evangelium of creation.

The Masculinity of the Christian

In the New Testament, Christians are referred to as the sons and daughters of God only in quotation from the Old Testament. Otherwise, they are referred to as the children of God, sometimes with an implication of immaturity, or proleptically as the sons of God, with emphasis upon what they are destined to become. The *fatherhood of God* became an Enlightenment commonplace: *Alle Menschen werden Brüder*. That God is our Father and we are his children was held to be the common belief of all religions. But God is rarely described as man's father in the Old Testament or in paganism, and "fatherhood" is clearly felt to be a metaphor, in the same way that God is the "father" of the dew. The begetting of the Son by the Father and the begetting of the Christian by God is a revelation of something humanity could never have imagined. The Son is truly begotten of God; he is not simply "like" God, the closest thing to God of any creature; rather he is the same substance (*ousia*) as God. He is the only-begotten; there is no other like him.

Yet Christians are also begotten in a sense that surpasses all metaphor and is almost impossible for reason to fathom.[18] The Son, by pouring forth the Holy Spirit, creates other sons. He conforms both men and women to his own image as Son, by that making them all God's sons (not daughters). God has no only-begotten daughter; he therefore has no daughters begotten of the Spirit, only sons. There is only one pattern for both men and women to be conformed to, that of the Son. In the Son, Christians become deiform, apotheosized, and achieve an intimacy and union with the godhead that is beyond the categories of natural reason. Christians are the children of God, growing into the image of the Son, that they may also become sons of the Father.[19]

Masculinity in the Early Church

The Christian, because he is a son of God, has a primarily masculine identity. In Christ there is no male or female; biological identity, like nationality and legal status, is ultimately irrelevant to whether one can become a son of God. Women as well as men are called to be sons of God and brothers of Jesus Christ. Hence, women are also called to participate in the essentially masculine process of initiation. The sacraments have always been open to women, as has martyrdom.

Christian Initiation

Various actions of the Church, especially baptism, the Eucharist, confirmation, and the laying on of hands came to be called *mysteries* in the East and *sacraments* in the West. Although Christianity is not simply a mystery religion, it decided to use a term, *mysterion*, which inevitably carried overtones of the mystery religions, to describe central Christian actions. Initiation is an important action in religions that have a concept of a realm that transcends the everyday world. These mystery initiations are closely parallel to masculine development. When Christianity called its key actions mysteries, it emphasized that in the life of the Church, which unites the believer with Jesus, the true initiation, the true mystery, was to be found. Some of the themes of the pagan mysteries were taken over into Christianity.[20]

The Western use of the term *sacramentum* to describe the liturgical actions of the Church carries military overtones. The *sacramentum* was the oath sworn by the soldier inducted into the army, and it transformed his life. He put aside all civilian concerns and henceforth devoted his life entirely to military affairs. Civilians were dismissed in soldier's slang as *pagani*, hicks, and Christians took over the term to describe those who had not enlisted in the army of Christ. Such use of military terminology emphasized the agonic nature of the Christian life, the struggle with Satan and all the forces of evil. The soldier has always been a potent image of the self-sacrificing savior.

Christian baptism is a rite of initiation. In defending masculine initiation rites, David Thomas notes that "Christianity is based upon a story of sufferings, followed by resurrection, redemption, and ascent into a better life that is an uncanny parallel of the narrative enacted in almost all ritual initiations."[21] Jesus's life is that of the hero and is therefore the consummation of masculinity. In baptism a Christian puts on Christ; he dies and is reborn with Christ. With Christ he descends into the abyss, confronts death—indeed dies—and is reborn to a new life.

Christian initiation is accomplished by the conformity of the believer to the death and resurrection of Christ. This is accomplished sacramentally by baptism, confirmation, and the Eucharist. Baptism is not simply an initiation in the sense of a beginning; it is also an initiation in the sense of a death to an old self and rebirth as a new self. This meaning is stressed in the New Testament: *unless you are born again* and *if we have died with Christ*, among other well-known passages. The early Church took over some of the symbols of the mysteries, which survived in the full rite of baptism at the Easter vigil: Death and resurrection were written in the heavens, in the daily and seasonal movement of the sun and moon, and especially at the moment in the great dance when the resurgent sun met the full moon at the vernal equinox, the promise of the resurrection that was to take place on earth.[22] The candles of the vigil allude to the *photismos*, the new light and understanding of the initiate—they may also allude to the torches of the searchers in the Eleusinian mysteries—and proclaim that here the true and final initiation can be found. The Spirit descends upon the initiate at confirmation, conforming him in principle to the crucified Christ. The initiate is united to the crucified and risen one by eating his body and drinking his blood in the Eucharist.

The Martyrs and the Monks

Beyond Baptism, Christian tradition has recognized an even deeper initiation, a stronger conformation to Christ. It is the baptism of fire, which "signifies a purification and a consecration, that is to say, a rite of initiation giving the right to a participation in the celestial Mysteries [i.e., the liturgy], just as baptism in water is the prerequisite for assisting in the earthly Mysteries."[23] This baptism of fire gives access to the divine light and is achieved through martyrdom or the equivalent of martyrdom, the life of the monk. The Christian is not simply a student of Christ; discipleship consists not simply in hearing and applying the teachings of Christ, as if he were simply another sage. To be a disciple of Christ is to imitate Christ, and the key event in the life of Christ was his death and resurrection. The Christian who is most fully conformed to that death and resurrection is the best imitator of Christ: the martyr therefore most clearly fulfills the Christian call.

Jesus responds to Philip, who has conveyed the Greeks' request to see him, that *unless a grain of wheat falls to the ground and dies it remains alone; but if it dies it bears much fruit.* Jesus by this indirect reply alludes to his own death, which would reconcile all men to God. The reunion of Jew and Greek in the Church was the first sign of the ultimate return of the cosmos to God. But Jesus implies something about his followers as well, whom he has told to take up the cross daily and follow their master. Luke describes the death of Stephen in terms parallel to Christ's death. In showing that Saul, who stood by consenting to the death of Stephen, becomes Paul the apostle, Luke also implies, as Tertullian later said, that the blood of the martyrs is the seed of the Church.

The theology of martyrdom developed very early under the pressure of martyrdom. The two great martyrs, Ignatius of Antioch and Polycarp of Smyrna, left their imprint on all later accounts of martyrs. The martyr is the new athlete, the new soldier. His passion is not passive, but active, a battle. The Church felt, therefore, that martyrdom was, properly speaking, a masculine activity. While awaiting execution in the year 202, Perpetua had a dream in which an angel came to her and anointed her so that she became, mystically, a man, exclaiming, "Facta sum masculus."[24] All Christians, including women, are called to be athletes of Christ, soldiers against Satan, and to act in a masculine fashion in the spiritual realm.

After the age of the martyrs, the monks became the new athletes of Christ,[25] the successors to the martyrs.[26] *The Teaching to Monks* (*Doctrina ad monachos*) ascribed to Athanasius even claims that the monk is more of a soldier than the martyr: "The martyrs were often consummated in a battle lasting for only a moment; but the monastic institute obtains a martyrdom by means of a daily struggle."[27] The Irish monks saw both the ascetic life and the life of the pilgrim as a form of martyrdom.[28]

Anthony battled demons in the desert in a "contest,"[29] in "many wrestlings" against "destructive demons."[30] Benedict finds warfare a natural metaphor for monasticism, and recurs to it frequently in his Rule. He addresses the one who by his own will, *abrenuntians propriis voluntatibus*, will be in the army, *militaturus*, with *fortissima et praeclara arma*.[31] Hearts and minds must be prepared for *militanda* in obedience. Cenobites are monks who are in *monasteriale militans*;[32] anchorites are those who have learned how to fight, *pugnare*, against the devil and can leave the column, *acie*, to engage in solo combat, *singularem pugnam*, to fight, *pugnare*, against the vices of mind and flesh.[33] Both slave and freeman are in the same rank, *aequalem servitutis militiam*.[34] The battle is fought against the devil.

Later monks continued to think of themselves as soldiers. The *Anonymous Life of St. Cuthbert* refers to God's soldier, *militis*.[35] Bede speaks of Cuthbert as an athlete and of his life as a warfare.[36] Cuthbert seeks out waste places as a scene of battle.[37] His withdrawal is not to seek peace but battle, the contest that is the way of life of a hermit.[38] Monks were "the champions of the Church who carry on the battle with evil spirits, and with the spirit of evil in the world. They are forever engaged in a wrestling match with their own passions; they are running a race for which they expect an incorruptible crown; the world is the arena in which they engage in a spirited contest with all that is opposed to the will of God."[39] The monastic life was an agonic life, one of conflict. The monk did not flee from human society to find safety in solitude, but like the hero went out into the wilderness to confront the forces of evil and fought them to rid himself and the world of all traces of evil.

The monk underwent an initiation to prepare him for the battle. The reception of the candidate was regarded as a mystery, a *mysterion*, closely parallel to the initiation of baptism.[40] The baptismal creed had a threefold affirmation of the Trinity and a corresponding threefold rejection of the world, the flesh, and the devil. Parallel to the baptismal liturgy, the monastic profession according to the customs of St. Pachomius required a threefold "renunciation of the world, his parents, and himself."[41] This may be the root of the medieval definition of monasticism as the life of poverty, chastity, and obedience. The candidate received a new identity as part of his initiation and was given a new name and new clothes, the habit of the professed religious. Monastic profession is a rebirth[42] and like baptism and martyrdom causes the remission of sins.

Monasticism set the spiritual tone of Christianity for the millennium after the age of the martyrs and before the rise of scholasticism. The greatest pope of this age was a monk, Gregory, and his greatest work was a commentary on spiritual struggle, the *Moralia in*

Job. Monasticism is not unique to Christianity: there were Jewish monks, the Essenes, and there are Buddhist monks. The spiritual man is known in many religions, and his life is a quest for initiation into the mysteries of life and death, the attainment of full manhood and masculinity. This pattern of spiritual life was comprehensible to all men, even if they did not choose to follow it. It was not seen as effeminate; it was a life of struggle and combat against invisible foes and one's own irrational fears and vices, both deadlier than any human enemy.

HEROIC CHRISTIANITY

Christians had to face the continued appeal of the ideology of masculinity in the pagan societies they confronted in converting Europe. The hero was the model of masculinity, and Christians had to explain to men who wanted to be heroes much more than they wanted to be Christians how a man could be both a hero and a Christian, how in fact Christ was the true hero, the true model for men. We are fortunate to have literary artifacts of this teaching in the literature of the Saxons and of the Anglo-Saxons.

Unknown poets reinterpreted Christianity for those whose souls were formed by the heroic ethos of Germanic paganism. On the continent, the *Heliand* depicted Christ as born in a hill-fort and working the miracle at Cana in a mead-hall.[43] The *Christ* and *The Dream of the Rood* retold the events of the Gospel in the heroic language of the Anglo-Saxons who had migrated to the British Isles. To be attractive to pagans, Christ had to be shown as a hero, and his apostles as loyal thanes.

The most extensive treatment of the pagan hero is in *Beowulf*. The relationship of the poem and Christianity is controversial, but its survival attests to an important fact: A monastic writer (and there were few others) thought *Beowulf* important enough to devote time and vellum to its preservation. Why was a monk interested in a pagan hero? The poem focuses on the grandeur of the hero, but also on the self-destructive nature of heroism and masculinity, perhaps hinting that heroism can be fulfilled only in the self-abnegation of Christianity and monasticism.

Oblivion is frightening to all human beings, but especially to the hero, whose energies are focused upon asserting his identity and attaining immortality through fame. The fear of oblivion, as we have seen, is concretized in the fear of being eaten, and it is this fear that finds expression in many folktales that resonate with this (predominantly masculine) anxiety, folktales that lie at the root of the story of *Beowulf*. In *Beowulf*, the hero is always in danger of being eaten. The sea monsters want to feast on Beowulf, "sitting around a banquet at the bottom of the sea,"[44] but instead he serves them with death: "I served them with my dear sword, as was fitting."[45] Grendel devours the retainers at Heorot, and Beowulf says that he will need no burial if he loses, because Grendel's stomach will be his tomb: "He will carry away my bloody corpse, intent on eating it . . . you will no longer need to trouble yourself about caring for my body."[46]

Beowulf is threatened more by Grendel's mother than by Grendel, although her strength is described as less than Grendel's as a woman's is less than a man's.[47] Femininity is a grave danger to the boy who wants to become a man. The boy must be "separated from his mother"[48] so that he can put on a new male identity. In descending into the lake and the cave, Beowulf descends, like all initiates, into the womb to be reborn. He must confront and defeat the threatening aspects of femininity: "The chthonian Great Mother shows herself preeminent as Goddess of the Dead, as Master of the Dead, that is, she displays aggressive and threatening aspects."[49] Such is Grendel's mother, who is never given a proper name. This lack of identity emphasizes that she is the threatening femininity that Beowulf must confront to establish his masculine identity.

Beowulf's central trial, his combat with her, is surrounded by references to water. The descent into the mere has overtones of descent into mother earth and death. The youth who is be initiated must confront "the monster of chaos," who is often "a water-monster" because water is an almost universal symbol (in the many versions of the Deluge) of the chaos and disorder that threaten the fragile con-

structs of man.[50] Eliade says that "initiatory death is often symbolized, for example, by darkness, by cosmic night, by the telluric womb,
the hut, the belly of a monster. All these images express regression to
a preformal state, to a latent mode of being (complementary to the
precosmogenic chaos) rather than total annihilation."[51] Beowulf
confronts Grendel at night, in a hall; he confronts Grendel's mother
in a cave in the earth.

Beowulf kills the Nicors who wished to eat him, Grendel, and
Grendel's mother, and he preserves the Geats from their enemies
during his lifetime. His actions are surrounded by motifs of salvation, especially the middle action, the descent into the mere and the
cleansing of the waters. The monster Grendel lives at the bottom of
a lake, and again we have here the combination of a primeval creature and a depth of water, that is, a reference to chaos.

The recognition of Beowulf as a hero comes not through the discernment of a hidden identity, but by public knowledge of his victories through their tokens: Grendel's arm and head, the giant sword,
the dead dragon, and the recovered treasure. The public knowledge
of his victories, his glory, is symbolized by bursts of mysterious light:
the sun shines after his victory over the sea monsters, the mysterious
burst of light in the cave after he kills Grendel's mother, and the
shining of the standard in the dragon's lair. Darkness is the ultimate
threat to the hero's identity. Oblivion is worse than the grave. Light
is a sign of victory over darkness (a natural symbol, but made prominent in Christian cultures by the light-darkness dualism in John's
Gospel), and *beorht beacen Godes* (the bright beacon of God) fills the
sky at moments of hope or victory. Beowulf's lasting memorial is his
tomb, built on a headland, that becomes a beacon,[52] a light that sig-
nals his triumph in death. The light of victory shines on the hero,
giving him fame—*kudos*, *kleos*, *dom* and *lof*—the only hope for deliv-
erance from total oblivion.

Light comes from fire, but fire is a greedy spirit that also consumes. Fire will consume Heorot, which awaits "the furious surge of
hostile flames."[53] The images identify the engulfing waters with the
fires of destroying enmity. The blade of the giant sword is consumed
by the heat of Grendel's mother's blood: "That sword, that fighting-

blade, began to dwindle into icicles of war. It was a marvel of marvels how it all melted away, just like the ice."[54] Fire consumes Beowulf's body at the end of the poem: "Now live coals must devour the commander of fighters."[55] Most ominously, "Heaven swallowed up the smoke"of Beowulf's funeral pyre.[56] The Geats are consumed by their enemies and vanish like the very race that buried the treasure.

Heroic society was built upon heroic self-will, kinship, and wealth.[57] Each of these contains its own destruction. The hero, even when he is young, is dangerous: "Indeed, his early endowments of strength, initiative, and courage are too great to be contained easily; he poses a threat to orderly life for other, more ordinary people."[58] Nevertheless, to protect his community, to live out the masculine role, a man must have a reputation for violence.[59] He must be a troublemaker, and it is sometimes hard to direct his hostility only against external enemies: "The young warrior must transmute his humanity by a fit of aggressive and terror-striking fury, which assimilated him to the raging beast of prey. He became 'heated' to an extreme degree, flooded by a mysterious, nonhuman, and irresistible force that his fighting effort and vigor summoned from the utmost depths of his being."[60] Beowulf shares many characteristics with the monsters he conquers, as he must if he is to conquer them. Grendel is very much Beowulf's shadow-self, an personification of the dangers and evils implicit in the heroic character.[61] Beowulf becomes *gebolgen*, swollen with fury, full of *furor, wut, fergus, menos*. All of these words describe the transformation of the man into the warrior, who is either superhuman or subhuman, but in any case non-human.

The second basis of society in *Beowulf*, the one whose potential for evil is clear in the second fight with Grendel's mother, is kinship or family, which is closely connected with femininity. *Mægth* (kinship) and *mæg* (woman) are, if not cognates, at least associated by sound. Women are peace-weavers: They knit together clans and reconcile differences, or at least they are supposed to. Beowulf expresses his doubts about the possibility of using marriage to patch up a quarrel.[62] Attempts to base lasting peace on kinship are as futile as attempts to terrorize enemies by heroic achievements. Beowulf's killing of Grendel does not end the slaughter in Heorot; it only leads to a feud. Grendel's mother is named only by her relationship, mother, and she keeps her hall under the waves, in a parody of Freawaru.[63] Germanic society was matrilineal, unlike other Indo-European societies. The female both knits together families and provides the connections that sustain feuds. *Beowulf* is full of feuds; indeed the digressions are mainly about feuds, and Heorot will eventually be destroyed in a feud.

The distribution of wealth in the form of gold, land, and food is the third major force for cohesion in heroic society. The owner of wealth is not supposed to rejoice in its mere possession, or else he gets a reputation for stinginess. Wealth is gained only to be given away. The circulation of wealth creates binding ties of gratitude. A king is a ring-giver, *beaggyfa*; his antithesis is the dragon, the miser, *avaritia*, who sits on gold and refuses to part with it. Yet, the dialectic of possession and giving is unstable.[64] One cannot give unless one possesses, yet possession of wealth is dangerous. It opens the way to avarice, to the hesitation to part with wealth and an eventual refusal to part with wealth. Wealth also attracts others who desire to possess it. Beowulf thinks that he is gaining happiness and safety for his people by gaining them the hoard. Yet the gold is useless, *unnyt*, to the Geats as it was to the dead race that had stored it in the ground.[65] It will only attract robbers and plunderers.

The person who put ink on vellum to preserve *Beowulf* came from an Anglo-Saxon, Christian culture; he was therefore writing in a monastic milieu, for an audience, whether clerical or lay, influenced by monastic ideals. England had been converted, in a wave of monastic evangelization, by Augustine, a monk, sent by a pope-monk, Gregory. Augustine knew from the violence that continued to plague England that the foundations of heroic society were flawed and that this society was demon-haunted. He also knew that the Christian, especially the monk, was a warrior, who conquered these demons with the weapons of poverty, chastity, and obedience. The monk was the new hero in a spiritual warfare, the real warfare, the archetype which earthly battle merely imitated.[66] The monk would want to enjoy some of the glory of the heroes of Germanic antiquity.

The three vows that distinguish monastic life and the forms of

religious life that derive from it are poverty, chastity, and obedience.[67] Through obedience, the monk gives up his own will; he obeys
a superior, in whose commands he hears the words of God. Through
chastity, he gives up sexuality and family life. Through poverty, he
gives up ownership of earthly goods, and holds all property in common with his brethren. Thomas Aquinas explains that the vows have
two purposes, first, in "tending to the perfection of charity," and second, "quieting the mind from outward solicitude. . . . The disquiet of
worldly solicitude is aroused in man in reference especially to three
things. First, as regards the dispensing of external things, and this
solicitude is removed from man by the vow of poverty; secondly, as
regards the control of wife and children, which is cut away by the
vow of continence; thirdly, as regards the disposal of one's own actions, which is eliminated by the vow of obedience, whereby a man
commits himself to the disposal of another."[68]

The first fight in *Beowulf* is a confrontation with the evils implicit in heroism, especially self-assertion and pride. Obedience addresses the "inordinateness of the human will," its tendency to assert
itself above everything, even God. Heroism is based upon the assertion of the self in the face of challenge and danger; heroism involves
pride, and is a form of egotism. The monk, by contrast, is self-
effacing and seeks to find his life by losing it. Obedience to the spiritual father in a monastery is for the sake of learning humility, which
conquers pride, the root of all sins. Benedict speaks of the twelve
steps of humility in chapter seven of his Rule.[69] Hrothgar, in his
parting advice to Beowulf, warns him of pride, "arrogance,"
oferhygda,[70] and gives him "twelve treasures."[71] Especially in the context of a warning about pride, an audience conversant with
Benedict's Rule would see the treasures as reminder of the twelve
steps of humility. The poet seems here, in his usual appositive manner, to be asking his audience to see the parallels between the monastic and heroic ways of life. There may be a similar dynamic in the
mentions of God's light,[72] which could refer to the *deificum lumen*[73]
of monastic life, and of "eternal gain"[74] which could refer to entrance
to the monastic life.[75]

The vow of chastity was as much a renunciation of kinship as of sexual activity. Nevertheless, there may be some hints of sexual activity in the fight between Beowulf and Grendel's mother. Any grappling of male and female, even in violence, has sexual overtones, and perhaps the sword that melts after the battle has a parallel in Riddle 20, in which the answer is either *sword* or *phallus*. Though finding sexual allusions in Beowulf's battle with Grendel's mother may seem far-fetched, the obscene riddle was favored by the Anglo-Saxons, who were amused by double-entendre.

Voluntary poverty exorcises the demon that lurks in gold. By giving up rights of possession, the monk attains both inner and outer tranquility. He owns nothing, and cannot be robbed. Yet his poverty allows him to enrich others with spiritual gifts. Only one who renounces the world can be trusted with the wealth of the world.

Monasticism, like baptism, was an initiation, and was a better initiation than Beowulf's. He did not confront, in his fights with the monsters, the deepest evils in the way the monk does in spiritual combat. Beowulf's death is a parallel to the death and rebirth of the Christian-monk, but he does not achieve the final victory. Beowulf conquers the dragon, but is destroyed in the fire, his funeral smoke mounts to heaven, and there is a great sadness in his end. He does not save his people, and the swallowing of the smoke is the oblivion that he has fought against in every battle. The monk, on the other hand, achieves this ultimate initiation. In his battle with the devil he receives a true baptism of fire, which "signifies a purification and a consecration, that is to say the rite of initiation giving the right to participate in the celestial mystery."[76] The baptism of fire is attained through asceticism and prayer, according to the teachings of Macarius.[77] The divine light from this fire, the *deificum lumen* (deifying light) of Benedict's Rule, was the object of the aspiration of the monk.[78] It is in monasticism that we must seek the ultimate significance of *Beowulf* for its Christian audience. Heroic glory is replaced by humble obedience; family by chastity; and wealth by poverty. Heroic society destroys itself because of its inherent self-contradictions. But even pagan heroes can be models for Christians who fight the good fight. Beowulf is praised by his own people because he was *manna mildust*, the gentlest of men,[79] and embodies the gentleness that was also the ideal of the monks, the meek who inherited the earth.

ANTECEDENTS OF MEDIEVAL FEMINIZATION

Did any early Christian developments contribute to the later medieval feminization of the Church?[80] Judaism was male-oriented (although heroines like Deborah and Judith were prominent), and Christianity had a more balanced emphasis on male and female, both fully heirs of the new covenant, and on ultimate meanings of the masculine and feminine. In the New Testament, women have a bigger role than in the Old Testament. Some men received their faith from women and were affected by this mode of transmission. Timothy received his faith from his mother and grandmother, Lois and Eunice, and his lack of masculinity was of some concern to Paul: Paul exhorts him to stand up, to stir up the spirit he received, to be a little more forthright and firm. Most of the initial converts to Christianity were among the godfearers, Gentiles who took up some of the practices of Judaism, and "pagan women in particular tended to become godfearers,"[81] because the demands of Judaism on men, especially circumcision, were much harsher. Celsus claimed that Christians were "able to gain over only the silly, and the mean, and the stupid, with women and children."[82] As Origen points out, however, Celsus is a snob and despises anything that appeals to the vulgar. If there was any disproportion of women in the church, it may have been that women, confined to the house, were also out of public notice and safer from persecution.[83] John Chrysostom, although he denigrates women as temptresses like Eve,[84] also occasionally refers to their greater piety[85] and implies they benefit from their seclusion from public life.[86]

As long as Christians had to face sudden and horrible death for their faith, the essentially masculine nature of the Christian vocation was clear. The Christian, male and female, as we have seen, was a soldier and an athlete. When the persecutions ended, virginity and celibacy replaced martyrdom as the emotional center of the church, the sign of its supernatural nature. Christians, being human, have a hard time thinking in a balanced, reasonable manner about sexuality. The apostolic teaching is that both virginity and marriage are good; but virginity is higher because it allows the person to be fully occupied with the affairs of God. A married person, having cares in this world, can easily allow those cares to obscure the *unum necessarium*. Virginity and celibacy also anticipate the new creation, when there will be no longer marrying and giving in marriage, because death and its concomitant, reproduction, will be no more.

Because of the emphasis on virginity as the equivalent of martyrdom, and perhaps because of a Platonic suspicion of the body, the Church began to see virginity as the supreme sign of the new life brought by Christ. Especially in the East, encratitic tendencies were strong. Some Syriac churches tried to limit membership in the church to virgins and celibates, and even the Greek Fathers strongly emphasized the importance of virginity as the precondition of perfection.

Virginity, in John Bugge's interpretation of the patristic texts, was praised because it was a means of escape from the world of sin, death, and reproduction.[87] The virgin attained a state of simplicity, like the simplicity of God. Origen added to this another strain of Platonism in his interpretation of the *Song of Songs*, in which he saw not only an allegory of the union of Christ and the Church, but an allegory of the union of the soul and God. This mystical marriage was open to both men and women, since the human soul was feminine in both. Athanasius spoke of virgins as "the brides of Christ."[88] Chrysostom speaks of virgins who see "only the Bridegroom."[89]

Two attitudes were associated with this. Marriage was not seen simply as lesser because belonging to the present age of the world, but as somehow evil. The vigilance of the Church against Manicheanism kept this attitude in check, but plainly there is a denigration of sexuality and marriage in the patristic church. What also happened, although not until much later, was that spiritual marriage became a substitute for carnal marriage, and Christ as the heavenly bridegroom became the object of erotic and even sexual longings.[90]

The basic pattern of masculinity and femininity in Jewish and Christian testaments is consistent with the pattern in other cultures. Masculinity was a spiritual quality: Men could fall short of it, and women could attain it. Mary's song of triumph recalls the story of Judith, who crushed the head of the enemy. What was new in Christianity was the invitation to both sexes to participate in the inner life of the godhead, to become sons of God and form a community which would be the bride of God, created by him and from him and revealing him. New depths of masculinity and femininity, of separation and communion, were revealed within the godhead, whose unity was now shown to be a Trinity of persons.

Before the year 1200, men and women played an equal role in the life of the church (of which the clergy was a minuscule part). Christianity had indeed found a place for femininity and given it a high value, but men perceived the religion itself as sufficiently masculine that they felt no need to distance themselves from it to attain a masculine identity. Indeed, the life of the monk was honored as a way to attain a masculine identity. The relationship of the sexes in the church showed no signs of imbalance. Although it is possible to gather misogynic statements from the Fathers, we should not take these too seriously. Many of the Fathers had difficult personalities, and were highly critical of everyone, both men and women. Even Tertullian and Jerome, although they could lambaste women for their worldliness, could also speak with reverence of female devotion. The Anglo-Saxon Church especially shows a harmony of men and women working together, both in the internal life of the church and in the monastic mission to their Germanic cousins on the Continent. Not until the High Middle Ages did something happen to the gender balance of the Church. Since then, men have disproportionately abandoned Christianity. Between the patristic and monastic eras and the modern era something happened to the Church to make it a world of women.

6

The Foundations of Feminization

MEN AND WOMEN, as far as we can tell, participated equally
in Christianity until about the thirteenth century. If anything, men were more prominent in the Church not only
in clerical positions, which were restricted to men, but in religious
life, which was open to both men and women. Only around the time
of Bernard, Dominic, and Francis did gender differences emerge, and
these differences can be seen both in demographics and in the quality
of spirituality. Because these changes occurred rapidly and only in
the Latin church, innate or quasi-innate differences between the
sexes cannot by themselves account for the increase in women's interest in Christianity or the decrease in men's interest. In fact, the
medieval feminization of Christianity followed on three movements
in the Church which had just begun at the time: the preaching of a
new affective spirituality and bridal mysticism by Bernard of
Clairvaux [1]; a *Frauenbewegung*, a kind of women's movement; and
Scholasticism, a school of theology. This concurrence of trends
caused the Western church to become a difficult place for men.

BERNARD OF CLAIRVAUX AND BRIDAL MYSTICISM

Like the light pouring through the great windows of Chartres, the brilliance of the High Middle Ages is colored by the personality of Bernard of Clairvaux. Like many great men, Bernard contained multitudes. As a monastic who united prayer and theology, he looked back to the patristic era, especially to Augustine. A monk who renounced the world, he set in motion the Crusades, whose effects are still felt in the geopolitics of Europe and the Middle East. A celibate, he introduced into Western spirituality an eroticism that developed into spiritualities he would have condemned.

Hence, Bernard was, at the same time, the instigator of religious war and the propagator of a spirituality that cultivated the affections, including the affection of eros, cleaving, if only in a small way, masculine and feminine spirituality. How men responded to his teaching I will discuss later. But Bernard's use of erotic language to describe the relationship of the soul and God was very appealing to women. Of Juliana of Mount-Cornillon, a thirteenth-century biographer wrote, "Since the writings of blessed Bernard seemed to her so full of mighty flame and sweeter than honey and the honeycomb, she read and embraced them with very much devotion, honouring this saint with the privilege of an immense love. Her whole mind was absorbed with his teaching: she took pains to learn it by heart, and fix in her memory, once and for all, more than twenty of the sermons in the last part of his commentary on the Song, there where he seems to have outstripped all human knowledge."[2]

The use of erotic language to describe the relation of the believer to God was not unprecedented, but Bernard, for reasons that will become clear, did not choose to acknowledge his intellectual debts. Bernard claimed that "if a love relationship is the special and outstanding characteristic of bride and groom it is not unfitting to call the soul that loves God a bride."[3] Realizing that this application needed defense, Bernard explained that

> although none of us will dare arrogate for his own soul the title of bride of the Lord, nevertheless we are members of the Church which rightly boasts of this title and of the reality that it signifies, and hence may justifiably assume a share in this honor. For what all of us simultaneously possess in full and perfect manner, that each single one of us undoubtedly pos-

sesses by participation. Thank you, Lord Jesus, for your kindness in uniting us to the Church you so dearly love, not merely
that we may be endowed with the gift of faith, but that like
brides we may be one with you in an embrace that is sweet,
chaste, and eternal.[4]

Having established the principle for the use of such language, Bernard then elaborated. He referred to himself as "a woman"[5] and advised his monks to be "mothers"—to "let your bosoms expand with
milk, not swell with passion"[6]—to emphasize their paradoxical status
and worldly weakness.[7]

Bridal mysticism has its patristic precedent in Origen, whose
heterodoxy makes him a dubious authority. Probably for this reason,
Bernard neglected to acknowledge the source of his ideas in Origen.
Origen's *Commentary on the Song of Songs* was "the first great work of
Christian mysticism."[8] Following rabbinical tradition that saw the
bride as Israel, Origen saw the Bride as "the Church"[9] or "the whole
rational creation"[10] and also (with no explanation for the extension)
as the individual soul. One suspects unexamined Platonic assump-
tions.[11]

The individualism of this interpretation was contrary to the
original image of the community as bride discussed in the previous
chapter. Yet Origen was very influential, and the ecclesiological interpretation of the *Song* slowly gave way to the individual interpretation in which the soul of the Christian is the bride: "the individual
soul of the mystic takes the place of the Church collective."[12]

Origen recognized the dangers of sensuality in his interpretation: "Do not suffer an interpretation that has to do with the flesh
and the passions to carry you away."[13] The *Song of Songs* for Origen is
about "the soul that seeks nothing bodily, nothing material, but is
aflame with the single love of the Word."[14] The soul as the bride of
God is an allegory in Origen and Bernard, but the allegory cannot be
extended to the individual soul precisely because it is individual. In
the New Testament, the bride is the Church. Even worse, this allegory was taken up into the increasing humanization of the relationship of the Christian and Christ, and the *individual* Christian
person, body and soul, came to be seen as the bride of Christ. Thus,

sensuality and spirituality joined hands. Female mystics took the language to heart, and developed "the sensual imagery" in the *Song of Songs* "much more openly than . . . in the official interpretation."[15] As Barbara Newman points out, "women with a talent for sublimation need not even give up their eroticism. Beginning in the twelfth century and increasingly thereafter, the brides of Christ were not only allowed but encouraged to engage in a rich, imaginative playing-out of their privileged relationship with God. Christ as a suffering, almost naked young man, was an object of the devotion of holy women."[16] This bridal status of holy women gave them an added cachet in the male imagination. As Abelard wrote to Heloise, she began to outrank him "on the day she became the bride of his lord while he remained a mere servant."[17]

Because of this extension of the metaphor of the *Song of Songs*, Bernard and the mystics who followed him used the language of marriage to describe the conformity of the soul to Christ, the transformation into Christ, and the deification of the Christian. Bernard believed that marriage was the highest type of human love and was therefore an apt symbol for the love of God and the soul. Likewise, Beatrice of Nazareth felt that "the divine Spirit modeled her soul according to his own image, and conformed it very appropriately to his own likeness with some proportional harmony" and speaks of this process as a "divine embrace and union."[18] Bridal mysticism with its implicit eroticism came to be the principal way in which the union of Christ and the soul was expressed, and it united with penitential practices. Ernest McDonnell summarizes the medieval development: "Without ceasing to be a means of expiating sins and suppressing unruly passions, penitential practices were more and more inspired and illuminated by the idea of *conformatio* or *configuratio* with the suffering leader of mankind, with the crucified Christ. With literal following of His acts and words as the basis of everyday life, these *mulieres sanctae* desired not merely to conform but actually to relive the passion, in all its excruciating horror."[19]

The language that expressed the union of the soul and God in erotic terms was highly congenial to women. As Valerie M. Lagorio in her survey of mystical literature concludes, "in the works of the women visionaries, one notes the prevalence of *Brautmystik*, the love affair between Christ and the soul, leading to espousal and marriage."[20] Birgitta of Sweden usually referred to herself in the third person as "the bride."[21] After 1300 in Germany, "It was chiefly among women . . . that the *Brautmystik* was received with fervor."[22] Mechtilde had a vision of Gertrude of Helfta: "[Mechtilde] saw the Lord Jesus as a Spouse, full of grace and vigor, fairer than a thousand angels. He was clad in green garments that seemed to be lined with gold. And [Gertrude] for whom [Mechtilde] had prayed was being tenderly enfolded by his right arm, so that her left side, where the heart is, was held close to the opening of the wound of love; she for her part was seen to be enfolding him in the embrace of her left arm."[23] Medieval eros, which delighted in bright colors and knights who received wounds of love, is prominent here. Christ had revealed himself to Gertrude "a youth of about sixteen years of age, handsome and gracious. Young as I then was, the beauty of his form was all that I could have desired, entirely pleasing to the outward eye."[24] Hildegard of Bingen carries the erotic imagery a little farther in her song "O dulcissime amator," in which she addresses Christ: "O sweetest lover, sweetest embracer. . . . In your blood, we are joined to you, with nuptial rites, scorning men, and choosing you."[25]

For Hildegard, and many others,[26] the bridal union of the soul and Christ is not simply higher than earthly marriage; it replaces it and takes on some of the physical eroticism of the missing sexual union. Margaret Ebner feels Jesus pierce her "with a swift shot (*sagitta acuta*) from His spear of love."[27] She feels her spouse's "wondrous powerful thrusts against my heart,"[28] and she complains that "[s]ometimes I could not endure it when the strong thrusts came against me for they harmed my insides so that I became greatly swollen like a woman great with child."[29] Jesus spoke to her these words: "Your sweet love finds me, your inner desire compels me, your burning love binds me, your pure truth holds me, your fiery love keeps me near. . . . I want to give you the kiss of love which is the delight of your soul, a sweet inner movement, a loving attachment."[30] She had learned of this kiss from Bernard: "I longed for and greatly desired to receive the kiss just as my lord St. Bernard had received it."[31]

Henry Suso, whose writings were known to Margaret, demonstrates the convolutions that men had to undergo to adapt this language to their spiritual situation. In the *Little Book of Eternal Wisdom*, the Servitor (an aspect of Suso) speaks of the "strange longing"[32] he feels for Wisdom, whom he sees as feminine, Sapientia. But then the Servitor says of himself that "the heavenly Father created me more lovely than all mere creatures and chose me for his tender, loving bride."[33] Wisdom then addresses the Servitor: "I place the ring of our betrothal on your hand, clothe you in the best garments, furnish you with shoes and confer on you the engaging name of bride, to have and to hold forever."[34] Revelation becomes a love affair. Wisdom says to the loving soul, "every sentence of Holy Scripture is a love-letter written by me exclusively for her."[35] The Eucharist becomes a love-union with the "beloved Spouse,"[36] "the table of divine sweetness where lovers are nourished by love."[37] The Servitor says, "my heart would be satisfied," "if I were granted the grace to receive into my mouth one single drop from the open wounds of my Beloved's heart."[38] The connection between bridal mysticism, Eucharistic devotion, and the devotion to the Sacred Heart are all present in this passage, which has sexual overtones that sound peculiar to the masculine ear.

This tone stems from the *Song of Songs*, the "Book of Love," as Suso refers to it, and dominates in his writings.[39] On occasion, Suso uses other metaphors, but the blood and flowers of his mystical eroticism of suffering suffuse everything he writes. The soul languishes for love of God; God suffers for his love of the soul. Suso prays to Mary to "spread over me your rose-colored mantle, dyed with the Precious Blood of your dear child."[40] Although it is difficult to grasp the personality of a medieval writer, Suso may not have been a fainting, languishing *dévot* in reality. His ability to switch suddenly from raptures to sober scholastic distinctions gives the impression that he was a stolid German soul, but that he thought he ought to be like the Servitor, ravished with love-longing.

In the few later mystical writings by male writers, the bridal metaphor is not dominant, but nothing of equal emotional intensity replaces it. Catholic mystics, such as Theresa of Avila and John of the Cross, employed bridal metaphors through the Counter-Reformation. John of the Cross was a great poet, and he handles the metaphor of the soul as bride with great skill. Thus, the incongruity of the metaphor is softened, but remains nonetheless.[41] Denys Turner summarizes the result of the predominance of bridal mysticism: "The Western Christian has traditionally been a female soul in love with her Bridegroom."[42]

THE MEDIEVAL WOMEN'S MOVEMENT

Male mortality in almost all societies is consistently higher than female mortality, despite the dangers of childbirth; but in the high Middle Ages the ratio of women to men may even have increased.[43] Society was confronted with the problem of a large number of unmarried women who had to support themselves, who did not live in households headed by men, and who developed a culture that had a feminine character. This was the *Frauenbewegung*, the women's movement.[44]

Women also had a new freedom of movement. After the twelfth century, society was orderly enough to allow women to live and travel on their own. Chivalry, the Peace of God, and growing commerce provided women sufficient security that they could visit famous shrines, such as the tomb of St. Thomas of Canterbury, and travel to hear famous preachers. But these preachers were often heretics. The Cathars were a constant danger, and new heresies threatened the church: "For the thirteenth-century Guglielmites, women were the only hope for the salvation of mankind."[45] The influence of such heresies among women drew the attention of church authorities to the lack of pastoral care for women not members of a household.

Women also responded in great numbers to the new spirituality preached by Bernard, but the Cistercians were appalled. R. W. Southern observes that "no religious body was more thoroughly masculine in its temper and discipline, than the Cistercians, none that shunned female contact with greater determination or that raised more formidable barriers against the intrusion of women."[46] Nevertheless, "the Cistercians' efforts to limit the number of nunneries joining the order proved unavailing."[47]

The new mendicant orders were also caught in this tidal wave of women. St. Francis of Assisi, in a somewhat uncharacteristic tone, observed, according to Thomas of Pavia, "the Lord has taken away wives from us, but the devil has given us sisters."[48] St. Dominic tried to keep his followers away from women. The earliest constitutions, written before Dominic's death in 1221, prohibit Dominicans from undertaking the *cura monialum*, the spiritual direction of women.[49] This prohibition seems not to have been based on Dominic's concern with preserving the Dominicans' celibacy, but on his fear that his followers would be overwhelmed by women's demands for attention and neglect their preaching to men.[50] In the end, the Papacy commanded the new orders, their reluctance notwithstanding, to take on the spiritual direction of women.[51] The secular clergy were generally corrupt, unlearned, and unimpressive; the monastic and mendicant orders were zealous, learned, and well respected. Women, despite the wishes of Francis and Dominic, became the main audience for the new mendicant orders. When Henry, the first Dominican prior of Cologne, died, he was mourned by "the women of Cologne."[52]

Even the veneration of saints was affected. The saints of the central Middle Ages, dominated by the Benedictines, tended to be men.[53] "Eleventh- and twelfth-century Christendom was a man's world."[54] This changed rapidly in the thirteenth century. The saints of the High Middle Ages, after 1250, tended to be clerics or women,[55] but "by the end of the Middle Ages, the lay male saint had virtually disappeared."[56] In the thirteenth century, the proportion of women anchorites also suddenly increased.[57]

This massive influx in the thirteenth century of women into religious life, whether in association with men's orders or as Beguines, did not escape notice. Caroline Bynum notes approvingly that

in contrast to the central Middle Ages, in which few female monasteries were founded, the twelfth- and thirteenth-century search for the *vita apostolica* attracted so many women to a specialized religious life that contemporary chroniclers themselves commented upon the phenomenon, sometimes with admiration and sometimes with trepidation. Women flocked to wandering preachers, like Norbert of Xanten and Robert of Arbrissel, and these preachers founded monasteries for them, never intending to establish bands of itinerant female evangelists. The number of Praemonstratensian and Cistercian houses for women grew at a speed that alarmed their orders.[58]

All classes were affected by this change: "The most spectacular manifestation of the sociological transfer of spirituality . . . is the transformation of an almost entirely male monopoly to an ever-increasing minority, sometimes even a majority, role for women."[59] Berthold von Regensburg noticed that women were more at church then men and preached to "you women, who are more merciful than men and go more willingly to church than men and say your prayers more willingly than men and go to sermons more willingly than men."[60] The feminization of the church was underway.

SCHOLASTICISM

Scholasticism revived Aristotle, who supplied both a new way of thinking about the Christian faith and a new approach to the relationship of masculine and feminine. Scholasticism's locus was the university rather than the monastery, but did not differ simply in locale from the older monastic learning. Its very purpose, training clerics in the service of the Church and state, not monks to read the Scriptures and sing the praises of God, was different. Prior to the rise of the schools, theology was based in the monasteries and united prayer and thought; it was part of the *lectio divina* and aimed at contemplation of God. The Scholastics thought according to the rules of logic and prayed according to the rules of faith, which was more and more a matter of the heart and emotions rather than the mind. Spirituality was thenceforth divorced from academic theology.

Thomas Aquinas, for example, is far more detached and logical than Augustine. In Augustine, the thirst of the soul for God is always present. In Thomas's theological writings all sense of a personal love for God is excluded. A skeptic or a religiously indifferent person could have argued from Thomas's premises and reached the same conclusions: "Theology henceforward claimed to be a science, and according to the Aristotelian ideal took on a speculative and even a deductive character. Like all sciences, it was disinterested; it was no longer concerned with nourishing the spiritual life, as the monastic theologians would have it do."[61] This split harmed both theology and the spiritual life, for neither profited by "the divorce between theology (now definitely a science) and mysticism, or at least the spiritual life. The province of the latter would then be purely religious sentiment."[62] Medieval theologians were of course believers, but a rift had been created, and the chasm would eventually open so wide that it is no longer surprising to have unbelieving professors of theology who leave religious practice to the simple *dévot*, who prays and pays the bills.

THE FEMININE AS RECEPTIVE

The Scholastics, as Prudence Allen has shown in *The Concept of Woman*, rediscovered and Christianized the Aristotelian analysis of the female. Aristotle followed Pythagoras in organizing reality into polar opposites, qualities that implied the existence of opposite qualities inferior to the first. As Aristotle observed in the *Metaphysics*, in a pair of contraries, one is the privation of the other: limit implies absence of limit, odd implies even, right implies left, rest implies motion, good implies bad, light implies dark, and male implies female.[63] Aristotle was especially interested in the contraries of form and matter, and he placed the male on the side of form, the female on the side of matter: "The female always provided the material, the male that which fashions it."[64] As the giver of form, man rules; as the matter that is given form, the woman obeys.

In the order of nature, the woman is therefore inferior to the man. Nevertheless, in the order of grace, Christian Aristotelians taught, the woman is above the man, precisely because of her natural inferiority: "Mary . . . herself became a kind of material for the formative power of God. Her perfect identity as nonresistant material for the working of the Holy Spirit led to her complete absorption of the wisdom of God. Therefore [for St. Albert the Great] it followed that Mary knew everything that God knew. She was the perfect philosopher, theologian, lawyer, physician, scientist, and so on."[65] What is true of Mary is true of women in general. Precisely because they are more like the raw material on which form is imposed, they are more open to the formation of the Holy Spirit. Men have a form already—a form which gets in the way of the shape of Christ that the Holy Spirit wishes to imprint on the human person. Women, relatively lacking in form, are more open to receiving another form. This analysis eventually permeated all medieval discussion of gender. As Ann Astell says, "In the metaphysics of sexuality, every person, male and female, is more feminine than masculine in relation to God—because receptive, dependent, and small."[66] The philosophical and theological explanation for women's greater devotion to Christianity was in place.

Thus, the Middle Ages saw the rise of a new, feminized piety. Caroline Bynum observes that women propagated "the most distinctive aspects of late medieval piety" and that "for the first time in Christian history we can document that a particular kind of religious experience is more common among women than among men."[67]

7

Feminized Christianity

AS MEN ABSENTED THEMSELVES from the Christian churches and found their spiritual sustenance elsewhere, the churches were left with congregations that were predominately feminine. Moreover, the Christian life itself was seen more and more as properly feminine—men had to become feminine in order to be good Christians—notwithstanding that the Christianity of the New Testament and patristic era saw the vocation of the Christian as masculine. The theology and spirituality whose pattern for following Christ was masculine was transformed when Christians began seeing their life-pattern as feminine. This feminized spirituality further identified the Church as the sphere of women (or of those men who were like women) and reinforced the male desire to keep a safe distance between themselves and a religion that threatened to emasculate them.

RECEPTIVITY AS CHRISTIAN

The Aristotelian analysis of masculinity and femininity provided medieval theologians with a philosophical explanation for the relative greater resistance men showed to Christianity, as well as a basis for the clerical cautions against women taking on masculine roles: If a woman were to become masculine, she would lose her emptiness and her openness to the Spirit. This Aristotelianism continues as the received, "traditional" explanation of the roles of men and women in Christianity. Karl Barth, accepting the Aristotelian formulation of masculinity as initiative and femininity as reception, stated: "As a living member of the church, man and all other superiors and subordinates in the community have no other option but to follow the example of women, occupying in relation to Jesus Christ the precise position which she must occupy and maintain in relation to man."[1] Manfred Hauke says of the Church as bride: "In receiving from Christ and cooperating with him. . . . Christian tradition gives precedence to the feminine for the purposes of representing the position of mankind before God (which is also definitive for males),"[2] and that "in relation to God, the soul is receptive, feminine."[3] F. X. Arnold has an explanation for "the special inclination which woman has for religion"—"the truly feminine, the will to surrender, the readiness to be receptive."[4] The essential element in a religious attitude is a "passive receptivity," because "in this readiness for self-sacrifice and in this cooperation of the creature, all that is truly religious in humanity is revealed."[5] Of Mary, George T. Montague says, "she is response and instrument."[6] Peter Toon writes "it is femininity rather than masculinity which symbolizes the right attitude of the whole person before God" because God wants from both men and women "a feminine response—that of humble reception of his initiative of grace and ready and willing submission to his gracious and perfect will."[7] Femininity is obedience, and active, assertive masculinity is an obstacle to grace. This notion has been such a commonplace that few questioned it before modern feminism.

Mary's obedience to Christ, not Christ's obedience to the Father (from which Mary's obedience draws its whole meaning), takes on a new prominence as a model for Christians. The early Dominicans attempted to preserve the peace of the community by softening rough masculine aggressiveness. The common good was founded "most of all on the monks' attempts to model their own orientation to the masculine Christ according to Mary's example of yielding, willing acquiescence."[8] St. Catherine of Siena heavily influenced the medieval Dominican Giovanni Dominici. He was characterized by "a lifelong identification with women's viewpoints: he was exceptionally close to his mother and most of his recorded spiritual counsel was written for nuns or laywomen."[9] St. Dominic's warnings had not been heeded, and we see a man dissatisfied with his own masculinity, who wants to become, in a spiritual sense, a woman.

Masculinity in this view is an obstacle to union with God. The logical consequence is that Christian men must renounce their masculinity. A modern Dominican, Brother Antoninus, wrote:

> *Annul in me my manhood, Lord, and make*
> *Me women-sexed and weak,*
> *If by that total transformation*
> *I might know Thee more.*
> *What is the worth of my own sex*
> *That the bold possessive instinct*
> *Should but shoulder Thee aside?*
> *What uselessness is housed in my loins,*
> *To drive, drive, the rampant pride of life,*
> *When what is needful is hushed acquiescence?*
> *"The soul is feminine to God."*[10]

Juli Loesch Wiley disagrees with the feminist claim that women have been kept from full participation in Christianity: "It would be closer to the truth to say, however, that it is *only* women who are admitted to the Christian mysteries. You see, any man who would participate must first become, symbolically, 'woman.' This is because, in traditional Christian terms, *all* souls are feminine."[11] In this tradition, which dates substantially from the twelfth century, the masculine humanity of Christ is irrelevant as an example for Christians. The feminine, obedient, responsive soul of Mary is the true model.

CONSEQUENCES OF BRIDAL MYSTICISM

Bridal mysticism did not disappear in the Reformation.[12] Edward Pearse follows Bernard: "God the Father gives Christ unto the Soul, and the Soul unto Christ; he gives Christ for an Head and Husband to the Soul, and he gives the Soul for a Bride or Spouse to Christ."[13] Puritan sermons used the dominant metaphor of the Christian as the Bride of Christ and the relationship between Christ and the Christian as that of a man and a woman. Cotton Mather, addressing the Puritans of the late seventeenth century, spoke of God's approach to the soul "under the Notion of a Marriage,"[14] applying passages from Scripture that refer to the church as bride to the individual Christian. Mather, while recognizing that the mystical marriage first referred to the Church, applied it also to each Christian: "Our SAVIOR does *Marry* Himself unto the *Church* in general, But He does also *Marry* Himself to every *Individual Believer*."[15] The Puritan Thomas Shepard stated that "all church members are and must be visible saints . . . virgins espoused to Christ."[16]

In the following century the Puritan Foxcroft in a funeral sermon spoke of the grave as a happy place in which "the Saints shall be impregnated" and from which they would arise "as some happy Bride from her Bed of Perfumes, call'd up to meet her royal Bridegroom."[17] The sweetness of Pietism, the Protestant version of the Baroque spirituality of the Counter-Reformation, has roots in bridal mysticism. Thomas Hooker preached that "Every true believer . . . is so joined unto the Lord, that he becomes one spirit; as the adulterer and the adultresse is one flesh. . . . That which makes the love of a husband increase toward his wife is this, Hee is satisfied with her breasts at all times, and then hee comes to be ravished with her love . . . so the will chuseth Christ, and it is fully satisfied with him. . . . I say this is a total union, the whole nature of the Saviour, and the whole nature of a believer are knit together; the bond of matrimony knits these two together, . . . we feed upon Christ, and grow upon Christ, and are married to Christ."[18] Hooker carries forward into New England Protestantism the central ideas of medieval mysticism: the total union of God and the soul, a union best expressed by the erotic imagery of marriage and the assimilation of eating.

Edward Taylor used bridal imagery throughout his meditations: "I then shall be thy Bride Espousd by thee/And thou my Bridegroom Deare Espousde shall bee."[19] The Christian must feel raptures toward his Savior, because "who/Can prove his marriage knot to Christ in's heart/That doth not finde such ardent flames oreflow?"[20] Taylor addresses his Lover, "Thy Pidgen Eyes dart piercing, beames on Love/Thy Cherry Cheeks sende Charms out of Loves Coast,/Thy Lilly Lips drop Myrrh down from above."[21] Erotic and even sexual metaphors for the relationship of Christ and the soul are used extensively by Puritan writers.[22] Amanda Porterfield notes of Taylor and his religious culture that "God was dominatingly male in the literature and consciousness of Puritans, and in his intimate spirituality, Taylor assumed a complementary feminine stance toward God."[23]

Jonathan Edwards, in eighteenth-century America, preached to young women of Christ, who "will be your lover, yea, he will be your glorious bridegroom. You are invited this day to the marriage feast of the king's son, not only as a guest, but as a bride." He pleads with women to "let him have your love who is fairer than the sons of men and is the most excellent, lovely, and honorable lover."[24] Wesley continued this imagery in *Jesus Lover of My Soul*. Catholic sentimental hymnology of the nineteenth century had a communion hymn, *O Lord I am not Worthy*, that referred to Jesus as the "bridegroom of my soul." Promise Keepers, a movement that is trying to bring men back into church life, has inherited this language. Its founder, Bill McCartney, claims that "we were created to be in a love affair with Jesus" and "Scripture tells us the *only* way to please God is to be passionately in love with Jesus Christ."[25] Evangelical Protestantism, despite its efforts to recruit men, is hampered by a tradition that not only emphasizes verbal expressions of emotion, but highly feminine emotions at that.

Alphonsus Ligouri in *The True Spouse of Jesus Christ* claims that "a virgin who consecrated herself to Jesus Christ becomes his spouse," for other Christians he is only "master, pastor, or father."[26] The original biblical image of the Church as the Spouse is almost forgotten, although Juan Gonzalez Arintero admits "The Church. . . is normally the *Bride* par excellence. . . . the title of Bride is also to be applied to all just souls."[27] But Alberto Calunga justifies the modern individualist interpretation: "[I]n the Old Testament Jehovah's relations with Israel began by his relations with the nation, but gradually

these became more individual; His dealings are with souls. . . . These
are then the true brides of Christ."[28] This low view of the Church is
more associated with American evangelicalism than Spanish Catholicism, but the reason for the popularity of St. Bernard among
evangelicals should now be clear. Arintero says the highest title of
Jesus is not Lord or brother (the ones used by St. Paul) but
"Spouse."[29] He gives a largely individualist interpretation of the *Song
of Songs*, in which he finds the mystical progress of the individual
soul.

The soul continues to be described by theologians as primarily
feminine because it is bridal and receptive to God.[30] The deepèst
relationship between God and the Christian is therefore bridal and
feminine. Hauke claims that "every Christian, of course, stands as a
receiver before God and thus fulfills the bridal role."[31] Therefore, it
is not unexpected that "women are more religious than men"[32] and
that the majority of Church members are women. Since she is feminine and receptive, Mary is "the first and exemplary Christian."[33]
Since he is masculine, Christ is apparently less suitable as a model
for Christians. This implication, which Hauke does not articulate,
may be the source of Protestant discomfort with Catholic
Mariology.

The transfer of the role of bride from the community to the soul
has helped bring about the pious individualism that has dissolved
ecclesiastical community in the West. The Church is the bride and
the object of the bridegroom's love, and individuals are the objects of
that love insofar as they are members or potential members of the
society of the redeemed. The Church should yearn for the presence
of her bridegroom, who consoles her and makes her fruitful in good
works and in new children. This imagery was natural to the Fathers,
but has been lost. Instead the individual is felt to be the center of
God's affections. For Latin Christians, the Church becomes a merely
juridical community whose structures are often obstacles to real interior piety. For Protestants, the juridical structure itself largely dis-
appears into voluntary denominationalism, and the only real concern
of Christianity is "Jesus and me."

For women there are many pitfalls. They may feel all too comfortable with bridal imagery, and the love they feel for Christ may be simply transferred from an earthly lover. Even worse, the combination of eroticism and the pain of the cross may produce what sounds like masochism and repel those who have an aversion to overtones of perverted sexuality.[34] The combination of bridal imagery with mistaken ideas of femininity forces Christian women to assume an attitude which is not really feminine and eventually provokes rebellion. Women are told they have a special obligation to obey a male clergy lest they be unfeminine and that their fulfillment as Christians should be a rapturous love affair with Christ.

For men the consequences have been disastrous. Bridal language used to describe a Christian's relationship with God has homosexual overtones to many men, unless they engage in mental gymnastics and try to think of themselves as women. "If monks wished to play the starring role in this love story," Barbara Newman says, "they had to adopt a feminine persona—as many did—to pursue a heterosexual love affair with their God."[35] But few boys like to be named Sue. Since normal men reject both homosexuality and femininity as incompatible with the masculinity for which they are always striving, bridal mysticism and the metaphors and attitudes to which it gave rise have placed a major obstacle to men's participation in the Church. Even among fundamentalists who have a balance of men and women in their congregations, women, not men, have religious experiences.[36] What is lacking in the West is a language of intimacy that expresses the closeness that men feel with men.

Maternal Mysticism

A woman relates erotically to a man not only as a husband and lover but also as a son and child. If the Christian should be feminine, as the Aristotelians maintained, he (or much more often, she) can relate as a mother to Christ. From this comes the devotion to the Christ child, and the importance of Christmas, which long ago eclipsed Easter as the greatest Christian feast in the Western church. The relationship of the Christian to the Christ child has a strong element of maternal eros. Amadeus of Lausanne described that "the little Jesus leaned on his mother's breast, and in her virgin lap reposed the eternal rest of the saints in heaven. Sometimes, his head supported on one or another of his mother's arms, he gazed with tranquil air on her whom the very angels long to look on, and, babbling gently, called that mother whom every spirit calls upon in need. She meanwhile, filled with the Holy Spirit, held her son breast to breast and pressed his face to hers. Sometimes she kissed his hands and arms and with a mother's freedom stole sweet kisses from his sacred lips."[37]

Gertrude had a vision of Christ at Christmas: "I took you out of your crib, a tender babe, wrapped in swaddling clothes. I pressed you to my heart where I gathered up onto a bundle of myrrh lying between my breasts all the bitterness of your childish needs."[38] Later Mary gives Gertrude the infant, "a darling little child who made every effort to embrace me."[39] This is so charming that any criticism of it looks morose and boorish. But when Gertrude sees Mary swaddling the infant, Gertrude asks "to be swaddled with you, so as not to be separated, even by a linen cloth, from him whose embraces and kisses are sweeter by far than a cup of honey."[40] The child frequently appeared to cloistered religious: "Dominican nuns typically saw the infant Jesus as a child with whom they played, joked, and kissed, who accompanied them when they were ill or dying, and for whom they cared in turn during Advent."[41]

This devotion took some odd turns. Many nuns in medieval convents had sacred dolls.[42] Margaret Ebner writes of one of hers: "I was sent a lovely statue from Vienna—Jesus in the crib, attended by four golden angels. One night I had a revelation in which I saw him in lively animation playing in the crib. I asked Him, 'Why don't you behave and be quiet and let me sleep?'.... I said, 'Kiss me, and I will forget that you have awakened me.' Then He fell upon me with His little arms and embraced me and kissed me."[43] Of another doll, Margaret says "I took the statue of the Child and pressed it against my naked heart as strongly as I could. At that I felt the movement of His mouth on my naked heart."[44] The problem is not the expression of suppressed maternal instincts, when the nuns cared for the dolls as if they were babies, or the occasional eroticism, when nuns felt the child kissing their breasts or when they kissed the foreskin,[45] but the attitude inculcated: that the only way or at least the best way to be a Christian was to relate to Christ as a woman relates to him.

JESUS AS MOTHER

Caroline Bynum has, through her thorough study of the medieval devotion to Jesus as mother, restored an awareness of this forgotten devotion.[46] Its most famous exponent was Julian of Norwich. For Julian, this Motherhood is dependent upon the quasi-identification of God and the Church, our Mother: "our Mother, holy Church that is Christ Jesus."[47] The love of a mother is one of pity, and it is the pity of God that led him to form the Church so that he could be a mother to his creatures: "A mother can give her child her milk to suck, but our precious Mother, Jesus, can feed us with Himself. He does most courteously and most tenderly, with the Blessed Sacrament, which is the precious food of true life."[48]

The devotion to Jesus as mother was based on a sound intuition about the nature of masculinity. In the pattern of masculine development, a man separated himself from the feminine so that ultimately he could achieve the degree of self-giving that a woman achieves in bearing and nursing a child. Therefore, when a man reaches that stage of self-giving, he can be described in feminine terms, although he has reached that stage in a way proper to masculine development.

This devotion focuses on the self-giving of Jesus, and it compares to the self-giving of a mother. The Church Fathers had compared the birth of the Church from the pierced side of Jesus to the birth of Eve from Adam's side. If someone gives birth, he is like a mother. If he nourishes with his own body, he is also like a mother. Masculinity involves nurturing, but a nurturing achieved in a willingness to suffer and die. In his death Jesus nourished his people; he fed them with his crucified body. He was the pelican, which struck its breast and bled to feed its young. He was a mother, as Julian of Norwich said, feeding with his body. In the usual medieval taste for developing a metaphor into an extensive allegory, preachers developed the various ways in which Jesus was like a mother. This devotion died out, but was replaced by another one which also stressed the mother-like qualities of Jesus, the devotion to the Sacred Heart.

THE SACRED HEART

The devotion to the Sacred Heart of Jesus flourished and has become one of the most popular in Catholicism. It too had medieval roots in the mysticism of love. The names associated with it in the Middle Ages are mostly women, St. Gertrude and St. Mechtilde. For Gertrude, Christ himself, "my sweetest little Jesus,"[49] is the archer of eros, and his heart is the one we are familiar with from St. Valentine's Day. Jesus tells Gertrude that he aims "arrows of love from the sweetness of my divine heart."[50]

In the sixteenth century, the devotion became more popular, and in the seventeenth century Margaret Mary Alacoque received revelations of the Sacred Heart, in which Jesus, "the Divine Spouse,"[51] "showed me, if I am not mistaken, that He was the most beautiful, the wealthiest, the most powerful, the most perfect and the most accomplished among all lovers."[52] Her heart was aflame with love for him as his was for her. He unites her to him in his sufferings so that she can join with him in saving sinners. He shows her "a large cross . . . all covered with flowers" and tells her "'Behold the bed of My most chaste spouses on which I shall make thee taste all the delights of My pure love.'"[53] She desires to be united with him through frequent communion, and in praying before the Eucharist, "How made me repose for a long time upon His Sacred Breast, where he disclosed to me the marvels of His love and the inexplicable secrets of His Sacred Heart."[54] Their union grows ever closer. One night, "if I mistake not, He kept me for two or three hours with my lips pressed to the Wound of His Sacred Heart."[55] To point out the dubious eroticism in these visions is not to deny their validity. The scholastic adage, that whatever is received is received according to the mode of the receiver, applies here. When Christ appeared to Margaret Mary, he spoke French; she also understood him to speak the language of love, the language in which women mystics expected God to speak.

This sacred eroticism is also prominent in the visions of Josefa Menendez (1890-1923). In her diary she says, "He drew me into his heart, and a stream of the precious blood escaping from it submerged me. 'For all that you give me,' he said, 'I give you my heart.' . . . 'My God, I am yours forever!'—And I went so far as to babble nonsense in my love. Then he answered: 'I, too, Josefa, love you to folly!'"[56] Josefa is so wedded to Jesus that her sufferings become redemptive; she becomes a Victim Soul. Like Thérèse of Lisieux, her prayers save sinners from hell.

Gabrielle Boussis (1874-1950) carried on an inner dialogue with Christ. He told her "I am the Ravisher. Don't struggle—and because you let yourself be caught, I will bring you into my secret garden among the flowers and the fruit. You will wear the wedding ring on your finger."[57] She lives in Christ and Christ lives in her: "I start my life on earth all over again with each one of you—my life wedded to yours —if only you choose to invite me."[58] In this wedding Christ and his bride interchange characteristics. She becomes a redeemer— and he becomes feminine. St. Catherine of Siena, in whose writings bridal mysticism is present but extremely subdued, says of a vision of Christ's heart: "She begins to feel the love of her own heart in his consummate and unspeakable love."[59] In almost all the depictions of the Sacred Heart, which became an iconographic theme at an unfortunate period for religious art, the nineteenth century, Jesus is soft, sometimes to the point of being effeminate.

The emphasis on the self-disclosure of Jesus's emotions through his verbal revelations to the women mystics is itself feminine. Men disclose themselves through their actions, women through their words. Women have a greater awareness of and loquacity about their emotions; men tend to cultivate an insensitivity to them and find it difficult to talk about them. This emotional insensitivity is a form of self-protection. If men have to undertake the dangerous tasks of society, a cultivation of emotions will interfere with their ability to carry out their tasks. For a man to talk freely and at length about his emotions sounds feminine, and that is what Jesus does in the visions in which he reveals his heart. Jesus in Scripture is much more reticent about his emotions; he reveals his anger, affection, and distress, but he does not talk about them. The style of the Gospels is closer to Hemingway's or the Icelandic sagas' than the romance novelist's. The Gospels are spare, and we are largely left to deduce emotions from the facts.

The emotions that Jesus talks about in the visions of his Sacred Heart are also emotions more proper to women than to men. He reveals his distress at sin, the pain he feels because of the disruption of communion between sinners and God; he talks of his deep and tender affection for souls. What he does not talk about is his anger at Satan, the wrath of God which is also the fire of his holy love, or his comradeship with those fighting against evil, both of which are prominent in the Gospels and are masculine emotions.

The eroticism upon which the devotion to the Sacred Heart is built might have produced a masculine Jesus. But what seems to have happened is that women (in part) constructed an image of Jesus as they wished men were: sensitive, willing to reveal themselves in speech, always ready to talk about their relationship. Such men are irritating to other men and strike them as effeminate. The masculine objection is not to love, but to self-revelation through words rather than actions.

THE BODY OF CHRIST

Most of all, the body of Christ in the Eucharist was the object of women's devotion. Juliana of Cornillon (1192-1258) called for the establishment of the feast of Corpus Christi. The observance of this feast grew out of the feminine piety of the city of Liège, a center of the Beguines, whom the clergy struggled to keep orthodox.[60] In 1208, Juliana had a dream in which she was called to propagate a new feast in the church, Corpus Christi. Urban IV, who was from Liège, saw the miracle of the bleeding host at Bolsena. The feast struck a responsive note, and was for centuries one of the most popular feasts of Latin Christianity. While the Eucharist had of course always been seen as spiritual food, there was a particularly feminine tone to this devotion because of women's close involvement in the preparation of food and because in nursing a woman becomes food for an infant.[61] Jesus, who feeds the faithful upon his body and blood, is on this view a feminine figure.

Women mystics lived upon nothing but the Eucharist. They saw a wounded man, or a baby, in the Eucharist.[62] Despite the desire women had for frequent communion,[63] an eros that delighted in seeing replaced the eating of the body and blood. Vision became the primary means of contact with the Eucharist, as the Beatific Vision was the culmination of human life in both the *Summa Theologiae* of Thomas Aquinas and the *Divine Comedy* of Dante. From this period comes the custom of elevating the host and of adoration of the host in a monstrance. Communion became less frequent, as the emphasis was placed on seeing the host. The Mass was viewed as a propitiatory sacrifice offered for the living and the dead, but the act of eating essential to the completion of the sacrifice was neglected.

Perhaps men neglected communion because for men the union with Christ's body achieved in the Eucharist had taken on uncomfortably erotic overtones. In a passage from Hadewijch we can see the erotic element in eucharistic devotion, as well as the relationship of eroticism to *Wesenmystik*:

> [Christ] gave himself to me in the shape of the sacrament. . . . After that he came himself to me, took me entirely in his arms, and pressed me to him; and all my members felt his in full felicity, in accordance with the desire of my heart and my humanity. So I was outwardly satisfied and fully transported. And then, for a short while, I had the strength to bear this; but soon, after a short time, I lost that manly beauty outwardly in the sight of his form. I saw him completely come to naught and so fade and all at once dissolve that I could no longer recognize or perceive him outside me, and I could no longer distinguish him within me. Then it was to me as if we were one without difference.[64]

Hadewijch is not exceptional. Miri Rubin noticed similar attitudes in other mystics: "The strong erotic tones which suffused the descriptions attributed to these women of their reception and incorporation of Christ into their bodies, drew from a long standing tradition of mystical imagery, but was also a new and direct erotic idiom of longing."[65]

AFFECTIVE SPIRITUALITY AND CHANGES IN DOCTRINE

Christianity, even in its forms that emphasize authority, has always had difficulty in dealing with spiritualities that may contain distortions. The foundational dogmas of Christianity were clarified in the intellectual conflicts of the patristic period, conflicts almost entirely involving men, and the analytic, logical approach has since been used by Church authorities in their attempt to evaluate spiritualities. Yet spiritualities are more systems of metaphors than deductions of syllogisms, and logic is not adequate to deal with them. Catholic authorities knew there was something exaggerated in the spiritualities of many medieval mystics, of Quietists, and of Jansenists. But they attempted to find false, heretical statements that encapsulated the errors, a very difficult project, because feelings rather than thought are at the heart of the matter. Indeed, no church has developed procedures for a fair evaluation of spiritualities. Differences among Protestants usually lead to the foundation of new denominations; Catholics used the clumsy instrument of the Inquisition and now discipline purveyors of false spirituality only if they fall into explicitly doctrinal errors.

As the Church became more and more feminized, the predominance of feminine emotions encouraged both mystics and the theologians who counseled them to attempt a subtle change in Christianity to make it conform more to the desires of the feminine heart. A change of emphasis here, a neglect of inconvenient Scripture there, and soon a religion takes a shape that, though difficult to distinguish from the Christianity of the Gospels, somehow has a quite different effect. Pantheism and universalism, for instance, are the heretical exaggerations of feminine attitudes, but how far can one go in stressing the immanence of God and his will to save before Christianity is left behind? When does bridal receptivity become passivity, and when does passivity become Quietism? There have been differences of opinion over where to draw the line. The authorities win in the textbooks, but the mystics have often won the battle for popular influence.

The Unity of the Soul and God

Since mystics were more often women, they stressed in their visions the feminine theme of unity. Peter Dinzelbacher notes that "from the sixth to the middle of the twelfth centuries visionary experiences was almost completely a masculine matter; whereas since the thirteenth century this charismatic gift predominantly belongs to women."[66] *Wesenmystik* (Being-Mysticism), which began among women, stressed the unity of the soul and God rather than the difference or distinction between them and was taught by the Dominican theologians Johannes Tauler, Meister Eckert, and Henry Suso, who all explained and justified the mysticism of the religious women they were directing.[67]

Eckert and Tauler, because they sought to understand, elucidate, and guide the mystical experiences of Christians who were all women, began to use language that caused acute discomfort in Rome. While these Dominicans were not heretics, they taught two things in particular which sounded offensive to pious ears, at least if those ears were masculine. The first was their search for a Godhead beyond the Trinitarian God, an undifferentiated unity from which all things, including Father, Son, and Holy Spirit, came and into which they would return. The second was the identity of the soul and God. These Dominicans used the theology of exemplarism derived from pseudo-Denys, and pointed out that the ideas of all things in the mind of God, the exemplars of existing things, were themselves identical with the divine essence. The Dominicans were probably seeking a philosophical ground for the entirely orthodox doctrine of deification in this second theme, the infinitely close and transforming unity of God and man, but they used language which made the union of the soul and God sound more like a numerical identity. Pantheism is the path along which feminine religious experience easily proceeds. The Beguines and Beghards throughout the fourteenth century evinced a "latent pantheism" that "went too far in identifying the mystic with God."[68] The first doctrine, the Godhead behind God, is of even more dubious orthodoxy, and has been revived by those who wish to escape a personal God, since it is difficult for us to imagine a person who is not either masculine or feminine, and it is difficult to maintain that the Scriptures put forth a feminine image of God.

From the feminine religious experience of unity Quietism is an easy development. Quietism, according to its enemies prevalent among the Beguines, declared that man's highest perfection consists in a sort of psychical self-annihilation and a subsequent absorption of the soul into the Divine Essence. From this comes Illuminism, the doctrine that the perfected soul, since it is God, or so closely united with him as to be indistinguishable from him, cannot sin. Such implications made Church authorities very uneasy, especially as the antinomianism lurking in such doctrines was also directed against secular authority.

PURGATORY

Purgatory was the keystone of medieval Catholicism. Although it has patristic roots, it was not developed in the first millennium and was never developed in the East, although the universal practice of praying for the dead presupposes something like purgatory. As LeGoff has documented, ideas about purgatory were elaborated only in the Middle Ages, although it was the people, and not the hierarchy, that provided the impetus for the attention to purgatory.[69] The hierarchy attempted to integrate this belief into the sacramental practices of the church. Mass could be offered for the dead. Endowments provided numerous benefices for priests, whose sole purpose was to pray for the dead. Indulgences could be applied to the dead, and indulgences could also provide a steady income for the church.

The impetus for purgatory was not only popular, it was specifically feminine. Barbara Newman says that "of all Catholic doctrines, none has been more deeply shaped by female piety than the notion of purgatory, which filled an overwhelming place in the visions, devotions, and works of charity undertaken by religious women."[70] Margaret Ebner had a great devotion to the Poor Souls and held continual converse with them.[71] The important role that purgatory played in the spiritual life of women is rooted in the feminine sense of connectedness, which causes women to seek to aid others even beyond the barrier of death and also causes them to be reluctant to admit that any are lost. The doctrine of purgatory is the orthodox (at least from a Catholic point of view) version of the Universalism that was rejected, in theory if not in practice, by the historic churches. As it is obvious that most Christians are sinners, some doubt must remain about their fate after death. Purgatory explained how salvation was possible for those who obviously had a lot to answer for in this world.

UNIVERSALISM

Julian of Norwich is but one Western visionary who expresses a hope for universal salvation, since she is told by Christ that "All things shall be well," and "you yourself shall see that all manner of things shall be well."[72] Julian marvels at this word of Christ's, because she knows of the eternal damnation of the demons and unrepentant sinners, but she is reassured by Christ that "what is impossible to you is not impossible to Me; I shall save My word in all things and I shall make all things well."[73] Julian has become the favorite mystic of Christian feminists.

Universalism was not in favor among orthodox clerics, but women felt its attraction. Gertrude of Helfta, like Isaac of Nineveh, was moved by compassion for all creatures: "When she saw little birds or other animals suffering from hunger or thirst or cold, she was moved to pity for the works of her Lord."[74] She feels this way because she is "like a bride who knows all the secrets of her spouse, and who, after living a long time with him, knows how to interpret his wishes." She is so united with God that her "soul, all on fire with divine charity, became herself charity, desiring nothing but that all might be saved."[75] Gertrude in a way becomes God; her love is so great "she did not hesitate to play the part of an equal with God, the Lord God of the universe."[76] Those who did not deny the existence of hell claimed that hell itself was a form of mercy to those who rejected God. Catherine of Genoa said "the suffering of the damned is not limitless, for God's sweet goodness sends his rays there, even in hell."[77] He does this by not giving men what they deserve: "Even in hell the soul does not suffer as much as it deserves."[78] Yet merely limiting the pains of hell was not sufficient for women mystics; they wanted to empty it of its denizens.

Hans Urs von Balthasar is a theologian noted for his orthodoxy, and is a favorite theologian of Pope John Paul II, who named him a cardinal just before von Balthasar's death. Yet von Balthasar created a minor controversy with his book *Dare We Hope "That All Men Be Saved"?*[79] He was influenced by the Swiss mystic Adrienne von Speyr, and in his chapter "Testimonies"[80] relies heavily on women mystics, especially of the Middle Ages. He quotes Mechtilde of Hakeborn, who influenced Thérèse of Lisieux. Mechtilde hears Jesus saying of Judas: "At this kiss, my heart felt such love through and through that, had he only repented, I would have won his soul as bride by virtue of this kiss."[81] In this sentence we see many of the themes of the mystics: the eros of the soul and Christ, the Sacred Heart, the hope for universal salvation, including even Judas. The women mystics were willing to undergo any suffering, to receive the stigmata, to go to hell, in order to save sinners. Von Balthasar notes that these experiences "stem from a fervent love of the Cross, from a wish to suffer together with Jesus for the redemption of mankind, and therefore gain a small share, in a manner pleasing to God, in Jesus' godforsakenness."[82] Von Balthasar's theology of Holy Saturday, in which the soul of Christ descends among the lost so that he may be also with them, and his consequent hope for universal salvation have their roots in the women mystics of medieval and post-medieval Western Catholicism.

THE RELIGION OF THE HEART

The religion of the heart flourished in both Protestantism and Catholicism, and the heart has been a feminine one. Herbert Moller characterized the popular religious atmosphere in European Christianity in early modern times.

> An analysis of the spiritual and emotional content of this mysticism reveals the invasion of feminine feelings into the sphere

of religion—love of Christ as the "bridegroom" of the feminine soul being the center of this mystical cult. It took various shapes such as quietism, the devotion to the Sacred Heart of Jesus, the cult of the Infancy, or a visionary intercourse with the Deity. The spiritual leadership of this religious and literary movement was assumed by men and women alike; the broad following, however, drew its strength in overwhelming numbers from among the feminine population. Mysticism was not restricted to any denomination. It pervaded Catholic Europe; it came to be the driving force of Protestant pietism; it flourished in numerous sects and conventicles; the "sacred poets" of seventeenth-century England addressed some of their deepest writings to women; finally is appeared, if only as a secondary trait, in Quakerism.[83]

This spirituality had its roots in the Middle Ages and its branches are still bearing fruit in our time.

This complex of tendencies—bridal mysticism, being mysticism, Universalism—has heavily influenced popular Catholicism. Anne Catherine Emmerich, a Catholic mystic who lived during the Napoleonic Wars and whose writings still enjoy wide popularity, said "I very often saw blood flowing from the cross on the Sacred Host; I saw it distinctly. Sometimes Our Lord, in the form of an Infant, appeared like a lightning-flash in the Sacred Host. At the moment of communicating, I used to see my Saviour like a bridegroom standing by me and, when I had received He disappeared, leaving me filled with a sweet sense of His presence. He pervades the whole soul of the communicant just as sugar is dissolved in water, and the union between the soul and Jesus is always in proportion to the soul's desire to receive Him."[84] Emmerich also has difficulties with the lack of universal salvation. One of her counselors said of her

she had . . . the habit of disputing with God on two points: that he did not convert all the big sinners, and that he punished the impenitent with everlasting pains. She told Him that she could not see how He could act thus, so contrary to His nature, which is goodness itself, as it would be easy for him to convert sinners since all are in His hand. She reminded Him of all that He and

His Son had done for them; of the latter's having shed His blood and given His life for them upon the cross; and His own word and promises of mercy contained in the Scriptures. She asked him with holy boldness, how could He expect men to keep their word, if He did not keep His?[85]

Emmerich was told she had gone too far, and she accepted the existence of hell, albeit unwillingly.

In Emmerich, all the tendencies of medieval mysticism continue, and we can also see in her relationship to the clergy the Aristotelian idea of the masculine as initiatory or governing and the feminine as responsive. She emphasized the importance of obedience to the lawfully constituted clergy, especially amidst the chaos of the Napoleonic wars. Obedience is of course a central Christian virtue: Christ became obedient unto death. For mystics obedience is especially necessary, lest they be led astray by their own desires or the suggestions of spirits other than the Holy Spirit. Yet the stress on feminine obedience presents us with the all too familiar picture of the modern church: a congregation of females being ordered around by male clergy. The presence of obedient, faithful men in the congregation, in proportion to their presence in the general population, would change the dynamics of obedience, and not create an atmosphere of subservient femininity in the church. Much of the contempt in which patriarchy is held by religious feminists arises from this peculiar demographic situation, in which a male clergy seems to be inculcating obedience in a female congregation so as to be served and not to serve.

This perhaps overheated world of mysticism is not a matter of the past in the Catholic Church. For decades, teenage seers at Medjugorje have received regular messages from Mary. Despite the disapproval of the local bishop of Mostar and the lack of enthusiasm in Rome, Medjugorje has become one of the largest pilgrimage centers in the world. It has also spawned numerous other miracles. Marina Warner recounts the events surrounding a statue of the bleeding Madonna in Italy: "Besides the priest, I could count only six men in the church, which must seat around two hundred. . . . Many of the women were brown, crooked, and gnarled, like cruel

Renaissance allegories of Vanity. . . . Later, during the rosary, a plaster statue of Our Lady of Fatima was passed around the congregation; each person, when her turn came to hold it, recited the first versicle of the Hail Mary. A younger woman whispered to me, 'It's so beautiful to cradle the Madonna as if she were a baby in your arms! Oh, you must do it!'"[86] We have entered the familiar world of medieval affective devotion. A priest involved in the affair is devoted to Luisa Piccarreta, who "survived on nothing but Communion wafers for sixty-five years."[87] It is still a world of women, and is still tinted with maternal eroticism (this time toward Mary). Such devotion is perhaps better than cold rationalism, but the unbalanced atmosphere is both a cause and result of the lack of men in the life of the church.

LANGUAGE

Walter Ong, having been formed in a masculine, Jesuit, clerical milieu does not seem to be aware of how feminized Christianity had become even before the 1960s, but he saw a rapid shift in the Catholic Church in the 1960s toward even greater feminization. He identified masculinity with struggle, the "agonic." The struggle with falsehood, for instance, has been, if not abandoned, at least toned down: "Down through Pius ix's Syllabus of modern error (1867) a conspicuously agonistic stance has commonly marked conciliar and papal doctrinal pronouncements. Indeed it has been a commonplace of theology that the Church needs heretics (adversaries) to sharpen its understanding of the truth it possesses. . . . But the agonistic can be a central or a peripheral concern: of late, it has moved from the center to the periphery. The tone of the decrees of the Second Vatican Council (1962-1965), while often forthright and firm, lacks the agonistic edge typical of many earlier church pronouncements."[88] The preferred model of church life is irenic, or conciliatory, or waffling; clarity is *declassé*. Ong detects this change in the liturgy:

> A statistically analytic recent study . . . has compared the sixteenth-century *Catechism of the Council of Trent* and *A New Cat-*

echism: Catholic Faith for Adults, the widely-used post-Vatican II
"Dutch Catechism," and found the former distinctively polemic in presentation of Catholic doctrine in high contrast to
the less agonistic approach of the latter. The old *Breviarum
romanum* had included in the round of its weekly readings all of
the 150 psalms: the new *Liturgy of the Hours* (1971), which replaces the *Breviary*, omits three execrative psalms calling down
God's wrath on the psalmist's enemies. . . . In similar nonago-
nistic style, instead of writing off the human city as inimical to
the heavenly kingdom, the *Liturgy of the Hours* now prays, "may
we work together to build up the earthly city, with our eyes
fixed on the city which lasts forever". . . . The duality is still
there, but the intensely agonistic stage of consciousness has
been superseded by another stage, and existence is not longer
defined so utterly by polemic.[89]

The contrasts of Christianity, grace and sin, life and death, have
been toned down with a considerable loss of emotional power.
Without this power, the popular appeal of the liturgy has declined
(even with a more accessible language) and church attendance has
plummeted.

The liturgical use of language can achieve emotional intensity in
different ways. The Byzantine liturgy has an intensely emotional element deriving from the theological hymns of the Syriac church, in
which the emotions of awe and wonder are evoked at the irruption of
the divine into the human. The Latin liturgy achieved intensity in a
different way. Building upon the biblical use of antithesis, the Latin
liturgy evoked strong contrasts, of good and evil, of joy and misery,
of hope and fear. The ICEL translators, as Ong noticed, systemati-
cally flattened these to the point that all emotional intensity is lost.
The consequent emotional flatness is disappointing in what is supposed to be the central action of the visible universe, the Divine Liturgy in which the sacrificial self-communication of God is made
present. The Anglican Elizabethan translation of the liturgy lasted
for centuries with only modest revision because it stayed close to the
rhetoric of the Roman Liturgy, especially in it use of contrasts and
antithesis, and its rolling periods, clause piled upon clause to achieve

an effect of sublimity and climax. The ICEL translation, because of its use of short sentences and lack of antithesis, has lost the emotional quality of the Roman liturgy. The consequent vacuum attracts those who try to fill it by spontaneous additions but do not have the skill of the ancient authors. Two recent and public results of the feminization of the church have been the use of what is called "inclusive language," and the use of women as priests, pastors, and ministers. If the church is composed mostly of women, women should be its rulers, according to modern democratic sentiment. The use of masculine terms to refer to Christians is also anachronistic: there are few men, and those that remain are often not very masculine.

Even the change from Latin to the vernacular was also a symptom of feminization, according to Ong. Latin had been a means of maintaining a Latin culture in the Roman Catholic clergy. A language restricted to men is common; it is a sign of masculine separation from the feminine world. After it became a learned language, Latin was learned almost exclusively by men. The system of education that used Latin and centered around Latin literature was centered around contest and disputation and was confined almost entirely to men. The disappearance of Latin was part of the demasculinization of the clergy. Ong notes that "within two years, 1967 and 1968, the School of Divinity of Saint Louis University (1) ceased using Latin as a method of instruction, (2) dropped the thesis method as a method of instruction, (3) dropped circles and disputations together with oral course examinations as integral parts of its program, and (4) admitted women students."[90] Catholic life, including its liturgy, has given up the attitude that the Christian is separate from the world, which is his enemy.

THE TRINITY

The doctrine of the Trinity is undergoing a rapid transformation. The masculine names of the first two persons have offended feminists, and some churches (including an occasional Catholic priest) are starting to baptize in the name of the Creator, the Redeemer, and the Sanctifier. These names specify the actions of the godhead *ad extra*, to the creation, while the point of the names of the Father, Son, and Holy Spirit is that the Christian is incorporated into the inner life of the Trinity. The Father is the Father of the Son, the Son the Son of the Father. The Spirit of Sonship comes upon the Son and constitutes him Son, and returns to the Father to acknowledge him as Father.

Some wish to preserve the scriptural names of Father and Son and still find a place for femininity inside the godhead. The Spirit, as we have seen, has an association with femininity, and therefore has been the recipient of the pronoun *she*. Even highly orthodox theologians are determined to make the Trinity feminine. The misidentification of femininity and receptivity provides the means. As David Schindler summarized Hans Urs von Balthasar's position, "The Father, as the begetting origin-without-origin, is primarily (supra-) masculine ([über-]männlich); the Son, as begotten and thus receptive (der Geschenlassende) is (supra-)feminine ([über-] weiblich); but then the Father and the Son, as jointly spirating the Spirit, are again (supra-)masculine; the Spirit, then is (supra-) feminine; finally, the Father, who allows himself to be conditioned in return *in* his begetting and spiriting, himself thereby has a (supra-) feminine dimension."[91] It would seem that von Balthasar and Schindler would agree with feminists that the Spirit should be called *she*. Although they attempt to preserve the names of Father and Son, the feminine aspects of both persons would seem to at least allow Mother and Daughter as alternative names. If the Second Person is feminine within the Trinity because of her receptivity, and we are incorporated by baptism into the Trinity, we can rightfully call the First Person Mother and be daughters of God. Such is the result of the attempt to apply Aristotelian categories to Christianity.

Men's and Women's Reactions

If men of normal or pronounced masculinity see that religion has somehow made its professional male representatives, the clergy, less masculine, they will feel a strong desire to stay away from the church. David Martin alludes to the situation in which clergymen find themselves: "There is the inevitable corollary that high female representation in church affects the self-image of the clergyman in a rather deleterious way."[92] It is not simply a matter of image. The only male group that is more feminine than the occupational group that includes the clergy (and artists and editors and journalists) in Terman and Miles's survey is that of passive male homosexuals.[93]

Feminism is multiform, but many strains are clearly incompatible with historic Christianity. In our time, theologians and church authorities adopt a tolerant attitude to feminist aberrations. Ironically, this may be because women are not taken seriously as moral agents; their errors are regarded as silly female notions that will pass. Nevertheless, feminism may be as much a challenge to Christianity as was Gnosticism (to which it bears a strong resemblance).

The mainline Protestant clergy is becoming a feminine profession.[94] In the Episcopal Church, since 1930 "the ratio of young male priests has dropped about 80 percent."[95] Feminist theologians are unearthing vast amounts of literature from the medieval and post-medieval periods (only a small portion of which I have cited above) that provides a distinctly feminine twist to Christianity. The "traditional" position is weakened by its acceptance of the identification of femininity and receptivity. This error can lead to distortions even of Trinitarian theology. It also does not provide a sound basis for women to understand their own femininity and its place in Christianity. The rejection of a distorted Christianity by feminists has roots in the attempt to identify femininity with receptivity and obedience.[96]

If the feminization of the Church continues, men will continue to seek their spiritual sustenance outside the churches, in false or inadequate religions, with highly damaging consequences for the church and society. Neither fascism nor criminal anarchy is conducive to Christian life. The inner life of the Church will also be weakened. The Scriptures and the writings of the Fathers will become more and more incomprehensible, and will be rewritten or ignored. Central Christian doctrines, such as the Trinity and the Atonement, are under severe attack, and may vanish from the popular consciousness of Christians, to be replaced by a self-worship that cloaks itself in Christian language. A Dominican Prioress quotes approvingly the Statement of Philosophy from the journal *Women of Power*, which upholds "the honoring of women's divinity."[97] Women reject "the practice of self-sacrificial love"[98] in favor of "self-realization."[99] Women reject obedience because they "are seeking a God with whom they can be one, not to whom they must be subject."[100] Jesus's atoning sacrifice vanishes and is replaced by "the vision that Jesus' phantasy enkindled when he walked among us."[101] The Church will survive feminism as it survived gnosticism, but its life and missionary impulse will be severely weakened.

The Old Testament warns of the dangers of uxoriousness. Men, from Adam to the Jews of Nehemiah's time, allowed their affection for women to persuade them to tolerate women's importation of the worship of false gods into the life of the Chosen People. Not every woman did so; many were loyal like Judith and Esther, but enough worshipped false gods to bring disaster upon Israel. In the first millenium heresy came from men, not women. In the second millenium, although men continue to develop and revive heresies, women have been the sources of serious distortions of Christianity. Typology may provide a clue to understanding the Old Testament, and both Catholics and Protestants have seen events of the Old Testament as paralleled in the life of the Church. Typology requires discernment of spirits, but it appears that Christian leaders are following the example of Adam, and give free rein to those women who have listened to the serpent: "Ye shall be as gods."

8

Countercurrents

THE FEMINIZATION OF THE CHURCH has not gone uncontested. The distortions in spirituality and practice were glaringly obvious to both Catholics and Protestants. Both the Reformation and the Counter-Reformation included unsuccessful attempts to shake off the feminine piety of the Middle Ages, return to the spirituality of the New Testament and the Church Fathers, and give greater emphasis to the church militant. The Jesuits represented a new masculine emphasis in the Roman Catholic Church, a return to patristic ideas of the inner life as a spiritual combat. Luther reminded Christians that the chief foe was the devil, who was more and more seen as active in human agents, whether they were papists or witches. In North America, the Penitentes of the Southwest continued or revived Spanish practices to form a vigorous and enduring Christian masculinity; Protestants used revivalist techniques to attract men to a new birth and a final transformation.

These attempts continued when, at the beginning of the twentieth century, business became the religion of the common man. The Men and Religion Forward Movement, for instance, used the techniques of modern advertising to bring men to Christ. Biblical and patristic revivals in the Roman Catholic Church tried to return the

Church to models of spirituality that existed before the feminization and sentimentalization of medieval piety, and the Second Vatican Council made these models official while trying to heal the split between religion and the public world. Recently, a handful of Catholic and mainline Protestant writers have acknowledged the lack of men. A recent movement, which is still developing, is the evangelical Promise Keepers, which has updated the revivalist tradition and has had much initial success.

MEDIEVAL CATHOLIC MASCULINITY

The Middle Ages were not totally feminized in their religious practices. The clergy remained all male, and the cultivation of a combative, agonistic style of scholastic rational theology appealed to men, although this theology was not very fruitful for the life of the Church. Its sterility gave rise to a call for a religion of the heart, in such movements as the Brethren of the Common Life, with its great product, *The Imitation of Christ*, and Lutheranism. Preaching was aimed specifically at men: the Bernard who called himself and his monks *women* and who popularized bridal mysticism was also the preacher of the First Crusade. Men also participated in the eroticism of religion in the chivalric veneration of Mary.

The Crusades

The element common to Bernard of Clairvaux's encouragement of both eros and violence was a humanization of religious emotion. Human emotions, erotic love and anger, were integrated into Christianity through their direction to the Celestial Bridegroom, on the one hand, and the enemies of the Church on the other, in particular heretics and Saracens. Christ often took on the attributes of an earthly bridegroom and was the object of more or less explicit erotic fantasies; the external enemies of the Church took on the attributes of the demons and became the object of a war of annihilation.

In addition to the *Sermons on the Song of Songs*, Bernard was the author, for the Knights of the Order of the Temple, of *On the New*

Christian Militia.[1] He felt some discomfort in both books, for he realized that he was innovating and that his innovations needed a defense. Bernard insists that "to inflict death or to die for Christ is no sin,"[2] and he defends the Christian knight against charges of manslaughter: "If he kills an evildoer, he is not a mankiller, but, if I may so put it, a killer of evil."[3] Bernard claims he does not mean "that the pagans are to be slaughtered when there is any other way to prevent them from harassing and persecuting the faithful, but only that it now seems better to destroy them."[4] Bernard cites John the Baptist's advice to soldiers to be content with their pay as implying the legitimacy of killing and goes so far as to characterize the knight who dies in warfare against the pagans as "a martyr"[5]—a theme taken up in modern times, when the soldier who dies for his country became the new Christ.

Chivalric Devotion to Mary

Male mystics and religious in the Middle Ages centered their spiritual life not on images of the feminine divine, but on Mary.[6] The problems of regarding God as in some way feminine posed too many emotional and intellectual challenges. Nor did men feel all that comfortable adopting a feminine stance before God. Some had the intellectual and poetic abilities to do it, but most felt an intense male fear of homosexuality, especially of passive homosexuality, of being used like a woman. It was easier to venerate the divine in Mary. The eros implicit in medieval devotion led to this development. Women's devotion to Christ was tinged with eros; that is why "women concentrate especially on the infant or adolescent Christ," while "monks refer more frequently to the virgin Mary."[7] Veneration of the Mother of God has a long history in Christianity, but it took a very odd turn in the Middle Ages at the same time that bridal and maternal mysticism came to dominate the life of women in the Church.

Femininity, because of its passivity, paradoxically opens women to the power of the Holy Spirit. They are like soft wax that more easily takes an imprint. Mary, above all, was passive and receptive

and took the imprint of the Spirit better than anyone else. She took
it so well that she sometimes looks very much like God. Hilda Graef
in her survey of Marian devotion notes: "This tendency to assimilate
Mary increasingly to the transcendence of God himself becomes
even more pronounced in later writers."[8] Mary became the Queen of
Mercy, the protector of sinners from the justice of Christ.[9] God was
attracted by her beauty and became her lover at the Annunciation.[10]
She held his hand from punishment; she rescued the impenitent
from hell; she knew everything from the first moment of her conception;[11] she was equal to God;[12] she was greater than God.[13] Christian
men had a quasi-erotic relationship with her. St. John Eudes in the
seventeenth century "saw Mary as the spouse of the priest; indeed at
the age of sixty-seven he drew up a formal contract of marriage with
her and henceforth wore a ring."[14] After being confronted by Pusey
with the beliefs concerning Mary that were propagated by Catholic
books of devotion, John Henry Newman, already a Catholic, replied
that "I consider them calculated to prejudice inquirers, to frighten
the unlearned, to unsettle consciences, to provoke blasphemy, and to
work the loss of souls."[15] The Second Vatican Council emphasized
the subordination of Mary to Christ and cautioned against "the fal-
sity of exaggeration."[16]

CATHOLIC REACTIONS

The changes I have summed up in the word "feminization" were not
unnoticed by contemporaries. Eckhart was (probably unfairly) condemned, and mysticism was suspected by the various Inquisitions.
Catholics who were already trying to return the Church to its early
purity were stung by the accusations of the Reformers, who claimed
that the reformed church was closer to the early church. Some medieval innovations made Catholics very uncomfortable. Obvious visual eroticism was an immediate target, and changed attitudes to art
can be dated almost to the year. The Jesuits tried to regain the monastic tradition of spiritual militancy. In the Spanish Americas, the
traditions of penitential fraternities revived and flourished. In the
twentieth century, Vatican II reacted against the sentimental devo-

tions that dominated Catholic life and against the related tendency to exclude the Church from public, that is, masculine, life. Two Jesuits, Walter Ong and Patrick Arnold, have diagnosed the feminization of the church and the consequences of the lack of men.

Suspicion of Eros in Religion

The Counter-Reformation reacted in part against the extreme feminization and eroticization of Catholic piety during the Middle Ages. Leo Steinberg documents both the eroticism and the reaction against it in *The Sexuality of Christ in Renaissance Art and Modern Oblivion*.[17] Christ's sexuality was central to much art because art needed a visual manifestation of the eroticism of bridal and maternal mysticism. Consequently, the genitals of the infant and of the crucified Christ were emphasized to an extraordinary degree. What was being emphasized was not so much Christ's sexuality as the human relationship to God, which according to mystics and theologians was essentially feminine. If the Christian was essentially feminine in relationship to a masculine God, the visual counterpart of that masculinity was of course maleness, and maleness centered upon the genitals. Yet the sexual overtones are inescapable, as the official guardians of Catholic art realized.

Reforming Catholics felt that something was wrong with this eroticism, and the change in attitude occurred very quickly. Renaissance nudes were given loincloths and pants. Michelangelo chiseled the leg off of Christ in a *pietà* because Christ's posture was too overtly sexual. In particular, the images that were redolent of homosexuality, in which the Father pointed to the genitals of the son, were abandoned. Mysticism in general came under suspicion, not simply because it provided a path to God apart from the sacramental, hierarchical church, but because the eroticism of mysticism was felt to be somehow offensive.

This reaction was only partial and did not destroy the main currents of popular devotion, though it purged eroticism of some of its most overtly sexual references. Since the eros of mother and child is not explicitly genital, it remained at the heart of Catholic piety. Furthermore, the religion of the heart, which was based upon medieval affective piety, continued to dominate the Catholic laity. The erotic focus on the emotions of the believer tended to identify him as feminine.

The Jesuits and Militant Spirituality

The Jesuits were prominent in Counter-Reformation Catholicism until the twentieth century. They were far more masculine than the medieval orders, all of which, in spite of their resistance, had been feminized in the thirteenth and fourteenth centuries. The Jesuits, unlike the Cistercians, Dominicans, and Franciscans, never had a female branch. As Robert Harvey notes, "With the exception of one brief episode . . . there was no consideration given to the founding of a female order in connection with the company of Jesus."[18] Although much of Ignatius's initial support came from women—his "efforts met with a greater response among the women than in any other quarter"[19]—he wanted his followers to steer clear of them: "All familiarity with women was to be avoided, and not less with those who are spiritual, or wish to appear so."[20]

Ignatius was a soldier[21] and remained one, although now "the new soldier of Christ."[22] His conversion was brought about by reading a version of the *Legenda aurea* that emphasized the chivalric nature of Christianity. After his conversion he tried to be a better Christian by following both the crusading and chivalric ideals. He nearly killed a Moslem who, by denying that Mary remained a virgin *in partu*, was not sufficiently respectful of Mary for Ignatius's taste: "At this, various emotions came over him and caused discontent in his soul, as it seemed he had not done his duty. They also aroused his indignation against the Moor, for it seemed that he had done wrong in allowing the Moor to say such things about Our Lady, and that he ought to sally forth in defense of her honor. He felt inclined to go in search of the Moor and stab him with his dagger for what he had said."[23] A divine sign spares the Moor, and Ignatius seems to look back upon this incident as a symptom that he was very immature in the spiritual life, that he did not yet understand what kind of service God demanded of him.

Ignatius, in his *Spiritual Exercises*, abandoned the tradition of bridal mysticism. He uses "bride" to refer only to the Church, not to the Christian.[24] Even in a passage in which he compares Satan to a "false lover"[25] who seduces the soul, he does not develop the logical parallel of God as a true lover who woos the soul. Instead, Ignatius returns to the older patristic and monastic models of spiritual warfare. He compares the Christian to a knight who is addressed by an earthly king: "It is my will to conquer all the lands of the infidel. Therefore, whoever wishes to join with me in this enterprise must be content with the same food, drink, clothing etc. as mine. So, too, he must work with me by day, and watch with me by night, etc., that as he had a share in the toil with me, afterwards, he may share in the victory with me."[26] This military experience, of being comrades and followers of an earthly prince, is the analogy that Ignatius chooses to help the Christian understand his role in the drama of salvation. Christ speaks to each Christian: "It is my will to conquer the whole world and all my enemies, and thus to enter into the glory of my Father. Therefore, whoever wishes to join me in this enterprise must be willing to labor with me, that by following me in suffering, he may follow me in glory."[27] The Christian is forced to choose between the two standards, "the one of Christ, our supreme leader and lord, the other of Lucifer, the deadly enemy of our human nature."[28] The Jesuits always felt that life was a struggle, whether a warfare with evil or a contest with self and God. Alonso de Orozco, echoing patristic and monastic language, warned "that he who would see the face of the most powerful Wrestler, our boundless God, must first have wrestled with himself."[29]

The Penitentes

The Penitentes of New Mexico are among the few groups of Catholics that have maintained a vital hold on the male laity for centuries. The Penitentes do not worship Jesus the Bridegroom, but, as they sing in one of their songs "Jesús confrado,"[30] Jesus the Brother, in whose suffering they participate as brothers. The Penitentes either continue or revive (documentation is lacking) the penitential traditions of medieval Europe.

The penitential fraternities were the successors to the Crusades, which had begun as a penitential exercise. Penance, and not killing, was their central spiritual value.[31] Those who did not go on crusade could join a confraternity, whose male members often did not get along well with the clergy.[32] Penitents engaged in a close imitation of Jesus, and took upon themselves the sufferings of the world. The Flagellants, making public an old private practice, whipped themselves through the streets "in order to avert God's anger by assimilating themselves with Christ through sharing in his sufferings."[33] These were all male.[34] In Europe these male religious organizations had died out: "The confraternities of penitents were absorbed by the third orders, which recruited their own members primarily among women."[35]

During Holy Week, the Penitentes, more properly the Brothers of the Confraternities of the Holy Blood, strip themselves to the waist, bloody their backs with flint knives or broken glass, beat themselves and each other with cactus whips, carry man-sized wooden crosses in solemn procession through the desert, temporarily crucify themselves, and spend the whole of Good Friday night in darkness, prayer, and sleepless vigil. All of this is to make real the adjurations, "Take up your cross and follow me" and "Put on Christ." They wish to identify and conform themselves more perfectly to the image of the living Christ, to become a version in flesh of the *santos*—the images of the holy ones—like the carved and painted figures the Penitentes' *santeros* (literally "saint-makers") fashion from the recalcitrant materials of the American desert.

The rites of initiation into the lay confraternities of the Penitentes are startlingly like the puberty rituals with which most societies mark the transformation of boys into men. The would-be *hermano*, or penitent brother, presents himself to the novice master, who determines the candidate to be of good character and not a flagrant public sinner. The novice undergoes a period of prayer and fasting and returns to the master for the solemn rituals of Holy Week. Novices generally strip to the waist and don short white cotton trousers, the *calzones*. The novice master, using the ritual flint knife or perhaps only a jagged piece of glass, makes three or four shallow gashes on the penitent's back. The free flow of blood both symbolizes the shedding of Christ's blood and serves a practical purpose during the next stage of the initiation, the flagellation. A prescribed number of strokes with the cactus-fiber whip follow, though the postulant may ask for more. The gashes prevent welts from forming and keep infection from setting in, so that the penance, though real and painful, does no lasting physical damage.

This stage of the initiation generally takes place within the nearly windowless, candlelit interior of the confraternity's chapel, the *morada*. From there, the brothers march in solemn procession along a route representing the Stations of the Cross, a symbolic journey as well as a physical one. Some of the brothers carry a piece of cactus inside their *calzones*; others carry full-size wooden crosses. Like their counterparts in Spain, many of the flagellants cover their faces with hoods, not to mask their participation in shameful rites (as pioneer Anglos thought), but as a precaution against spiritual pride. The brothers of the confraternity process to the accompaniment of sung, never spoken, prayers and the music of the *pito*, the liturgical flute. Generally the procession follows a nearly life-sized crucifix or figure of the suffering Christ, another of his mother, and sometimes more figures representing soldiers, the crowd, and the sorrowing women.

At the fourth station, where Christ meets his sorrowing mother, the *hermanos* stage the *encuentro*, the dramatic scene of that meeting. The statues of Jesus and Mary (Mary is often carried by women) are brought together and an *alabados* sung, voicing the sadness each of them feels at seeing the other's pain. Farther on, at the climax of the Holy Week paraliturgies, the brothers re-enact the Crucifixion in the same way, creating a drama that they understand both by observing and participating in it. They affix the figure of Christ to a cross and raise it aloft for all to see, life-sized, bloody, crowned with cactus thorns or nails and contrived with moveable arms, legs, jaws that can open and shut to simulate the last words, and sometimes even a concealed compartment in the side from which blood and water can be made to gush out. At the same time that the painted Christ is crucified, the postulant *hermanos* may be tied to their own crosses in sight of the crucifix, where they hang until their veins distend and their trunks turn blue from near-strangulation.

After they are taken down from their crosses, the brothers reenact the Deposition: the nails, the crown, the cloth draping the cross are taken down and given into the outstretched hands of the statue of the mourning Virgin, now become *Nuestra Senora de la Soledad*, Our Lady of Solitude. The dead Christ is laid first in her arms, and then in a special cradle and carried back to the *morada*, again, always accompanied by the appropriate songs of sorrow. Behind the solemn procession the brothers drag the figure of Death, a black-robed, skull-faced woman in a cart full of stones.

At the *morada*, the Christ is laid in state before the altar and the brothers sing a version of the office of *Tenebrae*, extinguishing the candles one by one until the *morada* is entirely dark. The forces of Chaos and Old Night are then given full symbolic play: the brothers wail, rattle the ceremonial rattles, and pray until dawn for their dead. Finally, at daybreak, they come out into the early morning light and sing the final hymn of rejoicing: Salvation is accomplished, for in celebrating Christ's death, they celebrate too his Resurrection.

As with all initiation rites for men, those who emerge successful, who attain to the fulfillment of manhood, are deemed fit to assume positions of societal leadership. Responsible, self-sacrificing leaders were in urgent demand in the Southwestern desert: The small farmers and landholders of New Mexico lay at the furthest outpost of Hispanic civilization. Their peripheral position, coupled with the various breakdowns of the civil order in Mexico and the gradual retrenchment of the Spanish empire, left the New Mexicans more or less to their own devices. The withdrawal of military support, the dwindling number of available clergy from Durango, and the dearth of rich and powerful landholders who might serve as a stabilizing class, forced the New Mexicans to invent new ways to meet their own liturgical and societal needs. The Brotherhoods filled the gap.

In the absence of priests, or with only occasional visits from clergy riding a long circuit, the confraternities provided the only liturgy available, and kept alive the community's life of prayer. Charitable works, feeding the hungry, clothing and housing the victims of the disasters of a harsh desert environment, protecting the weak, and burying the dead worked not only for the acquisition of virtue but for the stabilizing good of the society as a whole. Indeed, one can hardly distinguish between the two, and Christians might argue that the two goals are inseparable. The *hermanos* assumed a major role, if not the major role, in maintaining the civil order. The *hermano mayor*, the head of the *morada*, settled disputes and administered justice in practice, however much law and jurisdiction may have in theory lain with the King of Spain.

In Spain also, the public processions are one of the few occasions on which men feel they can display their religion. In the town of Monteros, the men never go to church, yet participate with enthusiasm in the procession of the *Señor de Consuelo*, a painting of the Crucifixion. Only boys are allowed the difficult task of carrying the large painting in its heavy frame through the streets. The painting is an emotional one: "One has only to look at the painting of the crucified Christ, his head hung pitifully sideways, his eyes downcast, to recognize that he is a man who has sacrificed greatly."[36] The boys, suffering under the weight, thereby "at once display power and suffering, [and] identify closely with the Son of God."[37] Men, in seeing the image of the crucified see the destiny of all men to be a sacrifice. They honor, in some sense, a "self-portrait, a supernatural image of themselves."[38] In Christ, as in men who fulfill their masculinity, there is a union of power and weakness, because men are strong only so that they may give of themselves to others, even to the point of death.

Twentieth-Century Catholic Outreach to Men

In a quiet way, the most effective Catholic outreach to men, or to be more precise, the most effective work that Catholic men have done with one another, has been through the Knights of Columbus. It was in some ways modeled after the non-Catholic fraternal orders that had been so successful in nineteenth-century America. Christopher J. Kauffman points out that "traditional notions of the male role permeated every aspect of Columbian fraternalism. The ceremonial 'rite of passage' was intended to imbue the member with a 'manly' sense of pride in his Catholicism and a strong dedication to defend the faith. The insurance program was a medium for expressing the breadwinner's economic responsibility for his family."[39]

On a more theological level, the *ressourcement* that preceded Vatican II was a cultivation of biblical and patristic studies, in an attempt to overcome the bifurcation between theology and piety that had begun with Scholasticism. Basil Pennington, a key figure in the *ressourcement*, set forth the purpose of the program: "There is a great need to reach back to the other side of the 'scholastic parenthesis' and pick up those currents of life which are more integrally and fully human, open to the divine and the divinization of the human."[40] The central thesis of *The Spirituality of the Middle Ages* is that Christian life had split into rationalist theology and pietistic devotion because of Scholastic hyper-rationalism, and that the two must be reunited, or, as von Balthasar put it, theology must be done on the knees.

The Church in the West had also become increasingly privatized after the Middle Ages. Religion was a matter of sentiment, and best confined to the home or the individual.[41] It had no relevance in a secular world governed by principles of reason that were accessible to all. The various churches reacted differently to this enforced privatization. The liberal churches, and some not so liberal, took up the Social Gospel. After various experiments with Catholic Action, the Catholic Church in Vatican II called for an *aggiornamento*, which would overcome the relegation of Christianity to the feminine world of the home: "Vatican II was an attempt on the part of the hierarchy to move the Church back over to the masculine, public side of the public/private split."[42] Again, there was an attempt to put a parenthesis around the developments that began in the twelfth century and to resume a relationship with society that had characterized the Church of the first millennium.

But, to date, the attempts of Vatican II to attain an *aggiornamento* by a *ressourcement* have not been successful. The extraordinary pontificate of John Paul II and the union of religious and nationalist fervor in Poland was almost certainly a key factor in the end of Communism in central and Eastern Europe. But the West continues to undergo a process by which religion is further feminized and public life further secularized.

A few Catholic writers, a very few, have noticed the lack of men in the church and have attempted to give both a diagnosis and a remedy. Patrick Arnold, in *Warriors, Wildmen and Kings: Masculine Spirituality and the Bible*, has made excellent practical suggestions. On the subject of the liturgy he says, "Butterfly, Banner, and Balloon Extravaganzas severely alienated many men. The most saccharine outbreaks of forced liturgical excitement featured fluttering dancers floating down church aisles like wood-nymphs, goofy pseudo-rites forced on the congregation with almost fascist authoritarianism, and a host of silly *schticks* usually accompanied by inane music." Arnold continues with the observation that a "liturgy that appeals to men possesses a quality the Hebrews called *kabod* ('glory') and the Romans *gravitas* ('gravity'); both words at root mean 'weightiness' and connote a sense of dignified importance and seriousness."[43] Nevertheless, Arnold's perceptions and attempts at prescribing solutions are vitiated by his obvious sympathy for homosexuality. The current attempts, within almost all Christian denominations, to normalize homosexuality will, more than anything else, convince heterosexual men that religion had best be kept at a great distance.

Little in Catholic circles portends any change in the current situation. Richard Rohr laments that "we seem to have resigned ourselves to church meetings where men are largely absent, to church ministry that is mainly done by women but overseen by a clerical caste, to an often soft devotionalism that attracts only a specific male clientele."[44] The last phrase is an allusion to the weak masculinity of men who tend to be attracted to church. Little in David James's survey *What Are They Saying About Masculine Spirituality?* shows promise for revivifying general male interest in Christianity. There is too much Jungianism, too much emphasis on male weakness and faults, and too few practical suggestions. The ascendancy of the feminist and homosexual agendas in the church blocks the way to any reconnection of men and the church.

PROTESTANT REACTIONS

The theological concerns of the Reformation are of course more important than its relationship to the feminization of the Church, but the gender question was not absent. Most scholars recognize the rejection of the religious feminine by the Reformation: "The Reformation substantially purged Christianity of its feminine elements, leaving men and women alike faced with a starkly masculine religion."[45] Paul Tillich claims that "the spirit of Judaism with its exclusively male symbolism prevailed in the Reformation."[46] The return to biblical and patristic models of spirituality led once again to a portrayal of the life of the Christian as a battle, a spirituality that was essentially masculine. In part the Reformation counteracted medieval feminization, but in part inadvertently reinforced it.

The Reformers

Luther, rejecting most of the comforting medieval devotions to saintly intercessors, mediators, and protectors, returned to a stark view of humanity caught between God and the Devil:

> The believer is never at rest, but is in incessant combat against the "flesh," the "world," the "devil." These three powers are opposed to God and his word. It is not always possible to distinguish them at the level of their action on Christians. The evocation of the devil by Luther is something more than a simple medieval heritage. If he spoke of the devil so often (and more deeply than was done in the Middle Ages), it is because he understood the whole of the history of the world as a battle of demonic power against God the creator and redeemer. Evil is not simply moral or a weakness of people, but transpersonal, bound to that mysterious power which Luther called, with the tradition, Satan or devil."[47]

Nor was this confined to Luther's own life; the hymn that became the battle cry of the Reformation, *Ein' Feste Burg*, portrayed the conflict between God and Satan vividly. The war was universal: "Christ and Satan wage a cosmic war for mastery over Church and world. No one can evade involvement in this struggle. Even for the believer there is no refuge—neither monastery nor the seclusion of the wilderness offer him a chance for escape. The Devil is the omnipresent threat, and exactly for this reason the faithful need the proper weapons for survival."[48] The Lutheran branch of the Reformation, because of its emphasis on *agon*, on struggle, led to a Christianity that was far more masculine than medieval Catholicism had been: "The overwhelming image of both God and the believer in Luther's writings is a masculine one. . . . True faith is energetic, active, steadfast, mighty. Industrious, powerful—all archetypally masculine qualities in the sixteenth (or the twentieth) centuries. God is Father, Son, Sovereign, King, Lord, Victor, Begetter, 'the slayer of sin and the devourer of death'—all aggressive, martial, and totally male images. With the home now the center of women's religious vocation, even the imagery of the Church becomes masculine, or at least paternal and fraternal."[49] The medieval preoccupation with Christ as the bridegroom had of course emphasized the masculinity of Christ, but it was the erotic aspect of masculinity that predominated in the Middle Ages. The Church had always been seen as the Bride, but in Lutheranism the Church became more of a fraternity.

But this note in the Reformation was to grow fainter, the tones of *Ein' Feste Burg* gradually replaced by *O, How I Love Jesus*. The feminine voice grew louder, while the masculine voice was muted, because the demographic composition of the church had changed since the patristic era. It was hard to maintain a masculine attitude in a church whose congregations were predominantly, sometimes overwhelmingly, female.

In its original European forms, all varieties of Protestantism emphasized the role of the father in the family. Luther and Calvin and the Anabaptists all agreed on the necessity of patriarchy. Calvin explained that the husband and wife were equal, but that the wife was functionally subordinate to the husband, whose authority was like that of Christ, an authority of service and sacrifice.[50] Such Christian patriarchalism has largely vanished from Protestantism except in such groups as the Amish, who anchor the identity of males in Christian fatherhood.

Revivalism

Revivalism had roots in Methodism, and it seems that early Methodism appealed about equally to men and women. In East Cheshire, Methodist societies had "about 55 percent female membership," which "closely matches the sex ratio as a whole in textile manufacturing centres."[51] Revivalism did not flourish in England, but became the predominant form of Protestantism after it had been transplanted to the colonies.

The series of revivals that began in the seventeenth century modified the demographic composition of the Church in America, which even in the seventeenth century was largely female. It also affected religious feelings and their expression. Bridal mysticism, although it was common to Puritan and pietist, did not flourish in America, which developed its own form of the religion of the heart: "Revivalism . . . was an emotionalized religion based on inner experience, but of a peculiar American type. Unlike the mystical movements of Europe, it did not center around asceticism and divine love, but rather around sin, repentance, and redemption; instead of stressing the humanity of Christ and the intimate love relationship between God and man, it aroused fear and trembling through hell-fire oratory."[52] Revivals served evangelism. In Hudson's classic definition, evangelism is "a theological emphasis upon the necessity for a conversion experience as the beginning point of a Christian life, while revivalism is a technique developed to induce that experience."[53] Revivalism was a call to change, which could take many forms and was given many names: "salvation, conversion, regeneration, or the new birth."[54] It could be highly emotional, but it could also be a decision based on consideration of the evidence, a business decision, a prudent spiritual fire insurance. But revivalism always involved the ending of one way of life and the beginning of another and therefore conformed to the pattern of death and rebirth by which men attain masculinity. Conversion is an experience comprehensible to men who follow the ideology of masculinity, who know that the meaning of life can only be found in a test that leads to a kind of death and a rebirth as a new type of being. Charles Grandison Finney, the preacher who began the Second Great Awakening, the wave of revivals that set the evangelical tone of American Protestantism, was a Freemason, and his conversion experience in 1821 closely resembled the fraternal initiation he had gone through when he became a Mason. Mark C. Carnes compares fraternalism and revivalism: "Both revivalism and fraternalism depend upon an agency outside the individual to generate a personal transformation; both depicted man as inherently deficient; and both invoked grim visions of death and hell to precipitate an emotional response that could lead men to an unknowable and distant God."[55] The anguish and the hellfire-and-brimstone sermons of the revivals were a change from the calm rationality, Unitarianism, and Universalism of the older churches.

In the First Great Awakening of the later eighteenth century, the one identified with the Calvinism of Jonathan Edwards, women made up the majority of new church members: "In over half of the churches the proportion of women at admission increased from previous levels or remained in line with the church's historical appeal."[56] But overall, the percentage of men joining the church increased over the low percentage of the pre-revival period: "On occasion, however, the Great Awakening did redress the severe imbalance of females over males in new membership, and in several towns even tipped it decidedly in the latter's direction."[57] Revivalist preaching obviously had a special appeal for men.

At the time of the American Revolution, the ratio of new male church members to new female members was at an all time low. Politics and, especially, war were far more attractive to men than the church was. Declension, or a falling off of membership, occurred primarily among men, and fears of male deism and atheism occupied the clergy.[58] During the Second Great Awakening, identified with Finney, the percentage of men who joined the church also increased,

but it was not as high as in the First. Women were the majority of
the participants in the revival: "Females were more receptive to the
revivalists' message than males."[59] This revival, unlike that of the
eighteenth century, appealed to the more mature: "Married adult
males were more likely to convert than young unattached males; females were more likely to convert than males; and of any single
group (considering gender and marital status), married females were
the most likely to convert."[60] That more married men than unmarried converted suggests that wives had more to do with male conversions in this Awakening than in the previous one.[61]

In the brief but intense revival of 1858, brought on by the tensions
that led to the Civil War, there was an unusually high percentage of
men. The *Christian Advocate* noted that often "the majority of the
converts [were] males."[62] Although the revival preached the old gospel, it used new methods: "It relied heavily upon businessmen, business methods, and the business outlook."[63] This was a harbinger of
Moody's approach and that of almost all later evangelists. In the
revivals of the twentieth century, men also seem to have been attracted to conversion at a rate that has exceeded that of non-revival
periods, although women have remained the majority of the converts. This relative success among males was not limited to Protestants, for whom revivals were almost an institution. The Roman
Catholic Church had a tradition of mission preaching which was
imported to America, and it also seemed to have more success reaching men than regular services.[64]

Nevertheless, the revivals did not reach the completely unchurched; they were most popular among church goers. Revivalists
were frustrated that churchgoers occupied the chairs and sometimes
asked them to stay away to make room for the unchurched. Those
who were not already members of churches often came from families
that had church members, or were children and adolescents from
Sunday schools. The down-and-outers, the utterly profane, the de-
ists and skeptics, did not go to revivals, and this group was primarily
male. Revivalism did not seem to have any long-term impact even
on more receptive males. If it added members to the churches in the
short run, it led to a falling off as enthusiasms cooled. Among

Catholics, priests who preached the parish missions knew that there was a large group of "mission Catholics" who came to church only for missions and then stayed away until the next mission. Conversion is a peak experience, and even men who want initiation find it impossible to live permanently on the mountaintop.

Muscular Christianity

A vague feeling that religion had become too feminized and a more conscious dislike of high-church foppery led to Victorian muscular Christianity.[65] This variety of Christianity shunned asceticism, especially celibacy and virginity, in which it detected perversion. Charles Kingsley despised Cardinal Newman and wrote *Water Babies* as a popular defense of Christian marriage and progeny and, beyond that, of the unity of church and world, sacred and secular.[66] Kingsley and his like-minded friends wanted men to be Christian without being too religious, because religion, in its ascetical Roman, monastic, Tractarian forms, was identified with femininity. Kingsley preached "godliness and manliness," but not "saintliness," which is "not God's ideal of a man, [but] an effeminate shaveling's ideal."[67] Kingsley disliked the popular images of St. Francis de Sales and St. Vincent de Paul, because "God made man in His image, not in an imaginary Virgin Mary's image."[68] Kingsley's charges, as we have seen, have some historical basis. Nevertheless, the Church of England belonged to Western Christianity, and was also feminized, although perhaps not as much as Roman Catholicism, especially in France.

Kingsley was an early proponent of the motto "Be All You Can Be" because manly potential should be fulfilled, not denied.[69] Kingsley advised a friend to preach to men "that Christ is in them, a true and healthy manhood, trying to form Himself in them, and make men of them."[70] Mysticism was abhorrent to Kingsley because it was effeminate. He disliked talk about Christ as the bridegroom of the soul, because it characterized the soul "as feminine by nature, whatever be the sex of its possessor."[71] Beyond these emotional objections to feminized religion lay a broad church emphasis on ethics, a "liberal religious awareness which crystallized . . . into a vigorously combative Christianity involving urgent ethical and spiritual imperatives."[72] Not the priest or the monk, but the Christian gentleman, was the ideal.[73]

The Men and Religion Forward Movement

In the Church of nineteenth-century America, men remained a distinct minority, even after the Awakening. After the turn of the twentieth century, Christian laymen began a crusade to bring men back into the Church, the Men and Religion Forward Movement, which reached its peak in 1911 and 1912. Gail Bederman, in her study of the movement, notes that

> the messages were often traditional, but the method of presentation was highly unorthodox. As often as possible, organizers bought ads on the sport pages, where Men and Religion messages competed for consumers attention with ads for automobiles, burlesque houses, and whiskey. . . . And the entire revival, from beginning to end, was occasionally depicted as one big advertising campaign. For example, *Collier's* announced that the Movement's experts "have taken hold of religion, and are boosting it with the fervor and publicity skills which a gang of salesman would apply to soap that floats or suits that wear."[74]

It stressed the image of Jesus as the Successful Businessman, the Super Salesman. In the National Cathedral in Washington, I came across a memorial tablet to an Episcopalian worthy, whose life was summed up, not as "Christian," or "Sinner," or "Devoted Father and Husband," but as "Investment Banker." Despite these oddities, the movement to a large extent had effect. All churches experienced an increase in male membership, the Episcopal church most of all.[75]

Like modern revivalism, the Men and Religion Forward Movement used business techniques. Unlike revivalism, it tried to bring men into a mainline Protestantism that did not emphasize emotional peaks, but a slow, steady acceptance of responsibility in the church and society. Its proponents covered a spectrum of orthodoxy.

Some were classic evangelicals, but the search for suitable church work for men led to an alliance of the proponents of the Social Gospel. Urban and political reform under church auspices was the heart of the Social Gospel, which also provided work suitable for men: the protection of the weak and interaction with the world of business and politics.

Bruce Barton, a popular writer of the early twentieth century, was generally favorable to the Men and Religion Forward Movement, but warned about its tendencies to churchiness. More committed to capitalism than orthodoxy, he seems to have had doubts about miracles, but he knew that Jesus was the model businessman. Barton lauds Jesus for the way he handled the apostles: "He believed that the way to get faith out of men is to show that you have faith in them; and from that great principle of executive management he never wavered."[76] Jesus was popular at the best dinner parties: "There was a time when he was quite the favorite in Jerusalem."[77] It is easy to mock Barton; but he had a serious purpose.

Barton noticed the almost total lack of attention to Joseph, who served as Jesus's earthly father, and traced it to the same tendency that leads Christians to portray Jesus as weak and willowy, instead of the strong carpenter he must have been: "The same theology which has painted the son as soft and gentle to the point of weakness, has exalted the feminine influence in its worship, and denied any large place to the masculine."[78] Barton pointed out that the human idea of Father, which Jesus applied analogously to his heavenly Father, was formed by Jesus's experience of Joseph.

Barton constantly attacked holy-card, Sunday-school Christianity for its betrayal of the masculine Jesus: "They have shown us a frail man, under-muscled, with a soft face—a woman's face covered by beard—and a benign but baffled look, as though the problems of living were so grievous that death would be a welcome release."[79] This is precisely how Jesus was shown in the widely-acclaimed *And Jesus Was His Name*: Jesus stands passive while his foes swirl around him. Barton instead delighted in the Jesus who is a warrior and hero, and noted that the way he motivated men was still a valid principle in modern times. Jesus used the "higher type of leadership which calls forth men's greatest energies by the promise of obstacles rather than pictures of rewards."[80]

Barton also criticized the clericalization of Christian life. Although the reformers had attacked religious life and had tried to convince all Christians they were called to a life of faithful obedience, clericalism crept back into Protestantism. To overcome this, we must "rid ourselves of the idea that there is a difference between *work* and *religious work*."[81] Christians have somehow gotten the idea that only work in or for the Church is pleasing to God, that only the work devoted "to church meetings and social service activities is consecrated."[82] This is a criticism of the Social Gospel and the attempts to make Christianity attractive to men by providing political and social reform work *within the Church*. Barton did not object to reform motivated by Christian faith and charity, but denied that it has to be under official church auspices to be Christian.

Barton proclaimed a message that has been taken up and amplified by both Opus Dei and Pope John Paul II, who would not share his naturalistic theological presuppositions. Barton wanted all Christians to realize that all work is worship; all useful service is prayer: "And whoever works wholeheartedly at any worthy calling is a co-worker with the Almighty in the great enterprise which He has initiated."[83]

More profound than Barton, Harry Emerson Fosdick sought to portray the masculinity of Jesus in *The Manhood of the Master*. Fosdick noticed the *coincidentia oppositorum*, the true sign of the supernatural, in Jesus, in "his heroic and revolutionary fearlessness, his capacity for indignation on the one side, and on the other this deep, friendly tenderness."[84] Jesus's wrath was fearful, especially since it was an expression of his love, the wrath of the Lamb. Remembering the love of Christ was important, Fosdick admitted, but "a man might better call on the mountains to cover him than to stand naked and defenceless before the indignation which that wrath creates."[85] Fosdick sounded a note of the twentieth century when he points out that Jesus was tempted, indeed was "the most tempted of all because he had the greatest powers to control."[86] Modern Christians, raised on an image of an effeminate Jesus, find the idea that he was tempted, especially in anything to do with sex (even if only by a marriage and children) sacrilegious, as was shown by the reaction to Kazantzakis's *The Last Temptation of Christ*.

The emphasis upon what Roman Catholics call the spirituality of work may explain the success of the Men and Religion Forward Movement, during which Fosdick wrote his book. The influence of the Men and Religion Forward Movement died out in the 1950s, but it may have led to the social health of the mid-twentieth-century American family. The father of the 1950s was the most family-involved father of American history and probably one of the most family-involved fathers in any modern culture. Religious practice, not coincidentally, also was at a peak in the 1950s.

Fundamentalism and Evangelicalism

One element in evangelicalism and fundamentalism that tends to preserve a masculine flavor is the strong tendency to think in dichotomies, a result of a close attention to Scripture. Parallelism and antithesis are very prominent in Hebrew writing and thought; men also tend to think in dichotomies; and dichotomies are also the raw material for conflict, which is again grounded more in the masculine experience of separateness and in masculine aggression.

Fundamentalism, according to Margaret Lamberts Bendroth, attempted to be self-consciously masculine and reacted against the effeminate liberal churches.[87] Why were the liberal churches effeminate? After all, both fundamentalists and liberals had predominantly female constituencies.[88] They were effeminate, according to the fundamentalists, because they refused to acknowledge the conflict, the battle between good and evil, in the world, and tried to make Christianity a mild religion of progress and enlightenment. Bendroth describes fundamentalism as "a means of separation, a way to declare superiority over the domesticated faith that shunned open conflict with the world, the flesh, and the devil."[89] The fundamentalists were more attuned to Scripture, which lays out a scheme of dichotomies whose conflict drives the course of world history, from the temptation in the Garden to Armageddon. Scripture is also a strong voice for separatism, calling men to come out of Babylon, in whatever incarnation she is present in history.

The evangelical wing of Protestantism is strongly influenced by revivalism and its crisis-spirituality, partially a conscious attempt to reach men. Evangelicals have therefore been in the lead among American Christians in attempts to reach men. Promise Keepers is in the revivalist tradition, with mass meetings to ask for a commitment to the faith. It focuses especially on married men, and among them on those who have some sense of responsibility and are willing to listen to spiritual advice on how to fulfill the responsibilities of marriage. But these men have already made a reconnection to the feminine in marriage, and it is this connection to the feminine that the leadership of Promise Keepers is using to bring men back into a relationship with the Church.

The long-range success of Promise Keepers is, however, not assured. Revivalist attempts to reach men may have some initial success, but they founder in their attempts to develop stable commitments. Men may be attracted by the crisis atmosphere, but they discover it is impossible to live day to day in a crisis. In addition, Promise Keepers faces the problem that the church life to which it is attempting to attract men is feminized. Evangelical church life may be less feminized than Catholicism or mainline Protestantism, but the underlying problem, that men feel that religion is feminine, is still present. Men who wish to connect to women, that is, married men, may submit to a partial immersion in the feminine atmosphere of religion, and it is always necessary to begin with the groups with which success is most likely. But the social and religious problem is not so much with married men as with men who do not have a permanent connection to women, unmarried and divorced men. These men are the locus of social pathologies and anti-Christian movements, and they are the ones it is hardest to reach through already-Christian women.

The faults of these attempts to connect men and Christianity are obvious to the modern reader, who often feels that any manifestation of masculine qualities in religion is offensive. Conflict cannot be removed from Christianity without changing the nature of the religion, but not all conflict is necessary or desirable. The Crusades poisoned relationships between the West and both Islam and Orthodoxy, provided a rationale for total war, and misled even Christians like G. K. Chesterton. Nor is this distortion confined to the "right" in ecclesiastical circles. Some of the Catholic clergy of Latin America grew weary of their role as chaplains to a women's society. They found themselves conducting devotions while upper-class Catholics ground down the poor. Even worse, a passive, obedient, suffering Christ was used as opiate for the masses. The cruel rich, liberation theologians thought, should feel the wrath of God. Machismo could be harnessed against the evil in society: "If social protest is man's work, they [liberation theologians] believe that the fiery Christ will replace the 'effeminized' version. Did not Christ chase the money changers from the temple?"[90] But such ambitions ended in disaster and an even worse oppression of the poor, as in Cuba and Nicaragua: "No matter how justified, social revolution in Latin America can spawn a new type of machismo, carrying violence, destruction, class hatred, and ultimately one-man or state despotism in its wake."[91]

Softer emotions also have their dangers. The chivalric devotion to Mary was a result of the distorted ideas of gender held by medieval and post-medieval theologians. The distortion is not simply one of language, as Pope John Paul II believes.[92] Scriptural metaphors contain meaning, and when they are so changed as to almost reverse their initial meaning, the preaching of the Gospel suffers. In fact, the focus on inner experiences and emotions, a focus common to early Jesuits, to Puritans, and to revivalists, creates a problem for men, who are taught to ignore and suppress their emotions in the service of the community. This type of inward focus and emotional self-awareness will necessarily strike men as feminine. The natural fear of being swallowed up in a feminine world and losing their masculinity drives men away from church. Revivals, both Catholic and Protestant, have temporarily increased the number of men, but over the long run, they do not stay. Nor will they ever stay as long as religious culture is geared to women and not also to men.

9

Masculinity as Religion: Transcendence and Nihilism

T HE AFFECTIVE SPIRITUALITY of the Middle Ages, we noted, had two dimensions. The first of these was, as we have seen, bridal mysticism and its variations, but the second was the militancy of the Crusades and chivalric devotion to Mary. When bridal mysticism came to dominate the life of the Christian church, the feminization of Christianity set the ideology of masculinity free from the faith.

Masculinity is a natural religion, and in many ways resembles the Christianity of which it is a foretaste. Can men worship a savior unless they know what it is to be a savior? A man wants to become a god. He wants to be a savior, protecting all those in his care, giving his own life to save theirs. In other words, he wants to transcend the limits of mere humanity, but that transcendence is dangerous. When he faces death a man can die the death of the body; but he can also die the death of the soul, the second death. All too easily he may be fascinated by darkness and become a partisan and emissary of death—a demon. The further masculinity consciously distances itself from Christianity, the greater the danger that it will make men agents of death—nihilists—because in nothingness they see the ultimate self-transcendence.

SACRED SEXUALITY

Until the end of the nineteenth century, masculinity had been thought of as manliness, a stoic ideal of reserve and self-control. Most of the founders of the American Republic, whatever their formal allegiance, were at heart more stoic than Christian. This ideal was an aristocratic one, but as civilization grew tiresome, both Europe and America experienced a new interest in the primitive, in the savage, in the uncivilized, in the passions of youth. Youth had the promise of contact with the elemental forces of life. This fascination with youth and the primitive was a product of Romanticism and eventually replaced the aristocratic ideal of manliness with a proletarian ideal of masculinity.

In America, the frontiersmen, Natty Bumpo and his successors, became the symbol of natural man, passionate and self-reliant. Gail Bederman examines the veneration of the savage and the primitive in American culture of the late nineteenth century, a veneration that also was present in European culture: Americans had the Indians, the Europeans, Africans and Polynesians.[1] Picasso used Polynesian masks as models of abstraction, as did Emil Nolde, revering in the primitive a violent energy that would shatter the effeminate bourgeois surface of European life. Nolde was among the first members of the Nazi party and was favored by Nazis who wanted total revolution, an unleashing of savage male energies. In America, the older forms of civilized manliness that emphasized prudence and self-restraint were replaced by an ideal of masculinity that saw savage sexual energy as a necessary component of complete manhood.

Young men have always shown a great enthusiasm for sexual intercourse, not only for the physical pleasure it gives, but perhaps even more because they think it shows they are men. Intercourse "is the ultimate self-validation, the undeniable proof of one's maleness and masculinity (which has always been a problem with men)."[2] But in the late nineteenth and twentieth centuries male sexuality has sometimes been given a quasi-divine status. Men have venerated their sexuality, and have experienced in it a transcendent world: "Sex has become the religion of the Western world, the bearer of most people's hopes of encountering something truly 'other'. . . . The search for the other, for the Eternal Feminine, Goddess or Whore, or the dark forces of the blood and semen, is the search for transcendence. Sex is the cry for the other, union with the transcendent."[3] Men are even willing to sacrifice themselves to their sexuality, preferring death to celibacy. In the Middle Ages, the minnesinger spoke of erotic love as if it were a religion. Wagner chose Tristan and Isolde as subjects for his opera because he too felt that romantic love was the ultimate experience of transcendence and that a love-death, *Liebestod*, was a way to escape the prison of self. But it is not so much romantic love as sexuality, and especially male sexuality, that has been deified.

Male sexual energy is deified because it is the sexual part of the self-sacrifice that gives masculinity its nobility. Men experience self-giving through separation in their role in sexual intercourse, because they give of themselves in ejaculation rather than receive in insemination. They attain the ability to do this at puberty, and many societies that have initiation rites therefore choose puberty as the time for these rites. G. Stanley Hall, a late-nineteenth-century educational psychologist, reversed the Victorian mistrust of sex. Hall believed that "it was no accidental synchronism of unrelated events that the age of religion and age of sexual maturity coincide."[4] Summarizing Hall's thought, Gail Bederman explains that "at sexual maturity, when a boy received the capacity for paternity, he ceased to exist merely for himself, and began to exist as a potential contributor to the divine process of racial evolution and the advancement of civilization. Adolescence was thus a holy time, when sexuality and spirituality burst upon a young man simultaneously, through the physiological second birth."[5] Testosterone replaced the Holy Spirit as the source of new life.

For Hall, the orgasm was a holy experience, because through it the man participated in the continuity of the race: "In the most unitary of all acts, which is the epitome and pleroma of life, we have the most intense of all affirmations of the will to live, and realize that the only true God is love, and the center of life is worship. . . . This sacrament is the annunciation hour, with hosannas which the whole world reflects. . . . Now is the race incarnated in the individual and remembers its lost paradise."[6] In Hall we see the worship of male sexuality, a worship which has found expression both in popular and high culture.

Hemingway and Lawrence, and others far less respectable, have participated in this worship. Lawrence worshipped male sexuality, seeing in it an experience of the divine.[7] Hemingway worshiped masculinity, "the code which is all we have in the place of God," and saw sexuality as a central part of masculinity. Violence and sexuality continue to be intrinsic to the American popular ideal of manhood. Although liberals who give lip service to feminism dominate Hollywood, most movies are aimed at the adolescent male and glorify violence and sexuality. Such films reinforce the popular culture and are responsible for the adulation that celebrity-criminals often receive. Society may find it hard to discipline young men whom it is sending to die in war, but even now in peacetime the sexual misbehavior of athletes is not only excused, but venerated. Feminism has made only a slight dent in this veneration among the middle classes, and none at all among the black proletariat. The search for self-transcendence in sexuality is especially pernicious, because it confuses the spiritual code of masculinity with physical maleness. A worship of the semen and the blood is a worship of dark gods and undermines the positive aspects of masculinity.

AIDS has given prominence to the homosexual as sexual hero. Homosexuals are far more promiscuous than heterosexuals, and when they infect themselves with a fatal venereal disease they become objects of worship, as in *Angels in America*. Indeed, Harvey Milk has been made into a saint with his own Byzantine-style icon. Homosexuals feel keenly the connection between love and death and routinely frustrate the public health measures that are designed to protect them. They have unprotected intercourse with partners they know are infected because they feel that only by a joint death can the barriers of the self be overcome. This is a perverse version of comradeship in war, which not unsurprisingly, as we shall see, shares gestures and language with homosexuality.

THE PLAYING FIELDS

Agonistic masculine play was the origin of civilization. In the modern world, sports are the emotional center of countless men. Sports are a traditional means to attain masculinity. The athlete is the one who faces and overcomes challenges and thereby escapes human limitations. The Greeks honored the transfiguration of the athlete: Pindar's odes celebrated the divinity that clothed the victor in the games. In modern America, the coach is the mentor who brings boys into manhood. He teaches them to endure pain, develop self-discipline, work as a team, and give themselves to others, and often (a sure sign of his initiatory role) instructs them in the mysteries of sexuality. Why athletic coaches (rather than, say, biology teachers) should be thought the appropriate teacher for sex education is a mystery from a pedagogical perspective, but entirely comprehensible if sports is the primary way a boy becomes a man.

Because sports provide an initiation into masculinity, they can easily become a religion. Sports are often the way the boy puts away the soft, sheltering world of the mother and her femininity and enters the world of challenge and danger that makes him a man.[8] Sports helped men be transformed and reborn: "In its pretense toward regenerative functions, it approximated a religious sensibility for men, albeit material and secular."[9] Team sports develop masculinity; they are "the civilized substitute for war"[10] and sublimate male aggression into channels less harmful than crime. They develop the virtue of comradeship, and teammates in sports like football become "blood brothers, men who assemble together to undertake dangerous exploits under conditions of duress and threat."[11] Michael Messner quotes a former high school athlete: "I'd say that most of my meaningful relationships have started through sports and have been maintained through sports. There's nothing so strong, to form that bond, as sports. Just like in war too—there are no closer friends than guys who are in the same foxhole together trying to stay alive. You know, hardship breeds friendship, breeds intense familiarity. . . . You have to endure something together— sweat together, bleed together, cry together. Sports provide that."[12]

Sports form character, "manly straightforward character, a scorn of lying and meanness, habits of obedience and command, and fearless courage."[13] For modern men, team sports are more transforming than religion because they provide a greater escape from the self. Paul Jones, a Dulwich boy who was killed in World War 1, claimed that in the attempts to develop team spirit, "Religion has failed, intellect has failed, art has failed, science has failed. It is clear why: because each of these has laid emphasis on man's *selfish side*; the saving of his *own soul*, the cultivation of his *own mind*, the pleasing of his *own senses*. But your sportman joins the Colours because in his games he has felt the real spirit of unselfishness, and has become accustomed to give all for a body to whose service he is sworn."[14] Sports on this view are a better school of charity than religion, for the ultimate test of charity is the willingness to die in war. Not only were wars won, but souls were saved on the playing fields of England.

A player who is "in form" has had a form descend on him as if from above; he is in "a state of grace. It is as if some transcendental power had given the player his blessing."[15] Although most players and spectators would not seriously call sports a religion, it nevertheless functions as one for them. It is "a secular means for tapping transcendental sources and powers, or restoring some fleeting contact with the sacred, or testing whether the gods are on your side or not."[16] Michael Novak regards sports as a natural religion.[17] Charles Prebish also thinks "*sport is religion* for growing numbers of Americans."[18] Religion enables man to transcend the secular, ordinary word; sports are the main way that many men attain this transcendence, whether directly as an athlete or vicariously as a spectator. In both cases, "the individual goes beyond his or her own ego bonds."[19] As Howard Slusher says, "Within the movements of the athlete a wonderful mystery of life is present, a mystical experience that is too close to the religious to call it anything else."[20] The dancer becomes the dance, and the athlete becomes the sport. He is transfigured; he may have a peak experience and the form may shine through him to the spectator, who sees the glory of transfigured being. Novak writes from his own experience of sport: "Athletic achievement, like the achievements of the heroes and gods of Greece, is the momentary attainment of perfect form—as though there were, hidden away from mortal eyes, a perfect way to execute a play, and suddenly a player or team has found it and sneaked a demonstration down to earth. A great play is a revelation. The curtains of ordinary life part, and perfection flashes for an instant before the eye."[21]

A strong agonistic element dominates all types of sports. The *agon* or struggle may be with another team or another individual or it may be with nature and the limitations of the athlete's own body. This contest distinguishes sports from art and perhaps explains why men tend to regard art as trivial and unworthy of masculine attention, even though ballet may be more physically demanding than even baseball or gymnastics. Pain is an inescapable part of sports and distinguishes it from the mere game (which art seems to be for most men). For the athlete, "true fulfillment arises in the confrontation and overcoming of self, not in fantasy but through pain and agony and the realization of life at a far greater and deeper level."[22] The mountain climber Maurice Herzog claimed that "in overstepping our limitations, in touching the extreme boundaries of man's world, we have come to know something of its true splendor. In my worst moments of anguish, I seemed to discover the deep significance of existence which till then I had been unaware."[23] Sports functions as the religion of many men in Western culture because it reveals the meaning of life.

This is not the same as *Sportianity*, as some deride the combination of sports and evangelical Protestantism in movements like the Fellowship of Christian Athletes.[24] Billy Sunday, baseball player turned evangelist, had no doubts about the nature of his religion: it was Christianity (in a muscular, aggressive form) and not baseball. For Christian athletes, sports are but a means to evangelize for their true religion, Christianity.[25] Sports can, like any human activity, be consecrated to God, although the competitive nature of sports creates some problems for Christian athletes. Yet Pope John Paul II, a dedicated sportsman, thinks that competition itself can be a good.

The transforming power of athletics can also be seen in individualist sports such as bodybuilding. We are fortunate to have an account of bodybuilding written by a literate, self-aware young man,

Sam Fussell. In 1983, Fussell graduated from Oxford and took a job in Manhattan in publishing before his planned enrollment in American Studies at Yale. This tall, thin, young scion of an academic family had been raised in Princeton, attended Lawrenceville and Oxford, and had been sheltered from urban American life. His size (six feet, four inches), skinniness, and academic demeanor made him a target. He came down with chronic diarrhea and pleurisy from his state of anxiety and fear. His parents had just divorced, and he had nowhere to go. He was tired of being hurt physically and emotionally by life and decided to take up bodybuilding.[26]

It was a change from Oxford and Princeton. Ever the academic, he researched the subject in bodybuilding magazines before he took the plunge. Yet the gym at the YMCA was not what he expected from the paeans to the wholesome nature of bodybuilding that filled the magazines he had read: it was full of homosexuals and maniacs who had built shells around themselves to protect themselves from reality. Fussell built himself up to 257 pounds. and was able to bench press 405 pounds. He left his publishing job to avoid getting fired for throwing a co-worker through a door. He moved to California, studied under professionals, and became a trainer in a gym. Filling himself with steroids, he entered shows, but fortunately lost. Perhaps it was the disappointment that brought him to his senses. He realized that he had started too late (twenty-six!) ever to have a great body, decided to quit, and return to the family tradition of writing.

Fussell (whose father, Paul Fussell, wrote *The Great War and Modern Memory*) uses throughout his book the metaphor of bodybuilding as military action. He speaks of men being in the trenches too long, and of a buttock scarred from steroid injections as looking like an aerial photograph of Ypres. Like the soldier in combat, Fussell descends into an abnormal and dangerous world, and there attains some wisdom. He is very ironic about himself and realizes the ersatz nature of this heroism, but he does come to understand the folly of building shells as protection from pain, is able to return to normal life, and warn others about the danger of the sport he rejects.

Bodybuilding is a profound warping of masculinity. Bodybuilders quote slogans reminiscent of Nietzsche: "That which doesn't kill you makes you stronger"; "Only the strong survive"; "No kindness forgotten, no transgression forgiven." They wear hats that say "Pray for War." When his mother came to visit him in the bunker apartment he had found, Fussell was wearing "military fatigues camouflaged to look like tree bark, spit-shined black combat boots, a T-shirt which read 'respect my spirit, for our spirits are one'. . . . A cardboard cutout of Arnold Schwarzenegger with loincloth and sword as Conan the Barbarian stood against one wall. . . . I could see from the look in her eyes that her worst fears were realized. All that was missing was a rifle and the President's travel itinerary."[27] For all its ridiculousness, bodybuilding is taken seriously by millions of men, for whom it has become a religion, a means to die to the old, weak self and to be reborn as the new, strong self, "the promise of metamorphosis."[28] Bodybuilding is only a hobby, and is non-political,[29] but other politicized forms of distorted hyper-masculinity have left their marks on the world-historical stage.

The controlled violence of sport often overflows into other types of violence. European football matches regularly end in mob scenes; soccer hooligans travel from country to country making life miserable for all who have the misfortune to be in their vicinity. A German woman told me of a case in point (totally ignored in the Western press). Visiting Leipzig when it was still under Communist rule, she arrived just after a football match, and the neo-Nazis who made up a large segment of the soccer hooligans had turned the city into a repeat of Kristallnacht. Not a shop window remained unbroken between the train station and the museum she was visiting. Even the Communist security apparatus was helpless to prevent this violence; nor is it rare. A 1969 soccer game between El Salvador and Honduras led to a riot and then to a shooting war that lasted one hundred hours. The toll was "6,000 dead and 12,000 wounded. Fifty thousand people lost their homes and fields. Many villages were destroyed."[30] War is sports pursued by other means.

Extreme Sports

Team sports like baseball and soccer and football no longer provide thrills adequate for the most daring athletes. Even standard mountain climbing and surfing have become *passé*. The adrenaline-driven have taken up sky surfing. They leap from airplanes with a surfboard, and ride air currents down thousands of feet until they finally deploy their parachutes. Others do illegal B A S E jumping—Building, Antenna Tower, Span, Earth. One person jumped from the center of the St. Louis Arch—and was arrested. Mountain climbing has given way to rock climbing of vertical faces, to mountain biking, to mountain running. Swimming has given way to scuba diving in caves, canoeing to kayaking over waterfalls. Death is courted in a thousand ways.

Most participants are in it for the adrenaline rush. Nevertheless, as they spend more and more time on the borders of life and death, participants begin to notice some highly unusual phenomena. Michael Bane decided to try the thirteen most difficult sports he could think of, risking death in various ways. When he was in the Iditarod bike race in the Alaska winter, he suddenly heard "a voice." "It is my friend Sandy back in Florida, and she appears to be praying." He is "dumbfounded."[31] At the race banquet, another racer asks Bane "Did you . . . hear any voices out there on the trail?"[32] He had also heard . . . something.

Bob Schultheis is an anthropologist, and the title of his book tells his story, *Bone Games: Extreme Sports, Shamanism, Zen, and the Search for Transcendence*.[33] While descending a mountain under the threat of death, he found himself becoming a "strange person."[34] He did "impossible things,"[35] his "old life" was "gone"; he was filed with "joy."[36] He died and was reborn—for a brief period. He discovered that skiers experience "stress-triggered ecstacy,"[37] that kayakers see helpful ghosts,[38] as did Lindbergh on his historic flight.[39] (He tried to duplicate the visions by controlled oxygen deprivation, but was never able to experience them again.) Western athletes experience rarely and intermittently a transformed state of being that shamans can achieve at will after long training.[40]

Is this purely subjective, albeit unusual? Or is there something Out There, at the "very edge of death"?[41] Schultheis considers the demonstrated effect that mind can have on body in yogis, but he wonders also about other possibilities. A reliable and truthful friend told of how, while mountain running, he admired Bear Peak and decided to run to the peak "as a kind of physical prayer to the peak, a ritual ordeal."[42] His prayer was heard. He felt an immense presence (possibly subjective): "Suddenly, several small sparrow hawks appeared around the mountaintop and began diving around him, so close that a couple of times he could feel the air blast from their wings. They wove around him, zooming away and then returning, again and again. . . . The sparrow hawks flew away as abruptly as they had appeared. Then from the four quarters of the sky, four ravens came flying; they approached the top of Bear Peak and then hovered in position, a hundred feet or so from where he stood: a hollow square, with him in the epicenter."[43] He tried to descend, but "one of the black birds flew around in front of him and blocked his way, hanging there in the air, cawing at him."[44] He went back. Four red-tail hawks came, and they too maneuvered around him, then four turkey vultures, and at last a golden eagle. He had had enough, and left.

Schultheis concludes that extreme athletes are "making a kind of religion."[45] He is correct. Men are seeking transcendence by achieving states of extreme stress in which life becomes transparent. The ascetic discipline required by this effort surpasses any undergone by the desert saints. Men will do anything, will come as close to death as possible, will even die because of their sport, if only they can have the possibility of tasting this transcendence through athletic mysticism.

BROTHERHOODS

Fraternal organizations originated in Europe with the independent, often anti-clerical, and sometimes anti-Christian groups that are loosely called freemasonic. The Masons are the prototype of the fraternal orders of the modern world. Masonry is generally considered a product of the Enlightenment in that it emphasized a mild theism free of denominational narrowness. Although it originated in the early eighteenth century in England, it seems to be more a product

of English hermeticism than of the Enlightenment.[46] English hermeticism was a by-product of the Renaissance which, in its Platonic
form, sought to revive the secret wisdom of the ancients, identified
with the mystery religion of the Thrice-Great Hermes, Hermes
Trismegistus, whence the name of the movement. Masonry took
over not only much of the mystifying language and arcane symbolism of this rather muddled movement (which also produced
Rosicrucianism) but also its character as a mystery religion.[47]

Masonry is a modern revival of the mystery religions. Like
Mithraism, and for much the same reason, "Masonry was a male institution."[48] Indeed, Masons proclaimed that the lodge was for
men, the church for women.[49] Both Masonry and the fraternal organizations that aped it used a confrontation with death, a necessary
part of a masculine initiation, as part of their initiation. While reno-
vating the International Order of Odd Fellows building in Baltimore
in the 1970s, contractors discovered several skeletons and reported it
to the police, who investigated and decided that the skeletons had
been legitimately obtained as part of an initiation ceremony. This
initiation can be more or less impressive and taken with greater or
lesser seriousness. That some Masons took it very seriously is clear
from the incident that gave birth to the anti-Masonic party of the
1840s, the murder of an ex-Mason who had threatened to reveal the
secrets of Masonry. The murder was not only perpetrated by Masons, but the murderers were protected from prosecution by fellow
Masons in government positions. The strength of Masonic feeling
was also shown by the decision of Sam Houston to release the captured Santa Ana, when he discovered that his Mexican foe was also a
Mason. Clearly Masonry had replaced Christianity as a serious spiritual bond among men.

In nineteenth-century America men found their spiritual sustenance in fraternal movements. The thousands of Masonic temples
and Knights of Pythias lodges and Independent Order of Odd Fellows halls that dot every American city and small town are relics of
that movement.[50] The fraternal orders had the primary purpose of
conducting initiation rituals.[51] These rituals were drawn from ancient mysteries (as revealed in romantic novels) and from puberty

rites of primitive societies, such as the American Indian,[52] although without the bloodshed that primitive rites often incorporated. The modern American lodge members were all male and kept their rituals secret from women. Through darkness, mysterious actions, speeches about pain and death, and even occasional confrontations with skeletons, men escaped shallowness and realized the seriousness of life. Men loved it and flocked to these fraternal orders throughout the nineteenth century, seeking initiation after initiation.[53] Men could not find the initiation they sought in Christianity, especially in its dominant liberal form. According to Mark Carnes, "Whereas for the liberals death confirmed the goodness of God, the perfectibility of man, and the moral values of Christian nurture, fraternal rituals taught than God was imposing and distant, that man was fundamentally flawed, and that human understanding of human and moral issues was imperfect. Only by experiencing the greatest of transformations—death—could man begin to comprehend the truths of human existence."[54] As liberal Protestantism abandoned the Puritan message of death and transfiguration, fraternalism took it up.[55] The evangelist Finney later perceived that for men "fraternal initiation could serve as a substitute for religious conversion."[56] In some ways fraternalism, because it emphasized the necessity of dying to a lower state and being reborn to a higher one, was closer to the orthodox Christianity than was liberal Protestantism, which had largely lost its sense of the drama of sin and redemption and tried to tame and domesticate Christianity by omitting or de-emphasizing the warfare with demons, the threats of hell, and the awesomeness of death, all of which are prominent in the New Testament.

Fraternalism was at best an ersatz religion and therefore resembles the Symbolist movement in Western culture. Fraternalism, like Symbolism, used traditional symbols detached from their historic context, whether they were Jewish (the Temple), Christian (the Bible), or pagan (the skeleton). All these symbols were fraught with meaning, but no one, least of all the Masonic specialist, could tell exactly what they meant. Nevertheless, the emotional pull of fraternalism was strong, and fraternalism declined in this century only after the real confrontation with death in war replaced the ritual confrontation in the lodge as the source of initiation for men.

IMITATIONS OF WAR

When war is absent, men seek "the moral equivalent of war" in their recreation. Boys' activities, of which the most successful is the Boy Scouts, are a remote preparation for war. For adults, military reenactments provide some of the thrill and even the pathos of war. Adult excitement and adrenaline rushes are available through combat games of varying degrees of seriousness. For those who want more realism, paramilitary groups and militias conduct exercises in pretend (and sometimes not-so-pretend) violence.

The Boy Scouts

The Boy Scouts were founded by Baden-Powell because recruits for the British army were too often found to be physically unfit—unfit, that is, for military service.[57] The British Scouts encouraged physical fitness by teaching boys to be observers and trackers. The Boy Scouts of America (BSA) do not cultivate this particular area of military expertise. Instead, the regimen of the Scouts is designed to teach boys how to endure moderate discomfort, cooperate with others, and ultimately save others. The BSA's disavowal of military intent is sometimes a little disingenuous. It is true that military discipline is not enforced, that drill (except to present colors) and paramilitary training are forbidden, and that the atmosphere of most scout encampments is military only in that it shares in "the havoc of war and the battle's confusion." Before America became involved in World War I, parents were assured that "Boy Scouts are looked upon as soldiers in the making. If by making soldiers is meant training boys for intelligent public service, cultivating character, self-reliance, mutual helpfulness, and the capacity to achieve success in the field of chosen endeavor, then the Boy Scout movement may properly be regarded as military. If by making soldiers is meant cultivating a spirit of pugnacity and the glorification of war, then the Boy Scout movement is non-military. These elements are not found in it."[58] But military recruiters place advertisements in *Boys' Life*, the scouting magazine, which in its articles often portrays the positive aspects of war—excitement and self-sacrifice.

Boys' Life holds the sacrificial ideal of manhood before its young readers, and shows them how fighting in war can be the ultimate sacrifice. One article tells the story of a mountain man, Alvin York, a "One-Man Army."[59] In his youth he "had been a wild character, a hard drinker and a brawler." Like the Trukese described by David Gilmore[60] and American blue-collar workers, York had been a rough character, but he had grown up and become a sober, responsible man, "a church elder." He followed the same path that the Trukese boys follow. After praying for guidance, he decided to go to war, to the Great War. It was not sheer belligerence that led him to fight, but a vocation from God. His aggressive spirit and his fighting skills sharpened in his youth would now be at the service of others: "He was a good shot, and his expert marksmanship would *save* [emphasis added] many American lives." Masculine aggressiveness is cultivated, not ultimately for the purpose of destruction, although destruction may be a necessary means, but finally for the purpose of salvation. The Germans had trapped five hundred American soldiers at the Argonne; "to *save* [emphasis added] them, the German machine guns had to be put out of action." During the attack on the Germans, York was "pinned down," and had to fire sixty yards uphill, "the most difficult shooting imaginable." York killed twenty-five and captured 132 Germans. For this he received the Congressional Medal of Honor. But a man does not fight for reward or for his own benefit. After the war, York was celebrated as a hero and offered jobs all around the United States, but he turned them down and returned to Tennessee where he "used his fame to help found a school to educate mountain children." A man lives not for himself, but for others, even in his aggressiveness.

Boys' Life has a regular feature, a cartoon panel which recounts "A True Story of Scouts" in which a Scout by his quick thinking and decisive action takes responsibility for a situation and saves someone from danger or death. The Boy Scout Honor Award is for those who save others from the danger of death while risking their own lives. One recipient earned it this way:

> Early Dec. 21, 1985, Webelos Scout Steven Beeson, 10, was awakened by a neighbor pounding on the door of his home in San Antonio, Tex.
>
> Crystal Santellana, 13, told Steven that her house was on fire and her two brothers, ages 2 and 6, were still inside the house. The 6-year-old had been playing with a lighter under the bed and started the fire.
>
> The room billowed with smoke, and flames burned through the floor in several spots. Steven quickly picked up the 2-year-old and took him outside, leaving him with Steven's older sister and Crystal. He went back in the house and rescued the 6-year-old and the family dog.[61]

My son's troop (in which I am an assistant scoutmaster) saved a family from rapids; their canoe had swamped, and was crushing the father against a rock. The scouts formed a human chain, pulled the canoe off the father, and brought everyone to shore. Once when I went on a weekend camping trip with my son's Scout troop, an Eagle Scout who had been in the troop and was now at the Naval Academy came along to help. He was returning directly to the Academy after the outing, so he had his uniform and white hat hanging in the rear of his car. It was a little visual reminder of the ultimate purpose of the Scout's training: to lead boys to accept responsibility and sacrifice, even, although this is rarely mentioned among men even in the military, to the point of dying for their country.

Military Reenactors

For adults who want to play war, military reenactments, especially of the Civil War, are popular. Initially, the male camaraderie and military ritual attract participants. But as men study their dramatic roles, by reading letters and memoirs left by the soldiers and by experiencing some of the hardships that soldiers undergo (marching, camp food, camping in harsh weather), something changes. As they become more immersed, mind and body, in the lives of the soldiers, reenactors gain a deep respect for soldiers who were willing to submit to a life of hardship, danger, and pain for the causes they believed in.

For some reenactors, role-playing comes to take on a ritual significance. They do not want the memory of those brave men to die and want to feel as close as possible a kinship with them. The physical hardships become a part of the appeal. In living through the weariness and cold and heat and filth that afflicted the original soldiers, the reenactors feel some sense of what it must have been to fight in the Civil War. They will march with blistered, bleeding feet and refuse well-intentioned offers of rides home, supporting each other instead and considering it a privilege to suffer in a small way like the soldiers they are imitating. One reenactor, whose interest began as an offshoot of his academic studies, says that after going through the experience of the reenactor he began for the first time to understand the Latin American piety that leads men to reenact the sufferings of Christ as closely as possible. The military reenactors take up their task voluntarily and rejoice in the fact that their own bodies become a physical memorial to those men they so admire. How much more would it be a privilege, an honor, a joy to suffer in the same way as the Redeemer, to feel in small the price he paid to redeem the world from death?

These sentiments are widespread among reenactors, although masculine inarticulateness about emotions prevents most from voicing them. Nevertheless, in a letter to the *Washington Post* in response to an article that described reenactment as entertainment, Ted Brennan speaks of his own reenactment experience. He admits that reenactment is "fun and educational," but far more important, reenactors "get a deeper appreciation about what our ancestors had to endure." Although the battles lack "blood and gore," they have plenty of "drills, heat, dust, smoke, and sore feet." Reenactors do not glorify war; with combat veterans, they know that "there is no glory in war—only pain, suffering, and death." They find something much more important than glory: a glimpse of the love that soldiers feel for each other, and even for their foes and comrades in suffering.

Brennan mentions a Confederate survivor of Pickett's Charge who said "how good it would be to cross that field just one more time with all those young, smiling fellows." Brennan claims that is what reenactors do: "We cross it for him, in his memory and in the memory of all those who fell that day and in the days since." Brennan refers to another veteran who "believed that heaven was a place where men could have a battle and when the smoke cleared, all of the fallen could stand up and shake one another's hands."[62] Such was the Viking idea of paradise. Valhalla, the Hall of the Slain described by Snorri Sturluson, in which warriors fight, die, and rise every day, contains an enduring appeal to men.

War Games

Military reenactment merges with war games, which have various degrees of seriousness. James William Gibson casts a jaundiced and leftist eye on freelance militarism in *Warrior Dreams: Paramilitary Culture in Post-Vietnam America*. He follows Klaus Theweleit's analysis of paramilitarism as an extreme manifestation of basic masculine patterns.[63] Men in America feel they have been betrayed by their own leaders and think they must band together to protect themselves and their families. Men must grow up to be warriors; war is "a primary rite of passage,"[64] "a relatively benign ritual transition from boyhood to adulthood."[65] They must leave behind the normal, safe world of women,[66] and plunge into chaos to confront the forces of darkness (Communists, terrorists, corrupt liberals). They may be scarred or die, but they are transformed and become gods, saviors. This is a religious world, a world of holy violence, in which men through sacrifice attain the mystery of communion.[67]

Gibson admits that this world appeals to deep masculine desires. He tried combat pistol shooting to see why it attracted otherwise sane and normal men and found that it was a religious experience of the type men crave. Combat pistol shooting was a *rite de passage*, "and like many initiation rites, it involved great physical pain."[68] The shooters were led into "'the zone', a state of altered sensory perception in which time is experienced as moving very slowly while eye-hand coordination dramatically increases."[69] War and simulations of war are appealing to men, and Gibson seeks a moral equivalent of war so that men in peace can still experience the "enchantment" that war holds out, "the travels, challenges, stories, and male initiation."[70] Gibson suggests wilderness adventure, but admits this "lacks war's seriousness."[71] Gibson's streak of leftist paranoia makes him exaggerate the threat that paramilitary organizations pose to public order. Yet Gibson is correct in identifying the deep appeal that this world view has for men and in characterizing paramilitarism as a form of religion.[72]

WAR AS HEAVEN—AND HELL

Societies that have harsh environments or hostile neighbors send their men to face these dangers, and modern societies are as harsh on males as primitive societies. In 1991, of those killed by accidents during work, 92 percent were men. The British census before World War I showed there were already a million more women than men. The Industrial Revolution was hard on men: machinery is dangerous. Industrial warfare is even harder and more dangerous. After World War I, the census reported two million more women than men, and the big gap in the male ranks was in the twenty to thirty-five-year-old cohort, which had vanished into the mud of the trenches—literally vanished, as half the dead were never even found.

David Jones's *In Parenthesis* is a long poem about a British soldier in World War II. The soldier, terrified by the prospect of going over the top, "wept for the pity of it all." His comrades try to get him to shape up: "You can't really behave like this in the face of the enemy and you see Cousin Dicky doesn't cry not any of this nonsense—why, he ate his jam puff when they came to take Tiger away."[73] It's the voice every man hears when he faces pain—"Be a big boy and don't cry."

The Spartans made their boys steal food or starve. A famous story tells of a Spartan boy who stole a fox and kept it under his cloak. When he was stopped by an adult, he refused to confess to the theft by letting the fox go. The fox ate into his intestines until he fell dead. He was held up as an example to other boys. Spartan mothers' words to their sons going off to battle were "with it or on it"; that is, come back victorious with your shield or be carried back dead on it. The British adopted this model in their public schools: cold water, bad food, and bullying toughened the boys. Boys may also undergo the informal discipline of the schoolyard or city street, or the hard labor of the farm, or the combative education based on debate and competition, prizes and humiliation.[74] Military schools often provide rites of passage in modern societies, an equivalent of the puberty rites in tribal societies.

Warfare is a further initiation into the mysteries of life and death, indeed the ultimate initiation. As Mussolini proclaimed, "War is to man what motherhood is to woman,"[75] and he was simply articulating what many soldiers have felt. From his experience in Vietnam, William Broyles came to realize that "war was an initiation into the power of life and death. Women touch that power on the moment of birth; men at the edge of death."[76]

David Jones draws parallels between the soldier and Christ. Jones used the machinery of the Arthurian legends to describe the experience of war, but beyond those was the death and resurrection of Christ. In one of his illustrations to the poem, Jones shows the lamb of God in the pose of the Easter lamb, but with the horns of the scapegoat, bearing the sins of the people, and driven out into the wilderness to die. The lamb is caught in the barbed wire of the battle field, and above him shines the Christmas star of Byzantine icons. The soldier is the new Christ, dying for the sins of his people.

But this transformation of the ordinary man into a savior-hero occurs in the context of war, which is a degrading horror. Even the work of anti-war poets such as Owen and Sassoon contains a disturbing implication: they hate war, but war brings out the highest and most beautiful form of human love.[77] Men may seek out war consciously or unconsciously as an escape from the suffocating selfishness of bourgeois society, as a way to transcend the calculation and boredom of materialism into the world of love and honor. But war is a cheat. In Evelyn Waugh's *The End of the Battle*, Mme. Kanyi addresses the hero, Guy Crouchback: "'It seems to me that there was

a will to war, a death wish, everywhere. Even good men thought
their private honor would be satisfied by war. They could assert their
manhood by killing and being killed. They would accept hardships
in recompense for having been selfish and lazy. Danger justified
privilege. I knew Italians—not very many perhaps, who felt this.
Were there none in England?' 'God forgive me,' said Guy. 'I was one
of them.'"[78] The soldier thus brutalized by war can become a milita-
rist; the warrior opens himself to the war god, the alien spirit that
can take possession of men in combat.[79] The history of Germany
after 1870 shows how a nation can descend into militarism. Ernst
Jünger's *Storm of Steel*, a German war memoir, inadvertently shows
why the French and British felt they had to fight to the end.

In the last German offensive in spring 1918, Jünger recognizes
that "the turmoil of our feelings was called forth by rage, alcohol and
thirst for blood."[80] There was another spirit in him, "the pulse of
heroism, the godlike and the bestial inextricably mingled,"[81] a spirit
not his own: "I was boiling with a fury now utterly inconceivable to
me. The overpowering desire to kill winged my feet. Rage squeezed
bitter tears from my eyes."[82] Christianity was no longer comprehensible: "Today we cannot understand the martyrs. . . . Their faith no
longer exercises a compelling force."[83] It is the Fatherland which is
his god, the idea that has been made sacred by the sacrifices of the
soldiers who die for it: "There is nothing to set against self-sacrifice
that is not pale, insipid, and miserable."[84] Self-sacrifice has become a
god—and therefore a demon. These emotions, disturbing and full of
portent as they are, are not even the worst products of militarism.
They were felt in the ancient world and fill the *Iliad*, *Odyssey*, and
Aeneid. Jünger sounds a modern note that is even more frightening.

Modern war produces a mechanical, inhuman objectivity and
detachment: "The modern battlefield is like a huge, sleeping machine."[85] Scientific war, which both sides experienced in its fullness
at the battle of the Somme, transformed the soldier into a machine:
"After this battle the German soldier wore the steel helmet, and in
his features there were chiseled the lines of an energy stretched to
the utmost pitch."[86] A famous German war poster captures the
transformation of the man into the soldier of scientific war.[87] It

shows a young man in a trench with barbed wire around him. He looks up with a hard and chiseled face. His eyes glow with an inhuman light. We catch sight here of the man-machine, the robot, that haunts the pages of modern fiction, the man who has sacrificed his humanity in the service of humanity, who puts on the new mechanical armor so tightly that he fuses with it.

Nevertheless, in Christian societies war is often identified with Christ's sacrifice. In the Great War, the identification of the soldier and Christ was nearly complete. Such was the image shown to the British public in World War 1 in one of the most popular posters: a dead Tommy (with a neat bullet hole in his temple) lies against the wall of a trench, with the figure of the Crucified overshadowing him.[88] Much had changed since the seventeenth century, when soldiers had been on the same social level as prostitutes. Even in Wellington's army, the officers were upper-class, but the soldiers were often rank criminals. But after the French Revolution, the ordinary man entered the army, whether voluntarily or by compulsion. The German volunteers of the nineteenth century had been the objects of national veneration. When confronted with a young man who volunteered to die to protect his family and friends, the public attitude was at first honor, then veneration, then, perhaps literally, adoration. George L. Mosse, in his analysis of the German attitude to the war dead, observes that for Protestant Germans "it was not only the belief in the goals of the war which justified death for the fatherland, but death itself was transcended; the fallen were truly made sacred in the imitation of Christ. The cult of the fallen provided the nation with martyrs and, in their last resting place, with a shrine of national worship."[89] The soldier was the new martyr.[90] His death, like that of a martyr, was a baptism of blood, able to wash out all the sins of a life and give immediate entrance into heaven and to heal the torn world. Even the Marxist Henri Barbusse wrote of the soldiers' "Gethsemene"[91] and saw their suffering as redemptive: a soldier "looked down at all the blood he had given for the healing of the world."[92]

Ludwig Feuerbach had told the world of intelligent skeptics that religion was but the projection of the highest and best qualities of humanity, that God was only man writ large. The war poets saw

Christ as the Soldier writ large. As Paul Fussell notes, the landscape and the place names of the Flanders battlefield forced the comparison of Christ and the soldier even on the common soldier. Flanders had names like Paaschendaele and was filled with wayside shrines, crucifixion groups that startled the Protestant soldiers of England. It was hard to avoid the comparison of the two.

In a letter, Wilfred Owen claimed that "Christ was literally in no man's land." What did he mean? He had apparently abandoned belief in conventional Anglican Christianity, although his mother had hoped he would follow a clerical career. And he had earlier written quasi-homosexual poems, in which he had expressed a wish to kiss the brown hands of the altar boy rather than the crucifix the boy held for veneration. But the real meaning of this eros Owen felt was revealed to him in the war. In his poem "Greater Love," he compares heterosexual eros unfavorably with the sacrificial love of soldiers for each other. In another letter, he recounted an incident in battle in which he cradled a young soldier in his arms as he bled to death. After a nervous breakdown caused by his being trapped for days in a shell hole littered with the body parts of a friend, he volunteered to go back to France because he thought he was a good officer and could help his men. He was killed by machine gun fire a week before the Armistice, and the news of his death reached his parents as the Armistice bells tolled.

Owen saw the soldier descending into hell and fulfilled his vocation as a poet by descending with him. The soldier, utterly forsaken by normal society, was thrust into a war that civilians could not imagine and left to die. He was degraded also by being forced to become a savage killer of other human beings. Owen curses all those who are indifferent to this suffering, and calls his future audience to remember the poor lads underground. It was perhaps in part the contemplation of such human suffering in the world wars that led the Swiss theologian Hans Urs von Balthasar to his theology of Holy Saturday, to his emphasis on the descent of Christ among the damned and the dead, to be one with the damned and the dead, and therefore to revive the importance of the Harrowing of Hell, which had been lost in the West after the Middle Ages.

Comradeship is the love that is the unexpected fruit of the hell of war. The word *comrade* has a faintly foreign sound to American ears. *Buddy* is the usual American term but it doesn't convey the seriousness of the tie as well as *comrade*. J. Glenn Gray was a philosopher who observed combat closely as an intelligence officer in Europe during World War II. He was able to analyze and articulate his emotions, giving a voice in his book, *The Warriors*, to all those soldiers who fought and died without being able to explain why they did it. He saw that the isolation of the human person within the shell of the self is a terrible burden and that in times of crisis almost anything, including death, is preferable to that isolation. Friendship overcomes the isolation in one way. It is a love based on a common interest or dedication to something outside the self. But comradeship is not quite friendship; it focuses on the other, on the comrade. Men experience a fusion of personality with the comrade, *a union which is not interrupted by death*. Gray notes that the Germans do not say that soldiers die—they fall. As a soldier, Gray realizes, "I may fall, but I do not die, for that which is real in me goes forward and lives on in the comrades for whom I gave up my physical life."[93] This fusion of personality is intoxicating, and veterans try to recapture the feeling at their reunions, although it seems that imminent danger is a necessary catalyst for this experience.[94]

Comradeship and homosexuality have a common element. Like lovers, comrades focus on each other, and the fusion of personality in the ecstasy of self-sacrifice is *like* (not the same as) that in the ecstasy of sexual intercourse. Comrades, like lovers, focus on each other's sexual identity, or to be more precise, lovers focus on sexual identity, comrades on gender identity, that is, on masculinity.

Thus, military poetry frequently uses language that sounds (especially to the post-Freudian ear) homoerotic. Sometimes it is, but more often, it is simply that sex and gender are closely connected. In praising the beauty of masculine self-sacrifice, poets, who use concrete language, often use physical and even sexual imagery. Wilfred Owen, again in "Greater Love", sees the love of a woman as less than the love of the comrade who is blinded or knifed to death in saving his fellow soldier: "Kindness of wooed and wooer/Seems shameless to their love pure." Sassoon and Owen were transient homosexuals, but the language they used was in the tradition of Victorian sentimentality and would not have been perceived as homoerotic by contemporary readers. Paul Fussell, in *The Great War and Modern Memory*, devotes a whole chapter, "Soldier Boys," to homoeroticism in the literature of that war,[95] but I think he places a mistaken emphasis on latent homosexuality. The two loves, one so honored that the soldier becomes Christ, and the other a disgrace and an abomination, find themselves forced to share the same language.

J. R. R. Tolkien transmuted his war experiences at the battle of the Somme into fantasy in *The Lord of the Rings*. Tolkien, when he wrote this book, was a devout Catholic and the father of several children, although his marriage seems not to have been happy. His closest relationships were with men. In the tradition of the poetry of the Great War, he draws upon erotic imagery to portray the love of comradeship which Frodo and Sam feel for each other, a relationship Tolkien said was modeled on that of the British officer and his batman (servant) in the Great War. When Frodo is captured by orcs, he is stripped and tortured. Sam surprises the orcs from behind and kills them: "[Sam] ran to the figure huddled on the floor. It was Frodo. He was naked, lying as if in a swoon on a heap of filthy rags; his arm was flung up, shielding his head, and across his side there was an ugly whip-weal. 'Frodo! Mr. Frodo, my dear!' cried Sam, tears almost blinding him. 'It's Sam, I've come!' He half lifted his master and hugged him to his breast. Frodo opened his eyes. . . .[Frodo] lay back in Sam's gentle arms, closing his eyes, like a child at rest when night-fears are driven away by some loved voice or hand. Sam felt that he could sit like that in endless happiness."[96]

Such language sounds unusual and suspect to modern ears, but Frodo's nakedness is only the visible representation of his vulnerability in his sacrificial and masculine role, and Sam's gestures of affection are an attempt to express the closeness of comradeship. As in the Renaissance and Baroque paintings of Jesus in which his genitals are at the focal point of the painting, it is not precisely sexuality, but masculinity and its connection to sacrifice that is of interest.[97]

The eros of homosexuality and the eros of comradeship resemble one another in that the focus is on the one loved, but the mode of union is different. In homosexuality, eros tries to achieve union through genital activity. But sexual union is achieved not in pleasure alone, but in the act of conception, in which man and woman literally unite in one flesh, that of the child. It is the possibility of conception that suffuses erotic love between man and woman with the hope that the prison of the individual personality can be escaped, that love can overcome loneliness and even death in the continuity of the generations. In the eros of comradeship, the personalities are fused because of the willingness of each to die for the other. It is a blood-brotherhood, a brotherhood attained only in blood, in sacrifice, and in death, or at least under the shadow and threat of these. A man is willing to die for his comrade because he feels an identity with him. It is not an identity based upon common interests or background; it unites men from different races, classes, nationalities, sometimes men who cannot even speak each other's language. The only common characteristic that unites comrades is their masculinity. Masculinity, at heart, is a willingness to sacrifice oneself for the other.[98]

THE FASCIST MALE

European fascism was self-consciously masculine. All varieties of European fascism cultivated the image of masculinity. The *Action Française* characterized the French situation in this fashion: "Democracy was equal to anarchy; it lacked the manly principles of action and initiative; it made the state the prey of rapaciousness and group interests; it was feminine, weak and evil."[99] The Italian Futurists were a group of artists who rebelled against the museum culture of early twentieth-century Italy. They wanted to escape from stultifying conventions, and to make an art out of the new industrial world, which was full of noise, motion, and violence. They rejected Christianity and women. Marinetti proclaimed in "The Founding and Manifesto of Futurism" that "we will glorify war—the world's only hygiene—militarism, patriotism, the destructive gesture of the anarchist, beautiful ideas worth dying for, and scorn for women."[100]

"Futurism exalted a militant masculinity which glorified conquest and war."[101] The Futurists hated pacifists, but welcomed and cheered Mussolini as they helped push Italy into World War I.[102]

The avant-garde in art was also the avant-garde of the fascist (in the generic sense) political movement in Europe. This alliance has long been a source of embarrassment to historians of art, who sometimes simply ignore the connection. The Expressionist painter Emil Nolde was a member of one of the first proto-Nazi groups and did not resign his membership until the end of the war. He, like Mircea Eliade (who was involved in Romanian fascism), celebrated the conjunction of modernity and the primitive that characterized fascist movements. The avant-garde (a term itself drawn from war) was embraced by the revolutionary Nazis who were more radical than Hitler. They wanted civilized constraints to disappear, so that the primitive power of sex, blood, and violence would be free to create a new culture, more in tune with nature than the desiccated Europe of the bourgeoisie.

Italian fascism was the least bloody of the totalitarian regimes of the twentieth century, and much of its totalitarian talk was bombast, an attempt to hold together an Italy riven by regional and local loyalties, in which the majority of the inhabitants did not even speak standard Italian. Mussolini found Italy a nation of waiters and wanted to leave it a nation of soldiers. He commanded, for instance, that local officials should wear uniforms and engage in physical exercise. Such fascists were more devotees of masculinity than of totalitarianism, and this put a strain on their relationship with their allies, the Nazis. Mussolini exempted Jewish veterans, their sons, and Jewish Fascist Party members (one out of three adult Jews) from the anti-Semitic laws that were the price of his alliance with Hitler. The Fascist army protected the Jews in the areas it occupied, and even threatened battle with the Germans to protect Jews. The anti-fascist war journalist and novelist Curzio Malaperte was in and out of prison for his opposition to Mussolini, but he testifies to the courage of the occasional fascist military and civil official who tried to protect Jews from Germans and from pogroms in Eastern Europe: "A Fascist who risks his skin to pull doomed Jews out of their murderer's hands

... deserves the respect of all free and civilized men."[103] Masculinity has always meant protecting the weak of one's own community, and the Italian fascists felt that Jews (unlike Ethiopians) were inside the European community.

German fascism was much more sinister, but it seems to be distinct from Nazism in that it was a celebration of masculinity rather than an ideology of race hatred masking total nihilism. Its immediate ideological ancestor is the Viennese Jew, Otto Weininger. Weininger anticipated many of the later psychological analyses of masculinity and femininity: he saw that femininity was the natural condition of all human beings, and that men were all originally bisexual, in that they contained the feminine in themselves, because of their birth from a woman and their early nurture from a woman. Weininger thought that women were the stronger sex and had an easier life: all they had to do to become women was to follow the logic of their own sexuality in reproduction. Men who chose to see reproduction as the fulfillment of their life, that is, the Jews, were effeminate men who had not taken up the challenge of transcendence.[104] Thus, Weininger rejected his own Jewishness, converting to Protestantism the day he received his doctorate. He also rejected the limitations of living in the body by committing suicide.

This type of masculinity escapes from femininity only to fall into the void. The complete pattern of masculinity contains both the escape from the feminine and the return to it. The hyper-masculinity which sees only the initial rejection and escape ends in nihilism, in a worship of the void and death. In these can be found the final confrontation with darkness, a confrontation which becomes a union, and a total and final rejection of the world of the feminine, of life and love and society.

Most European ideologies of masculinity do not go this far, but many of them have a strong tendency to nihilism. The final rejection of the feminine also explains why a tendency to homosexuality was a strong component of these attempts to regain masculinity. Heterosexual desire is the main force that keeps men from spinning off totally into the void and which therefore tends to reunite them with the world of women. If women must be totally rejected, heterosexual desire must also be rejected, and few men can be happy in permanent celibacy.

The immediate political roots of Nazism were in the Freicorps, the bodies of soldiers organized after World War I to keep order in a Germany on the edge of revolution. The corps were like other warriors, the Cossacks and the Tartars, who lived by plunder and killing. As Barbara Ehrenreich points out in her introduction to Klaus Theweleit's *Male Fantasies*, the fascist kills because he likes killing. It is not a substitute for something else, for instance, sex, but something desired in itself. Moreover, this desire is not a quasi-psychotic aberration, but based on a fundamental condition in the psychological constitution of the male. The Freicorps' "perpetual war was undertaken to escape women."[105] The fundamental fear of men is the fear of falling back into the feminine world of infancy: "It is a dread, ultimately, of dissolution—of being swallowed, engulfed, annihilated. Women's bodies are the holes, swamps, pits of muck that can engulf."[106] German fascists feared the loss of identity in the "other," in communism, in miscegenation between German and Jew. Anti-Semitism was not originally a prominent part of German fascism of the Freicorps variety, which was more like Prussian militarism, a celebration of the male as leader and protector. But males were insecure in a ruined and defeated Germany.[107]

Nazis promised to organize Germany as a *Männerbund*, a society that understood men's inner life and provided for it.[108] Josef Goebbels proclaimed that "the National Socialist movement is in its nature a masculine movement."[109] Hitler and the rituals of the Nazi Party gave the young men of Germany a substitute for the generation of fathers that had been lost in the First World War. Comradeship was held up as the highest form of love, and the German Christians who were not simply opportunistic anti-Semites tried to show that comradeship was to be found in its highest form in Christ, who lay down his life for his friends.

National Socialism, although it cloaked itself in a veneer of romantic nationalism (which did not deceive nationalists like Ernst Jünger) was at best racist, and at worst purely nihilist. Hitler valued Germany only as a means to achieve the dominance of the Aryan race, and the Aryan race only as a means to achieve absolute, unlimited, universal power. The lust for power is the only appetite that remains in the masculine abyss. The naked assertion of self in the will to power was the answer to the death of God. Indeed, the cruelties of Nazism were calculated ones: they killed their victims with the maximum of pain, so as to harden the executioners.

Nazism shows most fully the dangers inherent in masculinity. The male, to become masculine, must first move away from the normal, feminine, domestic world, face danger and darkness, and then return to the normal world transfigured by his experience. The motion away from the normal is dangerous. It should be a parabola, leaving the base line of the normal only to return to it, but it can become a hyperbola, plunging off forever into the nothingness of infinity. Initially, it can be very hard to see the difference between the two trajectories. Nor are they predetermined. The male has a free will and can choose one or the other. Nor can a society avoid the dangers of nihilistic masculinity by renouncing masculinity. Any society that faces dangers must have an ideology that convinces some to face those dangers voluntarily for the sake of others, and if a society is to survive, those who face the dangers must be men, not women on whom the biological continuity of society depends. Nor can nihilistic masculinity be defeated by femininity, in a renunciation of separation and difference in an orgiastic communion. If a man goes wrong and heads off into nothingness, he can be defeated only by a man who has faced the darkness and not been conquered by it. Ernst Jünger could have joined the Freicorps and become a Nazi; it was precisely his masculinity that saved him. He despised the Nazis as soft; they killed the weak. Germans who took masculinity seriously would eventually have found themselves in the position of the Italian Fascists who subverted the Holocaust.

The Heart of Darkness

The search for self-transcendence in war, a search that has captivated millions of men in our century, is a warning that masculinity contains a dangerous dynamic. Because a man feels that he must die to the old self, that he must somehow confront the mystery of life, including the mystery of evil, he is in danger of making death and evil and nothingness the end of his quest. Masculinity can easily become nihilism, a worship of the nothingness whose darkness and emptiness fascinate because they contain the promise of the final and ultimate death, a death that somehow seems necessary to complete rebirth. But the rebirth can be forgotten, and only death and emptiness remain.

Nihilism is not simply a philosophical error, but a religious one. Since for the nihilist the final truth of the universe is that it is a void, the good has no source outside the ego. To a nihilist the good is only what he wants. A soft nihilism is the ideal of modern European society, in which sex and possessions and amusements are the goal of life. Moral relativism is a disguised nihilism because it destroys the objective and imperious character of the good. A good that is not an absolute is no true good at all. A good that can be reduced to an instrumentality, that is not recognized as an absolute in its own right, becomes simply another means for the ego to pursue its ends. Soft nihilism is an easy path to hard nihilism: Weimar was the logical predecessor of the Nazi state.[110] Hard or revolutionary nihilism, in Herman Rauschning's perception, was the heart of Nazi ideology. The talk of blood and race and nation was a smokescreen, only a ruse for the masses to facilitate the pursuit of the true goal, absolute power.[111] The nihilist ends by adoring power; at the heart of the will to power is a void that nothing can fill.

Nihilism is a characteristically, but not uniquely, masculine fault. Women have been less affected by this particular fascination with the void or by the attraction of the power to do evil, although feminists have started to fall under its spell. For them everything is politics; facts are simply mental constructs to be manipulated in the service of their quest for power. But they are toying with fire. The man attracted to soft nihilism often falls into hard nihilism, because power is seductive and compelling. For many men, power is all that there is, the only reality in the world. It begins with the feelings of sexual power in adolescence, in which the body is filled with a force that seems to come from outside oneself but to fill and control the self.

As the muscles grow and harden, the adolescent male feels the power of his body and uses it to frighten other people. Swaggering male adolescents enjoy the looks on an adult's face, the fear or terror that their mere presence inspires.

This attraction to power can be disciplined and sent into socially useful channels, or at least channels that do not threaten to destroy society immediately. But the common element in the deformations of masculinity that result from an exaggeration of some masculine characteristics is their more or less explicit worship of power in crime, Satanism, fascism, Nazism—all of which are practical forms of nihilism.

The men who perpetrate the crimes of the twentieth century know they are damning themselves; but they are damning themselves, cutting themselves off forever from the mutual love of society, *out of love for and service to that society*. It is this mysticism of sin that has haunted the literature, politics, and even the theology of this century, but it has roots in the religious situation of Europe in which masculinity has become more and more alienated from Christianity. This perverted masculinity appeals to men because it is not a total lie, but a partial truth close to the real truth. Jesus is the embodiment of perfect masculinity in that he descends into death and hell, there to confront and conquer them and to return to his bride, the Church, as King and Spouse. But if a man in his own power tries to descend into hell, he finds there only a defeat, and is taken captive by the powers of darkness he wishes to conquer.

The Future of Men in the Church

MEN DO NOT GO TO CHURCH. They regard involvement in religion as unmasculine, and almost more than anything they want to be masculine. The basic ideology of masculinity is a given as long as men are born of women and societies face challenges. Even if it wanted men to abandon masculinity, the Church has no way to reach them to persuade them to do so. Nor should men abandon masculinity. For all its faults, it is a basic natural religion, a yearning for transcendence, a proto-evangelium built into the structure of human society. Since men continue to want to be masculine, they will continue (unless there are major changes in the Church) to put a greater or lesser distance between themselves and the Church. Is there any way that Christianity can reach men in a long-lasting and effective manner?

The churches should follow the medical motto, *primum non nocere*, first of all, do not make matters worse. Feminism and homosexual propaganda dominate the liberal churches, and both drive men even further away.[1] Apart from some groups of evangelical Protestants, whose commitment to Scripture has made them aware of the lack of men and led them to use tactics which have had at least initial effectiveness, all other varieties of Western Christianity are totally bent on expanding the role of women in the Church and choose to ignore the absence of the male laity. Homosexuals who want to change are welcome even (perhaps especially) in evangelical and revivalist churches, but Catholic and mainline Protestant churches that cultivate a gay atmosphere (Archdiocesan Gay and Lesbian Outreach, gay choirs, gay tolerance talks in schools) will keep heterosexual men away. Fear of effeminacy is one of the strongest motivations in men who will sometimes die rather than appear effeminate.

Christianity has within it the resources that allow it to appeal to men, to show that not only will Christianity not undermine their masculinity, but it will also fulfill and perfect it. James Ditties, a professor of pastoral theology at Yale, holds up the image of the Son, in all the charm of eternal youth, truly eternal, from a beginning without beginning to an end without end, as a model for all men. Adam seized at the possibility of being self-originate, of being father and nothing but father, but in Christ we are shown that even God is Son. Ditties is a rare writer who takes a positive approach to masculinity: "Authenticity for men—feeling 'saved' (in language that once meant more than it usually does now)—is to be found within those modes of living that appear most characteristic of men, not in being shamed or coached out of those modes."[2] Three masculine modes of living which can be studied to develop the practices and approaches that the Church needs are initiation, the struggle, and brotherly love.

INITIATION

In almost all societies, learning to be masculine also means being initiated into the religion of that society, since religion teaches the meaning of the mysteries of life and death. The holy is a masculine category: men develop their masculine identity by a pattern of separation, both biological and cultural, and to be holy means to be separated. The more transcendent God is, the holier he is and the more masculine he is. Judaism is a transcendent religion, as is Christianity, although especially in Christianity there are anticipations of the return to the feminine, of the wedding feast of the Lamb, which is the culmination of the masculine trajectory. Judaism was a masculine religion, and has remained so. The majority of the practitioners of Judaism in America are men, and there is no sense that the study of Torah is effeminate.

Christianity revealed that the masculine identity was open to all: in Christ there was no longer male or female all could become sons of the Father by the grace of adoption. In the first millennium the masculine character of Christianity was clear. The church of the martyrs gave way to the church of the monks, but it remained clear that to be Christian involved a profound and heroic struggle, which was perhaps more natural to men, but which was also opened up to women.

Men have a natural understanding of the process of and the need for conversion. They know from their childhood experiences and their inculcation in the ideology of masculinity the importance of dying to the old self and being reborn as a new self. All scholars who have compared the lives of men and women saints remark on the importance of conversion in men's lives and the relative lack of it in women's. St. Paul stands in contrast to Mary, St. Augustine to Monica. Revivalism bears out this hypothesis: it increases the percentage of men active in the Church, but it is not successful over the long run because the churches into which men are led by revival are still so feminized that the processes of gender identification take over, and converted men (and even more their sons) start putting distance between themselves and church life. Conversion can lead men into the Church, but the Church they enter must also have a spirituality that allows them to be both men and Christians—they cannot be real Christians unless they become real men. But at the heart of the Gospel is the call to become sons in the Son by entering into the life of the Trinity.

Gordon Dalbey, a United Church of Christ minister, observed Nigerian rituals in which boys are taken from the world of women and inducted into the world of men and the sacred realities of their tribe. He has formulated a Christian puberty ritual for boys to counteract the lack of male participation on the Church.

His suggestion for the ritual is this: The father, pretending to go somewhere else, goes to church to prepare to induct his son into manhood. With the pastor and other men, he arrives unannounced back at his house. His mother (uninformed about the event, which is for men only) is hesitant, but as the men outside sing *Rise Up O Men of God*, the boy breaks from his mother and joins his father and the men of the church. As he joins them, the men sing *A Mighty Fortress*. The men and boys then go to a campground for discipline and instruction which would include:

- An opening worship in which each boy is taught to memorize Romans 12:1-2, offering himself to God's service and opening himself to let God transform him inwardly during the initiation period;

- Time to remember the men from whom the boy comes: stories of his father and grandfather and American history;

- Time to remember the God from whom all men come: Bible stories and biblical standards of behavior;

- Learning to pray, both alone and with others;

- A time of fasting during which the boy is taught its biblical purpose;

- Teaching the nature of sexuality and how to relate to women with both compassion and strength;

- Aptitude testing for professional skills, followed by a general session in which the men sit as a panel and share frankly their jobs, inviting questions afterward;

- Rigorous physical exercise;

- Daily individual prayer, Bible reading, and journal keeping;

- Prayer and counseling for each boy to heal inner emotional wounds;

- Talks by much older, godly men about what life was like when they were boys, and what their faith has meant to them;

- A closing worship service in which the men call each boy

forward, lay hands upon him and pray for him to receive the
Holy Spirit as in the traditional rite of confirmation.[3]

The Boy Scouts have many initiatory motifs drawn from
outdoorsmen, Indians, and the military, and many churches sponsor
scout troops. An intensive scout program closely integrated with
instruction in religious beliefs, attitudes, and practices, such as
Dalbey suggests, can provide an initiatory experience for boys that is
not bizarre, but which achieves a real change in personality.

James E. Ditties is unusual among theologians in that he has a
sympathetic understanding of masculinity. In *Driven by Hope: Men
and Meaning,* he examines the masculine drive to transcendence—
what I have called the thirst for initiation. Because of the physical
and psychological development of the male, every "man experiences
life as given to him as incomplete."[4] This emptiness produces a desire for self-transcendence through death and rebirth. Men are always looking for this, upsetting the settled routines of life, going on
pilgrimages and adventures, changing careers, committing themselves obsessively to work or play or sex in a hope of finding the beyond there. Men seek power because they love: "We men are gripped
with a passion to control because we are gripped with a passion to
save."[5] Because he is a man, he knows that life is full of sorrow and
wants to protect those he loves from that sorrow. Every man is a
soldier and a priest. He wants to bring salvation, "to save life from
its sorrow by summoning the transcendent."[6] It is from these deeply
good roots that even male faults arise.

An understanding of masculine personality patterns can help
preachers and counselors develop a rapport with men. Explicit references to the difficulties that men face will help men realize that the
Church is not just for women. I remember a remark in a sermon I
heard years ago. The preacher spoke briefly of those who worked
long years in jobs they disliked so that they could support their families, and how this was a type of martyrdom, harder to bear because it
was hidden and unrecognized. Most men face this situation some-
time during their lives, and it helps to have someone offer a sympa-

thetic understanding, and to place this experience within the context of Christian life.

THE STRUGGLE

A truly masculine spirituality must include struggle. Jesus struggled throughout his life, struggles that culminated in the agony, that is, in the struggle in the garden. In another garden sinful man had fled from the holiness of God and refused to struggle with the mystery of outraged holiness and love. In this garden, the Son confronted the Father and wrestled with his will. He ultimately submitted, as Mary did, but he submitted after a question, a plea: *Let this cup pass from me.* The Trinitarian space between the Father and the Son allows there to be a potential space between the will of the father and the will of the son. This space, reflected in the distance of creation from the creator, could become a sinful space of rebellion and alienation leading down to hell. But it could also become a space in with the Other is confronted as Other, and accepted as Other. God was the God of Jesus Christ; he addressed him as my God (as distinct from your God), and to the Father as to God, the Son submitted in the garden, as he submits from all eternity. What was the cup? The torture and death of the cross? Yes, but in that torture and death all godforsakenness was tasted, all guilt, all suffering, all pain of the entire creation.

Insofar as men are Christian, they must be agonic, that is, they must participate in the struggle against evil. This struggle is close to the heart of Christianity, although it is not the very heart. Moreover, the struggle has been too often with merely external enemies. Many readers may agree with my description of the situation in which men are alienated from Christianity but fear that any attempt to reconnect masculinity and spirituality would lead to the corruption of Christianity. In a century of murderous violence in which even the pope wonders if God would send anyone to hell because men have already gone through hell on earth, the last thing we need is a religious war. Previous attempts to combine masculinity and Christianity sometimes ended in disaster. Bernard, in addition to preaching bridal mysticism, also preached the Crusade. Violence is always with us, but it is somehow worse when supposedly consecrated to the service to God. Luther, too, in his attempt to reform the church, unleashed murderous passions against the Jews. Although religious conflicts in our century have a strong sociological and political basis, it is difficult to deny the religious element in the Lebanese civil war, or the long agony of Ireland, or the bitter fighting and massacres in Bosnia.

The true struggle is not with flesh and blood. Christianity is indeed a great war and a great struggle with Satan, with ourselves, and also with God. Paul became the greatest apostle because he had kicked against the goads, because he had struggled with the Lord. He understood better than those who regarded the growing Nazarene movement with indifference what the claims of the new sect were, and he hated it. His soul was outraged at the blasphemy that a mere man claimed to be God, the totally Other, the Holy One. He was outraged because he realized the force of the claim. He was able to consent with his whole being because he came to know exactly what that claim meant, that Jesus was the Messiah of Israel, of all humanity, of the whole cosmos, and the expounding of this mystery had been entrusted to him in a special way.

Submissive obedience is held up as the model of the perfect Christian response. Mary's *Let it be* is seen as the model for all Christians; but her questioning of the angel before her concurrence is forgotten: *How can this be?* This questioning, this struggle with God is even more characteristic of men: Abraham bargained with God over the fate of Sodom; Jacob wrestled with God; Moses, the meekest of men, struggled with God over the fate of idolatrous Israel. When God wanted to destroy the people who had worshipped the Golden Calf and raise up a new people from Moses, Moses, instead of humbly submitting, told God to destroy him instead of destroying Israel. Much of the Old Testament is a wrestling with God, a struggle to understand how such things could be. How could God have ruled Israel through the often imperfect instruments of the Judges? How was David, an adulterer and a murder, yet a man after

God's own heart? How did Solomon, the wisest of men, fall into idolatry? Why was Israel, Gods chosen, torn up from the land promised to it and sent into exile? The prophets wrestled with God, knowing that they would be called to proclaim a message that the Lord would then not fulfill, leaving them open to the charge of being a false prophet. Jonah complained against God, voicing the frustrations of all the prophets.

This wrestling with God continued in St. Paul. Men often begin a friendship with a fight. Soldiers, in reflection on war, realize that they were closest to those with whom they were fighting. *To fight with* in English has a fruitfully ambiguous meaning. It can mean either to fight against someone or to fight at his side as a comrade. But the important thing is that, with a comrade and with an enemy, one has shared the struggle, one has tasted the perils of loss and death, and that taste binds friend and enemy together in a closer bond than the soldier with the civilians on his own side.

The interior life is the primary, although not the only, arena of struggle. The interior life has been largely seen as the province of the feminized spirituality that began in the Middle Ages. If the interior life seemed inescapably feminine, men who wished to be both Christian and masculine turned to the external struggle against evil. Spiritual warfare is a dangerous concept, but the most consistent promoters of it realize that the enemy is not human being, but is a spirit. The pacifist branch of the Reformation was dominated by the metaphor of spiritual warfare, as has been monasticism, which has been largely a pacific force. The front in spiritual warfare, the no man's land where the Kingdom of God confronts the Kingdom of Satan, runs through every human heart. Conversion is a summons to fight on this battlefield.

For all human beings, life is a struggle, but men know that it is their duty in a special way to be in the thick of that struggle, to confront the hard places in life and strive to know, in the fullest sense, what the mysteries of life and death are all about. Protestant Christianity in the historic churches has largely forgotten this. The tone of contemporary Catholicism, especially in America, too often is an irritating official optimism, in which administrative triumphs are trumpeted as if they were the Second Coming. In a recent celebration of Rome's honoring of a major ecclesiastic, the secular reporter was somewhat bemused by the self-congratulatory tone of the proceedings. The tone was hardly based on reality: the local church entrusted to this ecclesiastic had suffered a massive decline in church attendance, confirmation, and general infidelity to Catholic teaching, as well as more than the usual share of scandals. Narcissism is a major vice of the Church and is even held up as an ideal: the community comes together to worship itself. Venus's sign is a mirror. There has been little honest confrontation with the mystery of evil, and this lack of confrontation has led to a trivialization of Christianity that makes it especially unappealing to men who want to spend their lives not on verbal games and pleasant rituals, but on the serious matters that can yield an insight into the meaning of existence. The work of God in the world is the most serious business that a man can devote himself to, because eternal matters of salvation and damnation hang upon it. But sin and damnation have disappeared in an ecclesiastical atmosphere of universalism and self-fulfillment.

Churches that can preach the Gospel without the modifications that make it easy and bourgeois have a great advantage in reaching men. The rawer fundamentalist churches and the more traditional revivalist churches reach more men than liberal or latitudinarian churches. Unless the Church takes its own message seriously, as indeed a matter of the uttermost importance, it cannot expect men to take it seriously either.

BROTHERLY LOVE

What is the Gospel but a revelation of the mysteries of life and death? We learn that we can reach life only through death. Much of the effort of the Church seems to be in obscuring the Gospel, into distracting Christians into secondary and derivative matters, while losing sight of the *unum necessarium*. What has been missing in the preaching of the Church, although it is prominent in the canonical Gospels, is the element of brotherly love, but brotherhood understood not as vague affection, but as blood-brotherhood and comradeship. This self-sacrificial masculine love is deeply desired by men and is one of the things that makes war tolerable or even desirable. However, earthly wars are but a result of a far deeper conflict, the war in heaven in which we are called to participate.

Beyond the struggle, and already accompanying it and preventing it from becoming bitter and nihilistic, is the love that is at the heart of the Trinity, the Spirit of Sonship. The Spirit descends upon believers to make them sons, brothers of the Lord, whom he addresses as his friends. This intimate love bears some of the marks of eros, but not the eros of the Bridegroom. At the sight of beauty, according to Plato, the heart grows wings. The beauty that draws us upward is the glory of God shining on the face of Christ and that is a masculine beauty, one that has the color of the blood that is shed by men.

Eros and *Agape*, concupiscible love that seeks to fill an emptiness and the love of friendship that wills only the good of the beloved, are not incompatible. Eros can be a step toward agape. We love God because he is lovable, we desire Him because he is desirable. The pagans knew this, and this natural love for the good is sharpened by the self-revelation of God in Christ. The problem is that the Church in the West has expressed this eros in the language appropriate to the eros felt by women, whether it is the eros of the bride for the bridegroom or of the mother for the child. Such language is inescapably physical, because we are bodily beings, and even our abstractions are but bloodless metaphors drawn from our bodily experience. There is, I believe, a love between men that can be called eros (and which has nothing to do with homosexuality). It is found most clearly in the experience of comradeship, in which shared danger and the willingness of each to die for the other reveals the infinite preciousness of both body and soul. The love of Christians for Christ in the New Testament is this type of love. It is based on the sharing of danger and hardship, and makes men blood-brothers with Christ.

At the end of John's Gospel Jesus asks Peter three questions, questions whose significance is obscured by the usual English translation. Jesus asks Peter three times, "Do you love me?" Peter responds three times, "You know that I love you." But the Greek makes a distinction. Jesus first asks Peter, "Do you love me (*agapas me*)?" Peter responds, "Lord, I love you (*philo su*)." Jesus repeats the question again, and Peter responds the same way. The third time, Jesus asks, "Peter, do you love me (*philas me*)," and Peter responds exasperatedly, "Lord, you know all things, you know that I love you (*philo su*)."[7] After each question Jesus commands, "Feed my lambs," and after the third question foretells Peter's martyrdom in imitation of Jesus, when Peter would have to go where he would rather not go, that is, to the cross.

Agape and its related forms are the common words for love in the New Testament, and few distinctions are drawn, except in this one passage. To have *agape* for someone is in this passage of John contrasted with to have *philia* for someone, and *philia* seems to be the higher type of love. Jesus asks Peter if Peter loves him. It would make little sense for Peter to respond by using a weaker word, "Lord, you know that I have some regard for you." Peter uses a more intensive word, and it is this more intensive word that Jesus uses in the third question.

Philia in the New Testament means the type of love that brothers have for each other. If this is the connotation that *philo* has in this passage from John, a possible translation of the first two questions might be: "*Jesus*. Peter, do you love me? *Peter*: Lord, I love you as a brother, and of the third question, *Jesus*: Peter, do you really love me as a brother? *Peter*: Lord, I really love you as a brother (which is the highest possible love I can give you)." Peter loves Jesus as a brother not because they are both men or are both descendants of Abraham, but because they have the same Father, God. Christians are brothers, not because they are male human beings, but because they are sons of God, begotten of water and the Spirit, reborn, having received a new nature, participating in the nature of the Son of God, being conformed to him in his death and resurrection. Jesus predicts that Peter will fulfill his brotherly love by dying in the same way that his Lord and brother has died. This death is a reflection of the eternal distinction of the Father and the Son, a distinction that allows the Son to offer himself as a sacrifice to the Father. Because Peter is the brother of Jesus he shares in the same nature as Jesus and can die the same death as Jesus. Because he will do this, he can feed the flock of the Lord with the Eucharist, the body given and the blood shed.

Men are made for brotherly love. It is the escape from the prison of self in which all human beings are locked, but which afflicts men even more deeply because they flee from the connectedness of the feminine world precisely to live and die for others, including women. Men seek brotherly love at the workplace, in gangs, in fraternal organizations, in war, but rarely in church or anything to do with church. Although the New Testament is permeated by the brotherly love which men desire, a barrier prevents men from seeing it, and from seeing in Christ the Brother the meaning and fulfillment of the sacrifices that men make in order to become men. Unlike sexual love, brotherly love is not distorted or made perverse by suffering. Indeed the deepest brotherhood, as all men suspect, is not based on common natural birth but on shared suffering. Those who suffer together become brothers. The love that men show for each other on battlefields is heartrending. A man will fall on an exploding grenade almost without thinking to save his comrades. A man who has suffered with Christ becomes his brother.

THE CRISIS OF THE CHURCH in every age is a crisis of saints. There is no modern, accessible model of saintly lay masculinity in Western culture.[8] A man can be holy, or he can be masculine, but he cannot be both. Studies (such as this one) can only point out a problem and perhaps make the Church aware of its needs. It can correct wrong concepts, because misguided preaching and spiritual advice only makes the problem worse. But studies alone, commissions and articles and programs, will not themselves create the masculine saints, who alone can show to men that holiness is not the negation, but the fulfillment of masculinity. That can only be done by saints who are both dedicated to holiness, not by their own work, but by the work of the Holy Spirit, and who are fully masculine. These saints will be ordinary Christians, who come into contact with other men in sports, business, or the military.

The restoration of a balance in the Church between the sexes cannot be accomplished by public relations campaigns or revivals to attract men. Even if men are attracted, they will not long stay in a feminized church whether in its "conservative" or "liberal" forms. The current campaign to establish feminism and the toleration of homosexuality as the new orthodoxies can only drive men even further from the Church, as indeed seems to have happened in the past decade. The Church must develop a right understanding of the meanings of masculinity and femininity, an understanding that is consistent with human realities and with the data of Scripture. The Church must also find a way of evaluating the development of metaphor so that a change does not distort the message of the Gospel. Only then can it appreciate and preach the metaphors of Son, Bride, spiritual warfare, and the friendship with God that are intrinsic to the Gospel. Only then will men return to the Church, and the harmony of Adam and Eve in the new creation be at least in part restored. Then the Church will have a foretaste of the time when the Bridegroom will unite finally with the Bride, the Church, that uniting of all the sons of God in the communion of sacrificial love which shows to the world the inner life of the Trinity.

Notes

Introduction

1. Ronald A. Knox, *Enthusiasm: A Chapter in the History of Religion* (Westminster Christian Classics, 1983), 20.

2. Brenda E. Basher, *Godly Women: Fundamentalism and Female Power* (New Brunswick, New Jersey: Rutgers University Press, 1998), 46.

3. Evelyn Waugh, *When the Going Was Good* (Boston: Little, Brown and Co., 1984), 238.

4. Ibid., 239.

5. A noteworthy exception is Pope John Paul II, who writes that as his mother died when he was nine, "I do not have a clear awareness of her contribution, which must have been great, to my religious training" (*Gift and Mystery: On the Fiftieth Anniversary of My Priestly Ordination* [New York: Doubleday, 1996], 20). Instead the Pope was influenced by his father, "a deeply religious man. Day after day I was able to observe the austere way in which he lived. By profession he was a soldier and, after my mother's death, his life became one of constant prayer . . . his example was in a way my first seminary, a kind of domestic seminary" (ibid., 20).

1 Armies of Women

1. Tom Forrest, "Is the Church Attractive to Men?" *Origins* 17 (November 5, 1987): 382.

2. Barbara Leslie Epstein, *The Politics of Domesticity: Women, Evangelism, and Temperance in Nineteenth-Century America* (Middletown, Connecticut: Wesleyan University Press, 1981), 47.

3. Michael Argyle and Benjamin Beit-Hallahmi, *The Social Psychology of Religion* (London: Routledge and Kegan Paul, 1975), 75.

4. John K. White, "Men and the Church: A Case Study of Ministry to Men in a Medium Size Congregation" (D. M. Thesis, Trinity Evangelical Divinity School, Deerfield, Ill., 1990), 5-6.

5. Stephen B. Clark, *Man and Woman in Christ: An Examination of the Roles of Men and Women in Light of Scripture and the Social Sciences* (Ann Arbor, Michigan: Servant Books, 1980), 635.

6. Arno Gaebelien, "Good-Bye Darwinism," quoted by Margaret Lamberts Bendroth in *Fundamentalism and Gender, 1875 to the Present* (New Haven: Yale University Press, 1993), 66.

7. William Bell Riley, "She-Men, or How Some Become Sissies," quoted by Bendroth, *Fundamentalism and Gender*, 66.

8. Bendroth, *Fundamentalism and Gender*, 65.

9. Paul A. Carter, *Another Part of the Twenties* (New York: Columbia University Press, 1977), 53-54.

10. Barbara Welter, "The Feminization of American Religion: 1800-1860" in *Clio's Consciousness Raised*, ed. Mary S. Hartman and Lois Banner (New York: Harper and Row, 1974), 22.

11. Ibid., 42.

12. Ibid., 43.

13. Ibid., 89.

14. Ibid., 19.

15. Con O'Leary, *The Last Rosary*, quoted by Colleen McDannell, *The Christian Home in Victorian America, 1840-1900* (Bloomington and Indianapolis: Indiana University Press, Midland Book Edition, 1994), 120.

16. The efforts are described by Colleen McDannell in "'True Men As We Need Them': Catholicism and the Irish-American Male," *American Studies* 27 (1986): 19-36.

17. Claudia Nelson, "Sex and the Single Boy: Ideals of Manliness and Sexuality in Victorian Literature for Boys," *Victorian Studies* 62 (Summer 1989): 548.

18. Thomas Hughes, *Tom Brown's School Days* (New York, Puffin Books, 1983), 236.

19. Quoted by Norman Vance, *The Sinews of the Spirit: The Ideal of Christian Manliness in Victorian Literature and Religious Thought* (Cambridge: Cambridge University Press, 1985), 22.

20. Quoted in John Shelton Reed, *Glorious Battle: The Cultural Politics of Victorian Anglo-Catholicism* (Nashville: Vanderbilt University Press, 1996), 211.

21. John Shelton Reed, "'Giddy Young Men': A Counter-Cultural Aspect of Victorian Anglo-Catholicism," *Comparative Social Research* 11 (1989): 211.

22. David Hilliard, "UnEnglish and Unmanly: Anglo-Catholicism and Homosexuality," *Victorian Studies* 25 (1982): 181.

23. J. Eddowes, "The New Testament and Ritual: A Lecture," quoted by Reed "Giddy Young Men," 211.

24. Evelyn Waugh, *Brideshead Revisited* (Boston: Little, Brown, 1978), 26.

25. Pat Barker, *The Ghost Road* (New York: Penguin Books, Dutton, 1995), 67.

26. Hugh McLeod, *Religion and Society in England, 1850–1914* (New York: St. Martin's Press, 1966), 156.

27. For some other members of Uranian circles who were attracted to varieties of Catholicism see Hilliard, "UnEnglish and Unmanly," 197-199. His inclusion of Msgr. Robert Hugh Benson is probably unwarranted, although the Benson family was very odd. Benson's brother wrote novels which have become popular in modern homosexual circles, but the most famous, *David Blaize*, is a sympathetic celebration of attractive qualities (physical, emotional, and spiritual) in boys and young men. Although it mentions schoolboy homosexual experimentation, it does not hold it up as an ideal.

28. James R. Moore, *Religion in Victorian Britain*, Vol. 3, *Sources* (Manchester: Manchester University Press, 1988), 77.

29. Paul Johnson, "Anglicanism, Organic Sin, and the Church of Sodom," *The Spectator* 277 (22 November 1996): 30.

30. William Oddie, "My Time at Homoerotic College," *The Spectator*, 277 (7 December 1996): 21. Oddie says that when he was at St. Stephen's House at Oxford, he "estimated that fully two-thirds were openly homosexual" (20) as Anglo-Catholics especially tended to be homosexual. At St. Stephen's men were given women's names (21) (a custom at some Catholic seminaries in North America) and is now "a hotbed of radical feminism" (21). Cuddeson, still too peculiar, also had a reputation for homosexuality. Oddie sadly concurs that "in the Church of England sodomy is on the verge of becoming part of that Church's semi-official culture" (20). There are few men in the pews of Anglican churches.

31. William A. Christian, Jr., *Person and God in a Spanish Valley* (New York and London: Seminar Press, 1972), 136.

32. Ibid., 152.

33. Patricia Cayo Sexton, *The Feminized Male: Classrooms, White Collars and the Decline of Manliness* (New York: Random House, 1969), 97.

34. Lewis M. Terman and Catherine Cox Miles, *Sex and Personality: Studies in Masculinity and Femininity* (New York: Russell and Long, 1968).

35. Ibid., 201.

36. Ibid., 204.

37. Testosterone can fluctuate with emotions. Being successful raises testosterone levels in both men and women. Rosalind Miles notes in passing that "Dr James Dabbs of Georgia State University told the American Association for the Advancement of Science Annual Congress in 1989 that a survey of men in different professions showed that vicars displayed the lowest levels of testosterone, while 'actors and American football players' had the highest" (*The Rites of Man: Love, Sex and Death in the Making of the Male* [London: Grafton Books, 1991], 212). Perhaps men with low testosterone are attracted to being vicars; more probably the discouraging nature of the work and the low status they have among men produces the emotional state which in turn brings about low testosterone levels.

38. Terman and Miles, *Sex and Personality*, 220.

39. Ibid.

40. Ibid, 153.

41. Ibid, 9: "Most emphatic warning is necessary against the assumption that an extremely feminine score for males or an extremely masculine score for females can serve as an adequate basis for the diagnosis of homosexuality, whether overt or latent."

42. Charles S. Prebish, "Religion and Sport: Convergence or Identity?" *Religion and Sport: The Meeting of Sacred and Profane*, ed. Charles S. Prebish. (Westport, Connecticut: Greenwood Press, 1993).

43. Claire M. Renzetti and Daniel J. Curran, *Women, Men, and Society: The Sociology of Gender* (Boston: Allyn and Bacon, 1989), 262.

44. James H. Fichter, "Why Aren't Males So Holy?" *Integrity* 9 (May 1955): 3.

45. Argyle and Beit-Hallahmi, *Social Psychology*, 71.

46. Michael Argyle, *Religious Behaviour* (London: Routledge and Kegan Paul, 1958), 76.

47. C. Daniel Batson and W. Larry Ventis, *The Religious Experience: A Social - Psychological Perspective* (New York: Oxford University Press, 1982), 360.

48. Gail Malmgreen, "Domestic Discords: Women and the Family in East Cheshire Methodism, 1750-1830," in *Disciplines of Faith: Studies in Religion, Patriarchy and Politics* (London: Routledge and Kegan Paul, 1987), 56.

49. Kenneth Guentert, "Kids Need To Learn Their Faith From Men, Too," *U. S. Catholic* 65 (Feb 1990): 14.

50. David de Vaus and Ian McAllister, "Gender Differences in Religion: A Test of the Structural Location Theory," *American Sociological Review* 52 (1987): 472.

51. George Gallup, Jr. and Jim Castelli, *The People's Religion: American Faith in the 90's* (New York: Macmillan, 1989), 50.

52. Barry A. Kosmin and Seymour P. Lachman, *One Nation Under God: Religion in Contemporary American Society* (New York: Harmony Books, 1993), 210-11. See also Dean R. Hoge and David A. Roozen, "Research on Factors Influencing Church Commitment" in Dean R. Hoge and David A. Roozen, eds., *Understanding Church Growth and Decline, 1950-1978*, (New York: Pilgrim Press, 1979), 42-68; Gerhard E. Lenski's "Social Correlates of Religious Interest," *American Sociological Review* 18 (October 1953): 533-544.

53. Robert Moore and Douglas Gillette, *King Warrior Magician Lover: Rediscovering the Archetypes of the Mature Masculine* (New York: HarperCollins, 1990), xviii.

54. Argyle and Beit-Hallahmi, *Social Psychology*, 75. Jews were not included in one census, but evidence indicates that men are more observant than women. Argyle, *Religious Behavior*, 77.

55. George Barna, *Index of Leading Spiritual Indicators* (Dallas: Word Publishing, 1996), 87.

56. Lyle E. Schaller, *It's a Different World: the Challenge for Today's Pastor* (Nashville: Abingdon Press, 1987) 61-62.

57. George Barna, "The Battle for the Hearts of Men," *New Man*, 4:1 (January-February 1997): 42.

58. Patrick M. Arnold, *Wildmen, Warriors, and Kings: Masculine Spirituality in the Bible* (New York: Crossroad, 1991), 68; Kenneth L. Woodward, "Gender and Religion: Who's Really Running the Show," *Commonweal* 120:6 (22 November 1996): 10.

59. Jim Castelli and Joseph Gremillion, *The Emerging Parish: The Notre Dame Study of Parish Life Since Vatican II* (San Francisco: Harper and Row, 1987), 68–69.

60. Ed Wilcock, "How We Lost Our Manliness," *Integrity* 9 (May 1955): 12.

61. Fichter, "Why Aren't Males So Holy?" 3–4.

62. Fichter, *Social Relations in the Urban Parish* (Chicago: University of Chicago Press, 1954), 91.

63. Gallup and Castelli, *The People's Religion*, 50.

51 percent of men and 63 percent of women say that religion is not outdated and can answer all or most of today's problems.

58 percent of men and 69 percent of women say they have a 'great deal' or 'quite a lot' of confidence in the church as an institution.

51 percent of men and 69 percent of women say prayer is 'very important' to them.

33 percent of men and 45 percent of women say reading the Bible is 'very important.'

38 percent of men and 47 percent of women say attending church is 'very important.'

38 percent of men and 55 percent of women say that receive a 'great deal' of comfort and support from their religious beliefs.

64. George Barna, *Index*, 87. Barna's silent inclusion of women's greater interest in horoscopes shows that women's religiosity is free-floating, and might alight on something other than Christianity.

65. Peter L. Benson and Carolyn H. Eklin, *Effective Christian Education: A National Study of Protestant Congregations. A Summary Report on Faith, Loyalty, and Congregational Life* (Minneapolis, Mn.: Search Institute, 1990), 17. In the Christian Church (Disciples of Christ) 41 percent of the males and 35 percent of the females; in the Evangelical Lutheran Church in America, 58 percent of the males and 48 percent of the females, in the Presbyterian Church USA 44 percent of the males and 34 percent of the females, in the United Church of Christ 48 percent of the males and 33 percent of the females, in the United Methodist Church 43 percent of the males and 28 percent of the females, but in the Southern Baptist Convention 23 percent of the males and 23 percent of the females.

66. Ibid.

67. Edward H. Thompson, Jr., "Beneath the Status Characteristic: Gender Variations in Religiousness," *Journal for the Scientific Study of Religion*, 30 (1991): 381.

68. Cheryl Townsend Gilkes, "'Together and in Harness': Women's Traditions in the Sanctified Churches," *Signs: Journal of Women in Culture and Society* 10 (1985): 678.

69. David O. Moberg, *The Church as a Social Institution: The Sociology of American Religion* (Englewood Cliffs, NJ: Prentice-Hall, Inc., 1962), 397. This may be so because rural areas still have a stronger ideology of masculinity, which finds expression in farming and hunting, than urban areas, and as we shall see, masculinity and religiousness (at least of the Christian variety) do not get along well in our culture.

70. Ann Lee Starr, *The Bible Status of Women* (New York: Garland Publishing, Inc., 1987), 379.

71. Ibid.

72. David I. Macleod, *Building Character in the American Boy: The Boy Scouts, YMCA, and Their Forerunners, 1870-1920* (Madison, Wi.: University of Wisconsin Press, 1983), 44.

73. Ibid., 42.

74. Ibid., 43.

75. Starr, *Bible Status*, 380.

76. G. Stanley Hall, *Adolescence, Its Psychology and Its Relation to Physiology, Anthropology, Sociology, Sex, Crime, Religion, and Education*, Vol. 1 (New York: D. Appleton and Company, 1911), 225.

77. Carter, *Another Part*, 30.

78. Cortland Myers, *Why Men Do Not Go To Church* (New York: Funk and Wagnalls Co., 1899), xi.

79. Ibid., x. In fact the situation was worse for Catholics. The 1902 *New York Times* survey showed that 72.8 percent of Manhattan adults attending church services were women (McLeod, *Piety and Poverty*, 169). Some admit the gravity of the situation: *The Catholic Telegraph* once said that at the same communion rail there are everywhere ten young women for every one young man" (Carl Delos Case, *The Masculine in Religion* [Philadelphia: American Baptist Publication Society, 1906], 23).

80. Ibid.

81. Hugh McLeod, *Piety and Poverty: Working-Class Religion in Berlin, London, and New York* (New York: Holmes and Meier, 1996),169.

82. Howard Allen Bridgman, "Have We a Religion for Men," *Andover Review* 6 (April 1890): 391.

83. Ibid., 391.

84. Ibid., 389.

85. Ibid., 391.

86. "Is It Manly To Be Christian? The Debate in Victorian and Modern America" in *Redeeming Men; Religion and Masculinities*, ed. Stephen B. Boyd, W. Merle Longwood, and Mark Muesse (Louisville, Kentucky: Westminster John Knox Press, 1996), 80.

87. Frances Trollope, *Domestic Manners of the Americans* Vol. 1 (New York: Dodd Meade and Company, 1894), 103-104.

88. Quoted in Ann Douglas, *The Feminization of American Culture* (New York: Alfred A. Knopf, 1977), 98.

89. Quoted, ibid.

90. Joseph E. Kett, *Rites of Passage: Adolescence in America 1790 to the Present* (New York: Basic Books, 1977), 65.

91. Douglas, *Feminization*, 97.

92. Helen Lefkowitz Horowitz, *Alma Mater: Desire and Experience in the Women's Colleges from Their Nineteenth-Century Beginnings to the 1930s* (New York: Alfred A. Knopf, 985), 43.

93. Quoted Welter, "The Feminization of American Religion," 139.

94. Ted Ownby, *Subduing Satan: Religion, Recreation, and Manhood in the Rural South 1865-1920* (Chapel Hill: University of North Carolina Press, 1990), 129.

95. Ownby writes: "Records of twenty-seven evangelical churches reveal that between 1868 and 1906 women constituted about 62 percent of the churches' members" (Ibid., 129).

96. Whitney R. Cross, *The Burned-Over District: The Social and Intellectual History of Enthusiastic Religion in Western New York, 1800-1850* (New York: Harper and Row, Harper Torchbooks, 1965), 177.

97. Ryan, *Cradle*, 75. See also Curtis D. Johnson, "Women: Agents of the Gospel Message," in *Islands of Holiness: Rural Religion in Upstate New York 1790-1860* (Ithaca: Cornell University Press, 1989), 53-66.

98. Ryan, *Cradle*, 77.

99. Paul E. Johnson, "Women formed majorities of the membership of every church at every point in time. But in every church, men increased their proportion of the communicants during revivals, indicating that revivals were family experiences and that women were converting the men" (*A Shopkeeper's Millennium: Society and Revivals in Rochester, New York 1815-1837* [New York, Hill and Wang, 1978], 108). Mary E. Ryan says that "the proportion of females in the revivals was in excess of their presence in the population of the worship, it was slightly lower than their proportion of overall church membership. The preponderance of women also varied slightly over time, tending to decline in the middle of the revival cycle" (*Cradle of the Middle Class: The Family in Oneida County, New York, 1790-1865* [Cambridge: Cambridge University Press, 1981], 80).

100. Johnson, *Islands*, 55.

101. Richard D. Shields, "The Feminization of American Congregationalism 1730-1835" *American Quarterly* 33 (Spring 1981): 48.

102. Donald G. Mathews, *Religion in the Old South* (Chicago: University of Chicago Press, 1977), 47.

103. Epstein, *The Politics of Domesticity*, 45.

104. Ibid., 48.

105. Ibid., 49.

106. Ibid., 59.

107. Cotton Mather, *Ornaments for the Daughters of Zion* (Boston, 1692), 44-45.

108. Herbert Moller says: "While in New England immigration males outnum-

bered females three to two, the ratio was six to one in the Virginia immigration" ("Sex Composition and Correlated Culture Patterns of Colonial America," *William and Mary Quarterly*, 3rd series, 2 [1945]: 118).

109. Gerald F. Moran and Maris A. Vinovskis, *Religion, Family, and the Life Course: Explorations in the Social History of Early America* (Ann Arbor; University of Michigan Press, 1992), 66. Moran and Vinovskis show that over the course of the seventeenth century, church membership became more and more feminized; see *Religion*, 67, 85-90. They explain it as the result of the use of bridal metaphors in preaching (*Religion*, 98-99). By the onset of the Revolution, "the median percentage of women at admission had reached 65" (*Religion*, 101). Robert G. Pope notes the early decline of religious commitment among men: "The percentage if men among the new communicants is revealing: in 1632-1649 they represented 43 percent of the increment; in 1650-1669 this figure dropped to 35 percent; and in 1670-1689, to 33 percent. The same pattern holds for owning the covenant. By the final decade three out of every four half-way covenant members were women" (*The Half-Way Covenant: Church Membership in Puritan New England* [Princeton: Princeton University Press, 1969], 217-218). This is even more striking since over half the population was male.

110. Pope, *The Half-Way Covenant*, 218.

111. Grace Davie, *Religion in Britain since 1945: Believing without Belonging* (Oxford: Blackwell, 1994), 118.

112. Douglas Davies et al, *Church and Religion in Rural England* (Edinburgh: T and T Clark, 1991), 245-246). The others show low medium or medium religious commitment. Men showed a far lesser belief in life after death (30 percent) than did women (53 percent) (Davies, *Church and Religion*, 253). Or, for the more statistically minded, 27 percent of males showed low religious commitment, 29 percent medium-high or high religious commitment, as compared to 18 percent low and 43 percent medium-high or high religious commitment among working females and 15 percent low and 48 percent medium-high or high religious commitment among non-working females. See David Gerard, "Religious Attitudes and Values" in *Values and Social Change in Britain* (London: Macmillan, 1985), ed. Mark Abrams, David Gerard and Noel Timms, 70-71.

113. Davie, *Religion in Britain*, 118.

114. Peter Brierley, *"Christian" England: What the 1989 Church Census Revealed* (London: MARC Europe, 1991), 79. A even bigger drop has occurred among young men: "Roman Catholic men in their twenties fell considerable in the 1980s, and a smaller drop in women" (Ibid., 87). Among Anglicans the percentage of men 1979-1989 dropped 6% (Ibid., 85).

115. Davie, *Religion in Britain*, 118.

116. Ibid., 119.

117. Ibid, 119-20.

118. Eric Jacobs and Robert Worcester, *We British: Britain under the MORIscope* (London: Weidenfield and Nicholson, 1990), 81-82.

84 percent of women believe in God, but only 67 percent of men;

9 percent of women say they do not believe in God, but nearly twice as many men (16 percent) say the same

72 percent of women believe in sin and 66 percent of men

27 percent of men do not believe in sin and 21 percent of women

76 percent of women believe in the soul and 58 percent of men

14 percent of women do not believe in the soul, but 30 percent of men

69 percent of women believe in heaven and 50 percent of men

22 percent of women do not believe in heaven to 40 percent of men

57 percent of women believe in life after death and 39 percent of men

25 percent of women do not believe in life after death, to 45 percent of men

42 percent of women believe in the devil, to 32 percent of men

50 percent of women do not believe in the devil and 60 percent of men

35 percent of women believe in hell and 37 percent of men

55 percent of women do not believe in hell to 64 percent of men."

119. Ibid, 84.

120. Ibid, 76.

121. Ibid, 72.

122. Ibid, 73.

123. Ibid.

124. Gillian Rose, quoted in McLeod, *Piety and Poverty,* 151.

125. Richard Mudie-Smith, *The Religious Life of London* (London: Hodder and Saughton, 1904), 302. For the morning services 59,058 men and 82,975 women; for the evening services, 73,440 men and 132,232 women. There were major differences in denominations. The Church of England was the most feminized. For the morning services in London there were 46,343 men and 84,602 women, for the evening services 48,396 men and 96,680 women, almost a two to one ratio. For the larger Protestant denominations, the least feminized was the Salvation Army. It had 2,275 men and 2,138 women at the morning services, 4,411 men and 6,668 women at the evening services. The Roman Catholics in London had 18,784 men and 32,884 women at morning services, and 5,071 men and 9,890 women at evening services. The proportion of men among Roman Catholics was closer to that in the Church of England than that in the slightly less feminized, smaller Protestant denominations (442-46). Synagogues, by contrast, had 15,157 men and 4,375 women (265).

126. See "Women and Anglo-Catholicism" in Reed, *Glorious Battle,* 187-209.

127. S. A. Walker, quoted by John Shelton Reed, "'A Female Movement': The Feminization of Nineteenth-Century Anglo-Catholicism," *Anglican and Episcopal History* 57 (1988): 202.

128. John Charles Chambers, quoted in Reed, "A Female Movement," 202.

129. Reed, "A Female Movement," 204.

130. John Angell James, *Female Piety* (Pittsburgh: Soli Deo Gloria Publications, 1994), 262.

131. Quoted by Patrick Collinson, *Godly People: Essays on English Protestantism and Puritanism* (London: The Hambledon Press, 1983), 274.

132. Elisabeth Schneider-Böcklen and Dorothea Vorländer, "Die großen Kirchen—zumindest im Bereich der Bundesrepublik Deutschland - sind mit 80% Frauenanteil an der Zahl ihrer Mitarbeiter regelrecht, 'Frauenbetreibe.'" (*Feminismus und Glaube* [Mainz: Matthia-Grünewald-Verlag, 1991], 15). The situation has been of long standing. In the Protestant churches of Berlin, "a survey of attendance at morning services in 1913 showed that women also made up about two-thirds of the congregations counted—though women may have made up a higher proportion of the total churchgoing population, as there are some indications that (as in London) evening congregations were more strongly female than those in the morning" (McLeod, *Piety and Poverty*, 163).

133. Fichter, "Why Aren't Males So Holy?" 4.

134. In the basic Christian communities of São Paolo, 56.5 per cent of the middle-class membership and 66.2 per cent of the lower-class membership is female (W. E. Hewitt, "Basic Christian Communities of the Middle-Classes in the Archdiocese of São Paolo" *Sociological Analysis* 48 [1987]: 160).

135. Leo T. Mahon, "Machismo and Christianity," *Catholic Mind* 63 (Feb 1965):4.

136. Ibid., 5.

137. Carmen Lison-Tolosana, *Belmonte de los Caballeros: Anthropology and History in an Aragonese Community* (Princeton: Princeton University Press, 1983), 288.

138. Ibid., 295.

139. Stanley Brandes, *Metaphors of Masculinity: Sex and Status in Andalusian Folklore* (Philadelphia: University of Pennsylvania Press, 1980), 182.

140. Christian, *Person and God*, 134.

141. Lison-Tolosana, *Belmonte*, 309.

142. Ibid., 338.

143. Ruth Graham, "Woman versus Clergy, Women pro Clergy" in *French Women and the Age of Enlightenment*, ed. Samia I. Spencer, (Bloomington: Indiana University Press, 1984), 128.

144. Ibid., 130.

145. Gerard Cholvy and Yves-Marie Hilaire, *Histoire religieuse de la France contemporaine*, Vol. III, (Toulouse: Bibliothèque historique Privat, 1988), 377.

146. Fernand Boulard writes: "Le comportement des sexes, très contrasté dans les périodes anciennes, évolue nettement vers un rapprochement des taux. Le recensement dominical qui a couvert le diocèse de Versailles le 23 novembre 1975, a fait apparaître que le taux de masculinité (proportion d'hommes dans l'assembleé des pratiquants) s'établisssait presque partout entre 35 et 40% pour les plus de 25 ans; un peu plus faible dans les doyennés rureaux, il atteignait meme 50%, soit la parité absolue de la pratique des sexes, en quelques doyennés urbains. Or, en 1907-1908, dans l'arrondissement de Versailles, ce taux était de 15.6%' et vers 1880, moyenne de l'ensemble du diocèse, il n'atteignait pas 11%" (The behavior of the sexes, very different during former periods, has distinctly changed in the direction of a similarity of rates. The Sunday census which covered the diocese of Versailles on November 23, 1975 made it

clear that the rate of masculinity [the proportion of men in the assembly of practicing Catholics] has stabilized almost everywhere between 35 and 40% for those more than 25 years old; a little more weak among rural senior citizens, it attains an absolute part of 50% among some urban senior citizens. In contrast, in 1907-1908 in the neighborhood of Versailles, the rate was 15.6% and around 1880 for the whole diocese it did not reach 11%) (*Matériaux pour l'histoire religieuse du peuple français XIXe-XXe siècles* [Paris: Editions de L'Ecole des Hautes Etudes en Sciences Sociales, 1982], 19. However, the statistics in this book reveal a long-standing and massive difference in religious practice between French men and women.

147. Gabriel le Bras, *Etudes de sociologie religieuse*, Vol. 1 (Paris: Presses Universitaire de France, 1955), 124.

148. Ibid., 254.

149. Ibid., 180. "On remarquera l'abondance des pascalisants et le dimorphisme des sexes."

150. Ibid., 165.

151. "Les devoirs religieuse sont presque complètement négligés par les hommes ou pratiquée seulement pour la forme. Les femmes seul les observent géneralement." Cholvy and Hilaire, *Histoire*, 299.

152. Christianne Marcilhacy, *Le Diocèse d' Orléans sous l'episcopat de Mgr. Dupanloup* (Paris: Librarie Plon, 1962), 531.

153. The current situation in the Catholic Church, in which contraception is officially condemned but those who adhere to this doctrine are largely excluded from Catholic education and diocesan structures, may be due to the same strategy of not offending women.

154. "Que l'on y fasse une sérieuse attention; qu'on ne s'aliène pas la femme par d'imprudentes riguers; la chose est d'une immense gravité. La génération naissante est entre les mains de la femme, l'avenir est à elle. . . . Si la femme nous échappe—*le* nous *vise ses lecteurs prêtres*—, avec elle tout peut disparaître et s'abîmer dans le gouffre de l'athéisme, croyance, morale, et toute notre civilisation" Quoted by Langlois, Claude. "Féminisation du catholicisme," in *Histoire de la France religieuse*, Vol. 3, *Du rois Très Chrétien à la laicité républicaine*, ed. Jacques Le Goff (Paris: Editions du Seuil, 1991), 303.

155. Michelet, Jules, *Du Prêtre, de la femme, de la famille*, 4th ed. (Paris: Hachette, 1845), 8.

156. Ibid., 63.

157. Marcilhacy, *Le Diocèse d'Orléans*, 533.

158. Ibid.

159. See Marcilhacy, *Le Diocèse d'Orléans* 215 and Cholvy and Hilaire, *Histoire religieuse*, vol. 1, 256.

160. Rosemary Radford Reuther, "Christianity and Women in the Modern World," in *Today's Woman in World Religions*, ed. Arvind Sharma (Albany: State University of New York Press, 1994), 285.

161. Kosmin and Lachman, *One Nation Under God,* 220.

162. Mudie-Smith, ed., *The Religious Life of London,* 265.

2 Can a Man Be a Christian?

1. Mary Maples Dunn, "Saints and Sinners: Congregational and Quaker Women in the Early Colonial Period," *American Quarterly,* 582.

2. Tony Walter, "Why Are Most Churchgoers Women? A Literature Review," *Vox Evangelica* 20 (1990), 74.

3. Walter Rauschenbusch, *Christianity and the Social Crisis* (1907. Louisville, Kentucky: Westmister/John Knox Press, 1991), 367.

4. Ibid.

5. Rosemary Radford Reuther and Rosemary Skinner Keller, *Women and Religion in America,* Vol. 1, *Nineteenth Century* (San Francisco: Harper and Row, 1981), ix-x.

6. Simone de Beauvoir, *The Second Sex,* trans. and ed. H. M. Parshley (1953. New York: Everyman's Library, Alfred E. Knopf, 1993), 653.

7. Francis Trollope, *Domestic Manners of the Americans,* Vol. 1 (New York, Dodd, Mead, and Company, 1894), 103.

8. Trollope, *Domestic Manners,* Vol. 1, 113.

9. Ibid., 112.

10. Ronald A. Knox, *Enthusiasm: A Chapter on the History of Religion* (1950. Westminster, Md.: Christian Classics, 1983), 570-571.

11. Trollope, *Domestic Manners,* 102.

12. Cotton Mather, *Ornaments for the Daughter of Sion* (Boston, 1648), 45.

13. Quoted by Ruth Graham in "Women versus Clergy, Women pro Clergy," in *French Women and the Age of the Enlightenment,* ed. Samia I. Spencer (Bloomington: Indiana University Press, 1984),131.

14. Freud was working toward a distinction of physical sexuality and cultural gender identity, and there seems to be a consistent theory underlying his various observations. Judith van Herik has collected all the relevant passages from Freud and analyzed their significance for a theory of gender in *Freud on Femininity and Faith* (Berkeley: University of California Press, 1982).

15. Judith van Herik, *Freud on Femininity and Faith* (Berkeley: University of California Press, 1982), 55.

16. Ibid., 150.

17. Quoted in Reuther, *Women and Religion in America,* Vol. 1, 13.

18. Ann Douglas, *The Feminization of American Culture* (New York: Alfred E. Knopf, 1977), 47.

19. Ibid., 75.

20. James Alberione, *Woman: Her Influence and Zeal as an Aid to the Priesthood,* trans. by The Daughters of St. Paul (Boston: St. Paul Editions, 1964), 97.

21. Ibid.,p. 98.

22. Ibid.,p. 88.

23. Quoted in Douglas, *Feminization*, 108

24. Douglas, *Feminization*, 110.

25. Quoted in Douglas, *Feminization*, 121.

26. Douglas, *Feminization*,116.

27. For a compendium of outrageous things that Catholics have said about Mary see Hilda Graef, *Mary: A History of Doctrine and Devotion* (Westminster, Maryland: Christian Classics, 1985).

28. Sarah J. Hale, *Woman's Record* (New York: Harper and Brothers, 1860), xxxvi.

29. Nina Baym, "Onward Christian Women: Sarah J. Hale's History of the World," *New England Quarterly* 63 (1990): 253.

30. Hale, *Woman's Record*, xliv.

31. Ibid., 129.

32. Ibid.

33. Bridgman, "Have We a Religion for Men?" *Andover Review* 6 (April 1890): 389.

34. Quoted in *The Legacy of the Middle Ages*, ed. C. G. Crump and E. F. Jacob (Oxford: Clarendon Press, 1962), 402.

35. "Ad Omnes mulieres," quoted in Bede Jarrett, *Social Theories of the Middle Ages, 1200-1500* (New York: F. Ungar, 1966), 70-72.

36. Quoted in Crump and Jacob, *Legacy*, 432.

37. Quoted in Perry Miller, "Jonathan Edward's Sociology of the Great Awakening," *New England Quarterly* 21 (1948): 68.

38. Preface by Placid Jordan, in Gertrud von le Fort, *The Eternal Woman: The Woman in the Timeless Woman*, trans. Placid Jordan (Milwaukee: Bruce Publishing Co., 1961), viii.

39. Jordan, "Preface," in von le Fort, Eternal *Woman*, ix.

40. Von Balthasar sees the lack of men, which I think is in part a result of the Aristotelian theory he accepts, as a confirmation of his theory: "We should therefore not be surprised, but rather feel how fitting it is, that normally far more women than men participate in the celebration of the Church's Eucharistic banquet" ("Thoughts on the Priesthood of Women," *Communio* 23 [1996]: 707).

41. Manfred Hauke, *Women in the Priesthood? A Systematic Analysis in the Light of the Order of Nature and Redemption*, trans. David Kipp (San Francisco: Ignatius Press, 1986) 304. He concurs with Hans Urs von Balthasar who claims "every member of the Church, even the priest, must maintain a feminine receptivity to the Lord of the Church" (*New Elucidations*, trans. Mary Theresilde Skerry [San Francisco: Ignatius Press, 1986],198).

42. F. X. Arnold, *Woman and Man: Their Nature and Mission* (New York: Herder and Herder, 1963), 54-55.

43. Ibid., 55-56.

44. George T. Montague, *Our Father, Our Mother: Mary and the Faces of God* (Steubenville, Ohio: Franciscan University Press, 1990),85.

45. Friedrich Nietzsche, *Beyond Good and Evil*, 259, in *Basic Writings of Nietzsche*, trans. and ed. Walter Kaufman (New York: Modern Library, 1968), 393.

46. Ibid., 250.

47. Walter, "Why Are Most Churchgoers Women?" 87.

48. Ibid., 79.

49. Ibid., 87.

50. Ibid., 88.

3 What Is Masculinity?

1. J. M. Tanner, *Foetus into Man: Physical Growth from Conception to Maturity* (Cambridge, Massachusetts: Harvard University Press, 1978), 56. R. J. Stoller elaborates: "The biologic rules governing sexual behavior in mammals are simple. In all, including man, the 'resting' state of tissue is female. We can now demonstrate without exception, in all experiments performed on animals, that if androgens in the proper amount and biochemical form are withheld during critical periods in fetal life, anatomy and behavior typical of that species' males do not occur, regardless of genetic sex. And if androgens in the proper amount and form are introduced during crucial periods in fetal life, anatomy and behavior typical of that species' males do occur, regardless of genetic sex" (*Presentations of Gender* [New Haven: Yale University Press, 1985], 74).

2. Eleanor Emmons Maccoby and Carol Nagy Jacklin, *The Psychology of Sex Differences* (Stanford, California: Stanford University Press, 1974), 351-352.

3. For a review of current thought on possible biological influences on the characteristic behavior of men, see Perry Treadwell's "Biological Influences on Masculinity," in *The Making of Masculinities: The New Men's Studies*, ed. Harry Brod (Boston: Allen and Unwin, 1987), 259-286.

4. Elisabeth Badinter writes: "this very erotic relationship teaches the infant the nirvana of passive dependence and will leave indelible marks on the adult's psyche. But the consequences of this experience are not the same for the boy and girl. For the girl, it is the basis of identification with her own sex, whereas for the boy it is an inversion of later roles. To become a man, he will have to learn to differentiate himself from his mother and repress, within the deepest part of himself, that delicious passivity in which he was entirely and exclusively one with her. The erotic bond between mother and child is not limited to oral satisfactions. It is she who, by the care she gives him, awakens all his sensuality, initiates him to pleasure, and teaches him to love his body" (*XY: On Masculine Identity*, trans. Lydia Davis, [New York: Columbia University Press, 1995], 44-45.

5. Nancy Chodorow, The *Reproduction of Mothering: Psychoanalysis and the Sociology of Gender* (Berkeley: University of California Press, 1978), 169.

6. Irene Fast, *Gender Identity: A Differentiation Model* (Hillsdale, New Jersey: The Analytic Press, 1984), 69.

7. Fast claims that there is "a pattern of femininity found in men who have not successfully resolved issues of gender differentiation" (*Gender Identity*, 69). This unre-

solved conflict can result in a variety of disorders: extreme misogyny, because the female represents the infantile in the man, (Ibid., 69), sado-masochism, which is found far more frequently in males than females (Ibid., 70), and perhaps erotic disorders which cause the man to follow the mother's erotic gaze to a man (passive homosexuality) or to a boy (pedophilia). It is a sensitive subject, but the source of pedophilia among the clergy may be the same failure to achieve full differentiation from the feminine, a failure that causes some of them also to be attracted to religion, because they see it as a feminine activity. See also Ralph R. Greenson, "Dis-Identifying from Mother: Its Special Importance for the Boy," *International Journal of Psycho-analysis* 49 (1968): 370-374.

8. Margaret Mead noted "The boy learns that he must make an effort to enter the world of men, that this first act of differentiating himself from his mother, of realizing his own body as his and different from hers, must be continued in long years of effort—which may not succeed" (*Male and Female: A Study of the Sexes in a Changing World* [1944. Westport Connecticut: Greenwood Press, 1977], 151).

9. Ronald F. Levant says: "At an early age, then, boys are given the prize of a sense of themselves as separate individuals; in return, they are required to give up their close attachment to their mothers. Hence, as boys grow up, yearnings for maternal closeness and attachment (which never completely go away) become associated with the fear of losing themselves as separate. When such yearnings for maternal closeness begin to emerge into awareness, they often bring with them terrible images of the loss of the sense of identity" ("Toward a Reconstruction of Masculinity" in *A New Psychology of Men* [NY: Basic Books, 1995], 244). See Karen Horney, "The Dread of Women," *International Journal of Psycho-Analysis* (13) 1932, 348-360.

10. See Liam Hudson and Bernardine Jacot, "The Male Wound" in *The Way Men Think: Intellect, Intimacy and the Erotic Imagination* (New Haven: Yale University Press, 1991), 137-158.

11. Ibid., 49.

12. David Bakan, *The Duality of Human Existence: Isolation and Communion in Western Man* (Boston: Beacon Press, 1966), 15.

13. Ibid., 15.

14. Ibid.

15. Bakan writes: "The separated being is destined to die. The only way in which there can be any biological continuity is through the act of sexual intercourse, resulting in the birth of another separate (*Duality*, 51).

16. Ibid., 40.

17. Ibid., 141.

18. Hudson and Jacot, *The Way Men Think*, 57.

19. Walter Ong, *Fighting for Life: Contest, Sexuality, and Consciousness* (1981. Amherst: University of Massachusetts Press, 1989), 16.

20. David Gilmore in *Manhood in the Making: Cultural Concepts of Masculinity* (Haven: Yale University Press, 1990).

21. Ibid., 57. Peter N. Stearns says "One does not just become a man. A natural

passage of sexual maturation is not enough. In most societies, including our own, boys require a more extensive, arduous transition to manhood " (*Be A Man! Males in Modern Society* [New York: Holmes and Meier, 1990], 16).

22. Stoller, *Presentations*, 17.

23. Gilmore, *Manhood*, 121.

24. Ibid., 230.

25. Ibid., 229.

26. Michael Levin, *Feminism and Freedom* (New Brunswick: Transaction Books, 1987), 8.

27. Warren Farrell, *The Myth of Male Power: Why Men Are the Disposable Sex* (New York: Simon and Schuster, 1993).

28. Herb Goldberg, *The Hazards of Being Male: Surviving the Myth of Masculine Privilege* (1976. New York: Signet, 1987). See also James Harrison's "Warnng: The Male Sex Role May Be Dangerous to Your Health," *Journal of Social Issues* 14:1 (1978): 65-86.

29. Ibid., 5.

30. Farrell, *Myth*, 105. James Harrison concludes "the best available evidence confirms the psychosocial perspective that sex-role socialization accounts for a large part of men's shorter life expectancy" ("Warning," 65).

31. As Nicholas Davidson points out: "If toil and suffering have been women's lot, then have also been men's. It is no accident that women live longer than men, even in cultures that are said to oppress women (and may actually do so in some cases). Men have faced agony on blood-soaked battlefields, been worked to death in mines and on galley ships, and in all cultures die younger than women" (*The Failure of Feminism* [Buffalo: Prometheus Books, 1988], 50).

32. Goldberg, *Hazards*, 87

33. Richard A. Hawley, *Boys Will Be Men: Masculinity in Troubled Times* (Middlebury, Vermont: Paul S. Erikson, 1993), 17.

34. Ibid., 18.

35. Arnold van Gennep, *The Rites of Passage*, trans. Monika K. Vizedom and Gabrielle L. Caffee (London: Routledge and Kegan Paul, 1960), 10.

36. Ibid., 11.

37. Ibid., 15

38. Victor Turner, "Betwixt and Between: the Liminal Period in Rites of Passage" in *Betwixt and Between: Patterns of Masculine and Feminine Initiation*, ed. Louise Carus Mahdi, Steven Foster, and Meredith Little, (LaSalle, Illinois: Open Court, 1987), 9.

39. Alfred W. Howitt, *The Native Tribes of South-East Australia* (London: Macmillan, 1904), 532.

40. Van Gennep, *Rites*, 75.

41. Ibid., 72.

42. Bruno Bettelheim notes "some features of male initiation rites apparently are

designed to make men as much as possible like women" (*Symbolic Wounds: Puberty Rites and the Envious Male* [London: Thames and Hudson, 1955], 107).

43. Gilbert A. Herdt reports that one boy, Kambo, feared that he was developing a birth canal because of his homosexual activities, which were supposed to help him turn into a man: "That fantasy, a free floating anxiety that semen ingestion might effect female traits in a boy, is a prevalent response among young novices" (*Guardians of the Flutes: Idioms of Masculinity* [New York: McGraw Hill Book Company, 1981], 281).

44. Mircea Eliade, *Rites and Symbols of Initiation: The Mysteries of Birth and Rebirth*, trans. by Williard R. Trask (1958. New York: Harper Torchbooks, 1965), 26.

45. Bettelheim, *Symbolic Wounds*, 36.

46. Ibid.

47. Monika Vizedom, *Rites and Relationships: Rites of Passage and Contemporary Anthropology*. Sage Research Papers in the Social Sciences: Cross Cultural Studies Series, no. 90-027, Vol. 4 (1976), 43.

48. Bettelheim notes "among some groups of young men hurtful scarification was as important a part of adolescent ritual as it is in initiation. German students were more than willing to suffer cutting and bloodletting, proudly considering their the dueling ordeal as a demonstration of their manliness and their worthiness to belong to the group" (*Symbolic Wounds*, 99).

49. Turner, "Betwixt and Between," 11.

50. Rosalind Miles, *The Rites of Man: Love, Sex and Death in the Making of the Male* (London: Grafton Books, 1991), 44.

51. Ibid.

52. Ibid., 76.

53. Initiation is much more common among men. Bettelheim says "Nearly all students of initiation in preliterate society express the notion that initiation of girls is secondary to that of boys" (*Symbolic Wounds*, 246). That this should be so follows from the difference in development and relation to the mother that boys and girls experience, and to the fact that masculinity is an ideology that must be inculcated in boys.

54. Eliade, *Rites*, xiii.

55. Van Gennep, *Rites*, 105.

56. Harold R. Willoughby, *Pagan Regeneration: A Study of Mystery Initiations in the Greco-Roman World* (Chicago: University of Chicago Press, 1929. Midway Reprint 1974), 36-67.

57. Willoughby writes "Mithra himself had been for long centuries the god of battles, and his cult was an exclusively masculine one" (*Pagan Regeneration*, 152).

58. Franz Cumont, *The Mysteries of Mithras*, trans. Thomas J. McCormick (1903. New York: Dover Publications, Inc., 1956).

59. Eliade, *Rites*, 115.

60. Mircea Eliade, writes "For it is a fact that even Christianity, a revealed religion which did not originally imply any secret rite, which had proclaimed and propa-

gated itself in the broad light of day and for all men, came in the end to borrow from the liturgies and the vocabulary of the Hellenistic mysteries" (*Rites*, 121).

61. Mircea Eliade observes, "Le nombre de livres et études analysant les scénarios initiatiques camouflés dans les poèmes, les nouvelles et les romans, est considérable" ("L'initiation et le monde moderne" (The number of books and studies analyzing the serious of initiation hidden in poems, short stories, and novels, is considerable), *Initiation: Contributions to the theme of the Study-Conference of the International Association for the History of Religions Held at Strasbourg, September 17th to 22nd, 1964*, ed. C. J. Bleeker [Leiden: J. Brill, 1965], 12).

62. Frank S. Pittman III: "Before he is permitted to achieve victory, the hero must renounce his boyish selfishness, his fear of death and of humiliation, and even his desire for glory; he must be willing to give up his life for others" (*Man Enough: Fathers, Sons and the Search for Masculinity* [New York: G. P. Putnam's Sons, 1993], 183).

63. See Robert Randall, "Return of the Pleiades," *Natural History* 96 (June 1987): 43-52.

64. See Hope Nash Wolff, *A Study in the Narrative Structure of Three Epic Poems: Gilgamesh, the Odyssey, Beowulf* (New York: Garland Publishing Co., 1987).

65. *The Odyssey of Homer*, trans. Richard Lattimore (1965; New York: Perennial Library-Harper, 1975). Book and line numbers refer to this edition.

66. Howard W. Clarke, *The Art of the Odyssey* (Englewood Cliffs, NJ: Prentice, 1967) 9.

67. Ibid.

68. Gilmore, *Manhood in the Making*, 39.

6. George E. Dimock Jr., "The Name of Odysseus," in *Homer: A Collection of Critical Essays*, ed. George Steiner and Robert Fagles (Englewood Cliffs, NJ: Prentice, 1962) III.

70. Gilmore, *Manhood*, 38.

71. Wolff, *Study*. 57.

72. Ibid.

73. Dimock, "The Name of Odysseus," 53. But Odysseus is also the one who suffers much.

74. Wolff, *Study*, 57

75. Ibid.

76. As Catherine Callen King notes, "Homer wants us to see Achilles as having somehow having crossed the bounds of *human nature*. One such indication is the pattern of fire imagery, which, beginning with the divinely kindled fire that blazes from his head at the trench and continuing through the evening star that marks the end of his duel with Hektor, contributes to our seeing Achilles as an increasingly deadly elemental force. Another indication is the series of lion similes, which suggests that Achilles' deadly force is not only elemental but bestial as well" (*Achilles: Paradigms of the War Hero from Homer to the Middle Ages* [Berkeley: University of California Press, 1987],17-18).

77. P. L. Henry, "Furor Heroicus," *Studia Germania Gandensis* 3 (1961): 235.

78. See Henry, "Furor," 237.

79. See Doreen M. E. Gillam, "The Use of the Term 'æglæca' in *Beowulf* at Lines 893 and 2592" *Neophilologus* 61 (1977): 600-618.

80. See S. L. Dragland, "Monster Man in *Beowulf*," *Neophilologus* 61 (1977): 606-618.

81. Gilbert Lewis, "Payback and Ritual in War in New Guinea," in *War: A Cruel Necessity? The Bases of Institutional Violence*, ed. Robert A. Hinde and Helen F. Watson (London: I. B. Tauris Publishers, 1995), 34.

4 *God and Man in Judaism: Fathers and the Father-God*

1. Gerhard van Rad, *Old Testament Theology*, trans. I. D. M. G. Stalker (New York: Harper and Row, 1962), 146.

2. Stephen Sapp, *Sexuality, the Bible, and Science* (Philadelphia: Fortress Press, 19xx), 3.

3. See Sapp, *Sexuality*, 11.

4. Francis Martin notes that "while the Hebrew verb system distinguishes between masculine and feminine subjects, there is not one verb form in the Old Testament to be found in the feminine form when God is the subject" (*The Feminist Question: Feminist Theology in the Light of Christian Tradition* [Grand Rapids: William B. Eerdmans, 1994], 234).

5. Rudolf Otto, *The Idea of the Holy* (New York: Oxford University Press, 1958), p 26.

6. Julia Kristeva, *In the Beginning Was Love: Psychoanalysis and Faith*, trans. Arthur Goldhammer (1985. New York: Columbia University Press, 1987), 31.

7. Leo Strauss, "On the Interpretation of Genesis," *L'Homme*, 1981 (21): 10.

8. Ibid., 12.

9. Suzanne Heine, *Woman and Early Christianity: A Reappraisal*, trans. John Bowden (1986. Minneapolis: Augsburg Publishing House, 1987), 22.

10. Carol Myers, *Discovering Eve: Ancient Israelite Women in Context* (New York: Oxford University Press, 1988), 27.

11. George T. Montague, *Our Father, Our Mother: Mary and the Faces of God* (Steubenville, Ohio: Franciscan University Press, 1990), 18.

12. John W. Miller, *Biblical Faith and Fathering: Why We Call God "Father"* (Mahwah, New Jersey: Paulist Press, 1989), 149.

13. Ibid.

14. Ibid., 43.

15. Ibid., 44-51.

16. Perhaps there are psychological elements in the story. A father may also develop a Laertes complex, and be jealous of the child as the one who will replace him in the normal course of human life, reproduction, and death.

17. Whether the Psalms were written by the historical David or a literary construct "David" is unimportant in this context.

5 *God and Man in Early Christianity: Sons in the Son*

1. "According to the Philosopher, a thing is denominated chiefly by its perfection, and by its end. Now generation signified something in the process of being made, whereas paternity signifies that something is something completed; and therefore the name Father is more expressive as regards the divine person than genitor or begetter" (*Summa Theologica*, Q. 33, Art. 2, ad 2. in *Basic Writings of Saint Thomas Aquinas*, vol. 1, ed. Anton C. Pegis [New York: Random House, 1945], 326).

2. The central importance of the image of the Church as Bride is the subject of Claude Chevasse's *The Bride of Christ: An Inquiry into the Nuptial Element in Early Christianity* (London, Faber and Faber, 1940).

3. As William Oddie observes, "this balance of love, obedience, obligation, and sacrifice has not, within Christian civilization, always been observed. What is perhaps more striking, however, is how unquestioned in practice its acceptance has often been" (*What Will Happen to God, Feminism and the Reconstruction of Christian Belief* [San Francisco: Ignatius, 1988], 55). Oddie cites the behavior of the men on the Titanic. A group of Washington media people began jokingly visiting the almost-forgotten Washington memorial to these men on the *Titanic*. What began as a joke became a serious ritual and a tribute to the "courage and sacrifice and grace under pressure" of these men (Ken Ringle, "First Class Tribute: A Night of Remembrance for Titanic's Gentlemen," *Washington Post* April 16, 1996). As Oddie says, " the sinking of the Titanic remains as a kind of modern icon of the assertion of sacrificial and Christ-like male authority" (Ibid., 55).

4. Karl Barth: "He is not the saviour of woman as Jesus Christ is of his body the Church. " *Church Dogmatics*, vol. 3, *The Doctrine of Creation*, 54.1, trans. Harold Knight et al, (Edinburgh: T. T. Clark, 1960), 175.

5. David D. Gilmore, *Manhood in the Making: Cultural Concepts of Masculinity* (New Haven: Yale University Press, 1990), 230.

6. Ibid., 230.

7. Boff rightly claims that this association of Mary, the Church, and the Spirit is widespread among Catholic theologians. For citation see n. 34 (Boff, *The Maternal Face of God*, 266) and n. 54 (Boff, *The Maternal Face of God*, 267). See also Hauke, *Women in the Priesthood?* 277-296 and 316-317.

8. Kolbe's phrasing was "Spiritus Sanctus: 'quasi' incarnatus est: Immaculata" quoted by Leonardo Boff, *The Maternal Face of God: the Feminine and Its Religious Expressions*, trans. Robert R. Barr and John W. Diercksmeier (San Francisco: Harper and Row, Publishers, 1987), 96. See also Manfred Hauke, *Women in the Priesthood? A Systematic Analysis in the Light of the Order of Nature and Redemption*, trans. David Kipp (San Francisco: Ignatius Press, 1986), 277-296 and 316-317.

9. Boff, *The Maternal Face of God*, 93.

10. Otto, *The Idea of the Holy* (New York: Oxford University Press, 1958), 23.

11. See Leon Harold Craig, *The War Lover: A Study of Plato's Republic* (Toronto: University of Toronto Press, 1996), 65.

12. Thomas G. Weinandy, *The Father's Spirit of Sonship: Reconceiving the Trinity* (Edinburgh: T and T Clark, 1995), 17.

13. Ibid., 28.

14. Ibid., 35.

15. Hauke, *Women in the Priesthood*, 286.

16. Ibid., 287.

17. David L. Schindler, *Heart of the World, Center of the Church: Communio Ecclesiology, Liberalism, and Liberation* (Grand Rapids, Michigan: William B. Eerdmans Publishing Company, 1996), 8. Walter Kaspar says, "the Church is not only the image of the trinitarian *communio* but also its re-presentation" ("Church as *'Communio*,'" *Communio* 13 [Spring 1986], 108).

18. George T. Montague says "even the category 'metaphor' is inadequate., for our relationship with the Father is not just like Jesus' relationship with the Father; it is an actual, if created, participation in that relationship (*Our Father, Our Mother: Mary and the Faces of God.* [Steubenville, OH: Franciscan University Press, 1990], 55). The doctrine of deification is almost forgotten by western Christians, and its absence has been filled by the pantheistically flavored "god(dess) within" of feminism.

19. The New Testament is also aware of the dangers of masculinity. The Pharisees, whose name means separatists, emphasized the external codes of holiness, that separated them from pagans and Jews who did no observe the law, but neglected the interior code of holiness.

20. See Mircea Eliade, *Rites and Symbols of Initiation*, trans. by William R. Trask (Harper Torchbooks, 1965), 121; and Hugo Rahner, *Greek Myths and Christian Mystery* (1957. London: Burns and Oats, 1963).

21. David Thomas, *Not Guilty: The Case in Defense of Men* (New York: William Murrow and Company, Inc.), p 57.

22. See Rahner, Greek *Myths and Christian Mystery*, 110-112.

23. Carl-Martin Edsman, "le baptême de feu signifiera une purification et une consécration; le rite d'initiation donnant droit à la participation au mystère céleste, de même que le baptême d'eau est la condition requise pour assister a mystère terreste" (*Le Baptême de feu* [Leipzig, Alfred F. Lorenz, 1940], 135).

24. Edward C. Malone, *The Monk and the Martyr: The Monk as the Successor of the Martyr* (Washington, DC: Catholic University of America Press, 1950), 67.

25. Michael Novak writes: "Religions are built upon *ascesis*, a world that derives from the disciplines Greek athletes imposed upon themselves to gives their wills and instincts command of their bodies; the word was borrowed by Christian monks and hermits. It signifies the development of character through patterns of self-denial, repetition, and experiment" (*The Joy of Sports: End Zones, Bases, Baskets, Balls, and the Consecration of the American Spirit*, rev. ed. [Lanham, Md.: Madison Books, 1994], 29.

26. The early monks lived "'A life of martydom,' for monks are an army always engaged in battle with the obstacles to love" (Jean Leclercq, François Vandenbroucke and Louis Bouyer. *The Spirituality of the Middle Ages*, trans. by the Benedictines of Holmes Eden Abbey [London, Burns and Oates, 1968], 183.)

27. Malone, *The Monk and the Martyr*, 57.

28. Colgrave writes: "[T]hey sought to win the martyr's crown by extreme asceticism. In a seventh-century Irish homily, the writer describes three types of martyrdom: white martyrdom, which implies abandoning everything for God's sake; blue martyrdom, freeing oneself from evil desires by means of fasting and labor; and red martyrdom, enduring death for Christ's sake" (*Two Lives of Saint Cuthbert: A Life by an Anonymous Monk of Lindisfarne and Bede's Prose Life*, ed. and trans. by Bertram Colgrave [Cambridge: Cambridge University Press, 1985], 315.)

29. Athanasius, *The Life of Anthony and the Letter to Marcellus*, trans. Robert C. Gregg (New York: Paulist Press), 35.

30. Ibid., 69.

31. *The Rule of St. Benedict: the Abingdon Copy*, ed. John Chamberlain (Toronto: Pontifical Institute of Medieval Studies, 1982), 18.

32. Ibid., 20.

33. Ibid., 20-21.

34. Ibid., 22.

35. *Two Lives of Saint Cuthbert*, 98.

36. "Athleta, militiae celestis" (*Two Lives*, 180).

37. "At cum ibidem aliquandiu solitarium cum hoste invisibili orando ac ieiunando certeret, tandem maiora presumens, longinquiorem ac remotiorem ab hominibus locum certaminis petit." "But when he had fought there in solitude for some time with the invisible enemy, by prayer and fasting, he sought a place of combat father and more removed from mankind, aiming at greater things" (*Two Lives*, 214, 215).

38. "heremeticae conversationis agonem" (*Two Lives*, 266).

39. Malone, *Monk*, 90.

40. Monastic profession was regarded as "an irrevocable engagement, making the *conversio* a second baptism, a baptism of repentance, which, differing from the first, remits sin in virtue of the labour of mortification of which it is the beginning" (Leclercq et al, *The Spirituality of the Middle Ages*, 182). See also Malone, *Monk*, 121.

41. Malone, *Monk*, 126.

42. Paul Evdokimov points out: "The Old Slavic word for monk, inok, derives from inoi, meaning 'other,' which corresponds well to the symbolism of baptismal rebirth" (*Woman and the Salvation of the World: A Christian Anthropology on the Charisms of Women*, trans. Anthony P. Gythiel [Crestwood NY: St. Vladimir's Seminary Press, 1994], 106.

43. See *The Heliand: the Saxon Gospel*, trans. by G. Ronald Murphy (New York: Oxford, 1992).

44. *Beowulf*, ed. and trans. Michael Swanton, (Manchester: Manchester University Press, 1997), 61.

45. Ibid.

46. Ibid., 55.

47. Ibid., p. 95.

48. Eliade, *Myths*, 4.

49. Ibid., 62.

50. Jan de Vries, *Heroic Song and Heroic Legend*, trans. B.J. Timmer (London: 1963), 222. De Vries uses Mircea Eliade's analysis of myth in this analysis of the hero and initiation rituals (pp. 220-26).

51. Elaide, *Rites*, xiv.

52. *Beowulf*, 185.

53. Ibid., 39.

54. Ibid., 111.

55. Ibid., 183.

56. Ibid., 185.

57. See "Martyrdom and Monastic Profession as a Second Baptism," in Malone, O.S.B., *Monk*, 112-44.

58. Hope Nash Wolff, *A Study in the Narrative Structure of Three Epic Poems: Gilgamesh, The Odyssey, Beowulf* (New York: Garland Publishing, Inc., 1987), 57.

59. Gilmore, *Manhood*, 45.

60. Eliade, *Myths*, 84.

61. See Janet H. Dow's "Beowulf and the 'Walkers in Darkness'" *Connecticut Review* 4 (1970): 42-48.

62. *Beowulf*, 131.

63. Ibid., 95.

64. See Eugene J. Crook, "Pagan Gold in *Beowulf*," *American Benedictine Review* 25 (1974): 218-234.

65. *Beowulf*, 185.

66. For a complete discussion of this topic see "Martyrdom and Monastic Life as a 'Militia Spiritualis'" in Malone, *Monk*, 91-111.

67. The vow mentioned in the Rule of St. Benedict is obedience. Of the other two vows, Cuthbert Butler says "[s]ometimes these two vows have been added . . . but usually they have not been explicitly mentioned," *Benedictine Monachism: Studies in Benedictine Life and Rule* (London: 1919), 123. The three vows became explicit around the twelfth century, but the basic pattern was far older. For Gregory the Great, "[h]umility, continence, and generosity replace pride, lechery, and avarice," Carole Straw, *Gregory the Great: Perfection in Imperfection* (Berkeley and Los Angeles: University of California Press, 1988), 196.

68. *Summa Theologica* IIa-Iae, Q. 186, Art. 7, Sed Contra., trans. the Fathers of the English Dominican Province (Westminster, Maryland: Christian Classics, 1981).

69. *Rule*, 28-32.

70. *Beowulf*, 117.

71. Ibid., 123.

72. Ibid., 153.

73. *Rule*, 18.

74. *Beowulf*, 91.

75. It may have meant simply *to die* in a pagan context, but in the *Þidreks saga*, Heimir (Hama) enters a monastery.

76. Edsman, *Le Baptême*, 135.

77. Ibid., 153.

78. Ibid., 155.

79. *Beowulf*, 187.

80. Rodney Stark believes that a majority of Christian converts were women. In part, conversion may have been easier for women. Men had public religious duties which were hard to evade. But the modern suspicion that early Christianity was predominantly feminine appears to be largely a presumption that things were as they are now. Stark points to the conversion patterns for "new religious movements in recent times," but these may be a result of the very feminization I examine (*The Rise of Christianity: A Sociologist Reconsiders History* [Princeton: Princeton University Press, 1996], 100).

81. Susanne Heine, *Women and Early Christianity: A Reappraisal*, trans. John Bowden (Minneapolis: Augsburg Publishing House, 1988), 83.

82. Origin, *Contra Celsum* 3.45, in *Ante-Nicene Fathers*, Vol. 4, ed. Alexander Roberts and James Donaldson (Henrickson Publishers, Inc., 1995), 482.

83. Heine, *Women*, 94.

84. "Do not women still today convince their husbands to give much offence to God?" quoted by David C. Ford in *Women and Men in the Early Church: The Full Views of St. John Chrysostom* (South Canaan, Pennsylvania: St. Tikhon's Seminary Press, 1996), 90.

85. Ford, *Women and Men*, 94, 97-98

86. Ibid., 187.

87. John Bugge, *Virginitas: An Essay in the History of a Medieval Idea* (The Hague: Martinus Nijhoff, 1975). Bugge collects useful material, but his analysis is flawed by his tendency to see any trace of dualism or exaltation of virginity as "gnostic." The New Testament, despite its anti-gnosticism, contains a form of dualism and exalts virginity. The Fathers used all their rhetorical powers to praise virginity, because marriage has its obvious attractions, and part of the rhetorical strategy was to appeal to the Platonism that was the common atmosphere of the spirituality of antiquity. The Fathers adopted Platonic language without adopting all the presuppositions of that language.

88. Athanasius, *Apologia ad Constantinum*, 33.49, in *Historical Tracts of S. Athanasius*, trans. John Henry Parker (London: J.G.F. and J. Rivington, 1853), 185. Peter Brown observes that in the West the virgins were female, but in the East, male. See n. 13, *The Body and Society: Men, Women and Sexual Renunciation in Early Christianity* (New York: Columbia University Press, 1988), 262.

89. "On the Necessity of Guarding Virginity," quoted by Ford in *Women and Men in the Early Church*, 227.

90. The process started in monasticism, John Climacus wrote "I have watched impure souls mad for physical love but turning what they knew of such love into a reason for penance and transferring that same capacity for love to the Lord." Quoted by Brown, *The Body and Society*, 238.

6 *The Foundations of Feminization*

1. Despite the prominence of bridal mysticism in medieval and post-medieval spirituality, no one has done a full-scale study. See the article by Pierre Adnès, "Mariage mystique," in *Dictionnaire de spiritualité, ascetique, et mystique, doctrine et histoire*, vol. 9, (Paris: G. Beauchesne et ses fils, 1937-1995), col. 388-408.

2. Quoted by Jean Leclercq, *Monks and Love in Twelfth Century France: Pyscho-Historical Essays* (Oxford: Clarendon Press, 1979), 52.

3. Bernard of Clairvaux, *On The Song of Songs*, Vol. 1, trans. Kilian Walsh (Spencer, Mass: Cistercian Publications, 1971), 39.

4. Ibid., 86.

5. Ibid., 84. See Bynum, "Jesus as Mother and Abbot as Mother: Some Themes in Twelfth-Century Cistercian Writing," in *Jesus as Mother: Studies in the Spirituality of the High Middle Ages* (Berkeley: University of California Press, 1982), 110-169.

6. Bernard, *On the Song*, Vol.1, 27.

7. Caroline Walker Bynum observes "The male writer who saw his soul as a bride of God or his religious role as womanly submission and humility was conscious of using an image of reversal. He sought reversal because reversal and renunciation were at the heart of a religion whose dominant symbol is the cross—life achieved through death" (". . . And Woman His Humanity," in *Gender and Religion: On The Complexity of Symbols*, ed. Caroline Walker Bynum, Steven Harrell, Paula Richman [Boston: Beacon Press, 1986], 273).

8. R. P. Lawson. "Introduction," *Origen: The Song of Songs, Commentary and Homilies* (Westminster, Md.: Newman Press, 1957), 6.

9. Ibid., 38.

10. Ibid., 53.

11. Denys Turner sees "pagan neo-Platonism" (*Eros and Allegory: Medieval Exegesis of the Song of Songs*. [Kalamazoo, Michigan: Cistercian Publications, 1995], 32). Eugene S. Miao also sees Platonism, and points to "the lamentable part played by the mystical interpretation of the Canticle of Canticles in assisting the identification of the Eros motif with the Christian idea of Agape" *(St. John of the Cross: The Imagery of Eros* (Madrid: Playor, 1973), 51. Maio follows Anders Nygen (*Eros and Agape*) in finding all human love for God unChristian, but this is bizarre. A feminized Eros is what is objectionable; the Eros (for such it is, if eros is a love for something which a person is not and therefore has not) of friendship, brotherhood, and comradeship between man and Jesus is held up as a model in the Gospel.

12. Nelson Pike, *Mystic Union: An Essay in the Phenomenology of Mysticism* (Ithaca: Cornell University Press, 1992), 68.

13. Origen, *Commentary*, 200.

14. Ibid., 38.

15. Pike, *Mystic Union*, 68.

16. Bynum "Religious Women," 131.

17. Barbara Newman, *From Virile Woman to WomanChrist: Studies in Medieval*

Religion and Literature (Philadelphia: University of Pennsylvania Press, 1995), 6.

18. *The Life of Beatrice of Nazareth*, ed. and trans. Roger De Ganck, with the assistance of John Baptist Housbrouck (Kalamazoo, Michigan: Cistercian Publications, 1991), 197.

19. Ernest W. McDonnell, *The Beguines and Beghards in Medieval Culture with Special Emphasis on the Belgian Scene* (New Brunswick, NJ: Rutgers University Press, 1954), 51.

20. Valerie M. Lagorio, "The Continental Women Mystics of the Middle Ages: An Assessment," in *Roots of the Modern Christian Tradition*, 81. Leclercq et al concur, "It was chiefly among women . . . that the Brautmystik was received with fervor" (*Spirituality of the Middle Ages*, 373).

21. Birgitta explains: "One should know that this most humble handmaid of God never presumed to call herself or have herself called the bride of Christ, or his channel, because of vainglory or transitory honor any temporal advantage, but at the instruction of Christ and of blessed Mary, his most worthy mother, who both called her so" (*Birgitta of Sweden: Life and Selected Revelations*, ed. Marguerite Tjader Harris, trans. Albert Ryle Kezel [New York: Paulist Press, 1990], 71).

22. Leclercq et al., *Spirituality*, 374.

23. Gertrude of Helft, *The Herald of Divine Love*, trans. and ed. Margaret Winckworth (New York: Paulist Press, 1993), 82.

24. Ibid., 95.

25. Hildegard of Bingen, *Symphonia: A Critical Edition of the Symphonia armonie celestium revelationum* [*Symphony of the Harmony of Celestial Revelations*], trans. and ed. Barbara Newman (Ithaca: Cornell University Press, 1988), 220.

26. Bridal mysticism is ubiquitous in medieval and post-medieval mystics. In Beatrice of Nazareth it is explicitly erotic and dominant. At her profession, "she sweetly rested in the arms of her spouse" (*Life*, 100). Christ "pressed her soul wholly to himself in the sweetest embrace" (*Life*, 195). She receives communion "as if she were mad with excessive desire" (*Life*, 225).

27. Margaret Ebner, *Major Works*, trans. and ed. by Leonard P. Hindsley (New York: Paulist Press, 1993), 156.

28. Ibid., 135.

29. Ibid., 150.

30. Ibid., 122.

31. Ibid., 96.

32. Henry Suso, "The Little Book of Eternal Wisdom," in *The Exemplar: Life and Writings of Blessed Henry Suso*, Vol. 2, ed. Nicholas Heller, trans. Sister M. Ann Edward (Dubuque, Iowa: The Priory Press, 1962), 6.

33. Ibid., 17.

34. Ibid., 19.

35. Ibid., 36.

36. Ibid., 98.

37. Ibid., 231.

38. Ibid., 98.

39. Ibid., 242, 253.

40. Ibid., 343.

41. For at study of the use of the bridal metaphor by these two Carmelites, see Elizabeth Teresa Howe, *Mystical Imagery: Santa Teresa de Jesús and San Juan de la Cruz* (New York: Peter Lang, 1987), esp. 161-169. For both saints, "spiritual marriage symbolizes the culmination of the mystic's quest" (Ibid., 168). The conformity to God is not the Scriptural image of being conformed to the Son, but in John of the Cross's phrase, "Amada en el Amado transformada."

42. Turner, *Eros and Agape*, 25.

43. David Herlihy writes: "There is…a body of scattered but consistent comment which indicates that between the early and late Middle Ages, women had gained a superiority over men in life expectancy" ("Life Expectancies for Women in Medieval Society" in *The Role of Women in the Middle Ages*, ed. Rosemarie Morewedge [Albany: State University of New York, 1975], 11). The climate had improved in the high Middle Ages, when grain could even be grown in Iceland, and improved food supplies may have helped women more than men, because pregnancy made women more susceptible to the consequences of malnutrition.

44. See Herbert Grundmann, *Religious Movements in the Middle Ages*, trans. by Stephen Rowan (Notre Dame: University of Notre Dame Press, 1995). esp. 75-88. See also R. W. Southern. *Western Society and Church on the Middle Ages* (Harmondworth, Penguin Books, 1970), 318-331, and Ernest W. McDonnell, "Social Origins: The *Frauenfrage*," in *The Beguines and Beghards in Medieval Culture with Special Emphasis on the Belgian Scene* (New Brunswick, NJ: Rutgers University Press, 1954), 81-100.

45. Stephen E. Wessley, "The Thirteenth-Century Guglielmites: Salvation through Women," in *Medieval Women*, 289.

46. Southern, *Western Society*, 314.

47. Sally Thompson, "The Problem of the Cistercian Nuns" in *Medieval Women*, ed. Derek Baker (Oxford: Blackwell: 1978), 240.

48. "Dominus a nobis uxores abstuli, dyabolus autem nobis procurat sorores" (quoted by Grundmann, *Bewegungen*, 262, f. 149). Somehow this quote was omitted from the English translation, *Religious Movements*.

49. The decision reads "prohibemus ne aliquis fratrum nostrorum de cetero laboret vel procuret, ut cura vel custodia monialum seu quarumlibet aliarum mulierum nostris fratribus commitantur" (we prohibit either to labor or to seek out that the care or custody of nuns or of any other women be committed to our brothers) (quoted by Roger De Ganck, *Beatrice of Nazareth in Her Context* [Kalamazoo: Cistercian Publications, 1991], 21, note 89).

50. Grundmann says of Dominic: "On his deathbed, in his last conversations on the order, he pressingly warned his brethren against association with women, particularly with young women. Was he only warning against the moral attitude of individual friars? Is it possible that the founder, preoccupied with questions about the future of his order in these last utterances, had been discussing whether the order should incor-

porate further women's communities, placing friars to oversee and supply them, withdrawing from the order's primary duty of preaching?" (*Religious Movements*, 94-95).

51. According to Grundmann, "The women themselves sought to join the large orders, and the curia was concerned to make this possible; the orders, however, fought it, trying by all means available to avoid the obligation of receiving and administering women's communities" (*Religious Movements*, 90).

52. Grundmann, *Religious Movements*, 98.

53. Donald Weinstein and Rudolph M. Bell state: "Among Benedictines, however, very few women were celebrated as saintly. Of the 134 Benedictine saints in our sample, 106 died in the eleventh and twelfth century, and of this latter figure only 11 percent were women" (*Saints and Society: Christendom, 1000-1700* [Chicago: University of Chicago Press, 1977], 223).

54. Weinstein and Bell, *Saints*, 223.

55. Joan Coackley, "Friars, Sanctity, and Gender: Mendicant Encounters with Saints 1250-1325" in *Medieval Masculinities*, ed. Clare A. Lees (Minneapolis: University of Minnesota Press, 1994) 92.

56. André Vauchez has analyzed the processes for canonization and the canonizations in the Latin church. His figures show a shift from the twelfth to the fourteenth century in the ratio of lay men to lay women. From 1198 to 1431, 55.5 per cent of the canonization of lay Christian were of women, and 44.5 of men. However, "parmi les procès de canonisation de saints laïcs, 50% au XIIIe siècle concernent des femmes contre 71,4% au cours de la periode ultérieure. Aprés 1305, les laïcs dont la sainteté est reconnue par l'Eglise appartiennent deux fois sur trois au sexe faible (among the processes of canonization for lay saints, 50% in the thirteenth century concerned women as opposed to 71.4% during the course of the later period. After 1395 the saints whose sanctity was recognized by the Church belonged two out of three times to the weaker sex)." Vauchez continues that the Curia canonized women recommended by the mendicant orders, and that "La sainteté laïque masculine. . . disparait complétement de l'horizon de la Curie" (Lay masculine sanctity disappeared completely from the horizon of the Curia) (*La Sainteté en Occident aux derniers siècles du moyen age* [Rome: Ecole Française de Rome: 1981], 317.

57. Anne K. Warren, "English anchoritism was already biased toward women in the twelfth century. It became sharply female in orientation in the thirteenth century" (*Anchorites and Their Patrons in Medieval England* [Berkeley: University of California Press, 1985], 20). Female anchorites were always more common than male anchorites in England, although Warren notes that the proportion of men increased toward the Reformation.

58. Caroline Walker Bynum, *Jesus as Mother: Studies in the Spirituality of the High Middle Ages* (Berkeley: University of California Press, 1982), 14.

59. Jean Leclercq, "Introduction: The Roots of Modernity," in *The Spirituality of Western Christendom*, Vol. 2: *The Roots of the Western Tradition*, ed. E. Rozanne Elder (Kalamazoo: Cistercian Publications, Inc., 1984), xiii.

60. Berthold von Regensburg preached: "Ir frouwen, ir sît barmherzic unde gêt

gerner zuo kirchen danne die man unde sprechet iuwer gebete gerner danne die man unde gêt zu predigen gerner danne die man" (*Predigten*, Vol. 1, ed. Franz Pfeiffer [Vienna: Wilhelm Braumüller, 1862], 41). In another sermon, Berthold continues in the same vein, and says that women are "erbaumherziger, danne die man und betet gerner, mit venie, mit danne die man, mit kirchgengen, mit riuwe, mit ûf stên, mit salter lesen, mit vigilie. Mit maniger guottæte sît ir bezzer (More merciful than men and more willing to pray with prostrations than men, with visits to church, with quiet, with standing, with reading the Psalter, with vigils. With many good deeds are you better) (*Predigten*, Vol. 2, 141).

61. Jean Leclercq, François Vandenbroucke and Louis Bouyer, *The Spirituality of the Middle Ages*, trans. The Benedictines of Holmes Eden Abbey (London: Burns and Oates: 1968), 225.

62 Ibid., 242.

63. Aristotle, *Metaphysics* 1055b, 25-29 in *The Complete World of Aristotle*, Vol. 1, ed. Jonathan Barnes (Princeton: Princeton University Press, 1984), 1667.

64. Aristotle, *Generation of Animals*, 738b in *The Complete World of Aristotle*, Vol. One, ed. Jonathan Barnes (Princeton: Princeton University Press, 1984), 1146.

65. Prudence Allen, The *Concept of Women: The Aristotelian Revolution 750 BC - AD 1250.* (1985. Grand Rapids, Michigan: William B. Eerdmans Publishing Company, 1997), 383.

66. Anne W. Astell, *The Song of Songs in the Middle Ages* (Ithaca: Cornell University Press, 1990), 13.

67. Bynum, *Jesus as Mother*, 172.

7 Feminized Christianity

1. Karl Barth, *Church Dogmatics*, Vol. 3, 2, *The Doctrine of Creation*, 54.1, trans. Harold Knight et al. (Edinburgh: T & T Clark, 1960), 175.

2. Manfred Hauke, *God or Goddess? Feminist Theology: What Is It? Where Does It Lead?* trans. David Kipp (San Francisco: Ignatius Press, 1995), 135-36.

3. Hauke, *Women in the Priesthood?, A Systematic Analysis in the Light of the Order Creation and Redemption,* trans David Kipp (1986. San Francisco: Ignatius Press, 1988) 304. He concurs with Hans Urs von Balthasar who claims "every member of the Church, even the priest, must maintain a feminine receptivity to the Lord of the Church" (*New Elucidations*, trans. Mary Theresilde Skerry [San Francisco: Ignatius Press, 1986],198).

4. F. X. Arnold, *Woman and Man: Their Nature and Mission* (New York: Herder and Herder, 1963), 54-55.

5. Ibid., 55-56.

6. George T. Montague, *Our Father, Our Mother: Mary and the Faces of God.* Steubenville, Ohio: Franciscan University Press, 1990), 85.

7. Peter Toon, *Let Women Be Women: Equality, Ministry and Ordination* (Gracewing: Leominster: Fowler Wright Books, 1990), 100.

8. William Hood, *Fra Angelico at San Marco* (New Haven: Yale University Press, 1993), 21.

9. Ibid.,p. 22.

10. Brother Antoninus (William O. Everson), "Annul in Me My Manhood," in *The Crooked Lines of God* (Detroit: University of Detroit Press, 1962), 86-87.

11. Juli Loesch Wiley, "In Defense of God the Father," in Helen Hull Hitchcock, ed., *The Politics of Prayer: Feminist Language and the Worship of God* (San Francisco: Ignatius Press, 1992), 319.

12. Amanda Porterfield writes: "Puritans defined grace as a kind of intercourse between God and the saint that signified the saint's espousal to God and thereby her salvation, and they sometimes pictured this intercourse in a way that aroused erotic feelings that could be interpreted as the stirrings of grace" (*Female Piety in Puritan New England: The Emergence of Religious Humanism* [New York: Oxford University Press, 1992],14).

13. Edward Pearse, *The Best Match; or the Souls Espousal to Christ, opened and improved* (London, 1673), 33.

14. Cotton Mather, *Ornaments for the Daughters of Zion* (Boston, 1691), 63.

15. Cotton Mather, *A Glorious Espousal* (Boston, 1719), 11.

16. Quoted by Amanda Porterfield, *Feminine Spirituality in America: From Sarah Edwards to Martha Graham* (Philadelphia: Temple University Press, 1980), 24.

17. Quoted by Richard Godbeer, "'Love Raptures': Marital, Romantic, and Erotic Images of Jesus Christ in Puritan New England. 1670-1730," *New England Quarterly* 68 (1990): 366.

18. Thomas Hooker, *The Soul's Exaltation: A Treatise Concerning the Soul's Union with Christ, the Souls Benefit from Union with Christ, the Souls Justification* (London, 1648) quoted in Moller, "Sex Composition, and Correlated Culture Patterns of Colonial America" *William and Mary Quarterly*, 3rd series, 2 (1945): 150.

19. "Meditation. Cant. 4.8. My Spouse," in Donald E. Stanford, ed., *The Poems of Edward Taylor*, (New Haven: Yale University Press, 1960), 39.

20. "Meditation. Can. 1.2. Let him kiss me with the Kisses of his mouth," *Poems*, 257.

21. "Meditation. Cant.5.13. His Lips are like Lillies, dropping sweet smelling Myrrh." *Poems*, 303.

22. See Godbeer, "'Love Raptures,' 355-384.

23. Porterfield, *Feminine Spirituality*, 29-30.

24. Jonathan Edwards quoted in Perry Miller's "Jonathan Edwards' Sociology of the Great Awakening," *New England Quarterly* 21 (1948): 68.

25. Bill McCartney, "God is Calling Us to a Higher Love," in *Go the Distance: The Making of a Promise Keeper*, ed. John Trent (Colorado Springs, Colorado: Focus on the Family Publishing, 1996),13.

26. Alphonsus de Ligouri, *The True Spouse of Jesus Christ*, trans. and ed. Eugene Grimm (1929.Rockford, Il; Tan Books, n.d.), 18. Alphonsus quotes the patristic justification for this usage, but he denigrates marriage in a way that would have aroused

the suspicion of the anti-Gnostic propagandists among the Fathers. Christians seem unable to praise marriage without denigrating virginity (the fault of Luther) or to praise virginity without denigrating marriage. Since most Christians marry, and since almost all Christians have several years in which they must practice chastity before marriage, everyone has a chance to feel he is living in an impossible spiritual state.

27. Juan González Arintero, *The Song of Songs: A Mystical Exposition*, with a preface by Alberto Colunga, trans. James Valender and José L. Morales (Rockford Il: Tan Books, 1992), 21.

28. Ibid., 8.

29. Ibid., 22.

30. See Karl Barth, above, xxx.

31. Hauke, *Women in the Priesthood?*, 338.

32. Ibid., 94. Hauke, it must be admitted, says this in the context of women's greater integration of personality, a characterization of femininity that is closer to the

33. Ibid., 300.

34. Ron Hansen has used this eroticized spirituality as the basis for his novel, *Mariette in Ecstasy* (New York: HarperCollins Publishers, Harper Perennial, 1991). Mariette, a (fraudulent?) stigmatist, moves in a conventual world of pain and sexuality. She is taught "'We know from Church teaching that the soul has no true pleasure but in love. And we know from our experience that extreme bliss can only come from extreme passion'" (ibid., 60). The nuns enact a play based on the *Songs of Songs* (ibid., 82–85) . After she is stigmatized, her confessor wonders "'And why are there so many women and so few men?'" who are stigmatists (ibid., 127). Mariette dreams (?) she is being raped (by whom? the devil?) (ibid., 145). Mariette dreams of talking with Christ, and she sleeps with him: "And I share in him as if he's inside me. And he is" (ibid., 168). All this is only a slight distortion of the eroticized spirituality held up as a model for sanctity from the Middle Ages to the present.

35. Barbara Newman, *From Virile Woman to WomanChrist: Studies in Medieval Religion and Literature* (Philadelphia: University of Pennsylvania Press, 1995), 138. Bynum also observes: "religious males had a problem. If the God with whom they wished to unite was spoken of in male language, it was hard to use the metaphor of sexual union unless they saw themselves as female" (Bynum, *Jesus as Mother: Studies in the Spirituality of the High Middle Ages* [Berkeley: University of California Press, 1982], 161) which some of them did: "We also have many examples of monks describing themselves or their souls as the bride of Christ" (Bynum, *Jesus as Mother*, 161).

36. Brenda E. Basher speculates about the fundamentalist churches she studied: "both the emphasis on religious experiences in the female enclaves and the dearth of religious experiences in overall congregational life may be an entailment of each group's gender habits with its theological and social ideals rather than a consequence of gender-based social power conflicts. The male-imaged deity and heterosexual norms create an environment in which women who seek religious experience are actually performing their gender, while men perform theirs by declining to pursue such conduct" (*Godly Women: Fundamentalism and Female Power* [New Brunswick, New Jersey,

1998], 122). Basher assumes, as the fundamentalists may also assume, that "religious experience" is innately erotic, and therefore for men it would have homosexual overtones, because the Deity is male.

37. *The Cistercian World: Monastic Writings of the Twelfth Century*, trans. and ed. by Paul Matarasso (New York: Penguin Books, 1993), 145.

38. Gertrude of Helfta, *The Herald of Divine Love*, trans. and ed. Margaret Winkworth (New York: Paulist Press, 1993), 115.

39. Ibid., 117.

40. Ibid.

41. Ulinka Roblack, "Female Spirituality and the Infant Jesus in Late Medieval Dominican Convents," *Gender and History* 6 (1994): 41.

42. Ibid., 43.

43. Margaret Ebner, *Major Works*, trans. and ed. Leonard P. Hindsley (New York: Paulist Press 1993), 134.

44. Ibid.

45. Roblack, "Female Spirituality," 46, 50.

46. Bynum, *Jesus as Mother*, 110-159.

47. Julian of Norwich, *The Revelation of Divine Love in Sixteen Showings*, trans. M. L. del Mastro (Ligouri, Missouri: Ligouri Publications, 1994), 172.

48. Ibid., 168.

49. Gertrude, *Herald*, 211.

50. Ibid., 47.

51. *The Autobiography of Saint Margaret Mary Alacoque*, trans. The Sisters of the Visitation (Rockford, Il: Tan Books and Publishers, 1986), 41.

52. Ibid., 40.

53. Ibid., 62.

54. Ibid., 67.

55. Ibid., 82.

56. José de Vinck, *Revelations of Women Mystics From the Middle Ages to Modern Times* (New York: Alba House, 1985), 87-88

57. Ibid., 160.

58. Ibid., 165.

59. Catherine of Siena, *The Dialogue*, trans. Suzanne Noffke (New York: Paulist Press, 1980), 64.

60. Liege was dominated by feminine spirituality. Miri Rubin observes of men such as Jacques de Vitry and Jacques Pantaléon, the future Urban IV: "The men witnessed the spirituality of their female neighbors or charges and compared it with their own; some extraordinary friendships were struck between monks and beguines, and this mutual fascination was to develop further when the mendicant and beguine communities were to meet in the thirteenth century" (*Corpus Christi: The Eucharist in Late Medieval Culture* [Cambridge: Cambridge University Press, 1993], 167.

61. Caroline Walker Bynum, *Holy Feasts and Holy Fasts: The Religious Significance of Food to Medieval Women* (Berkeley: University of California Press, 1987).

62. Miri Rubin writes: "narratives of encounter with a child in the host dominated the fantasies of women, especially by those attached to the eucharist. These could be violent and pathetic like Jane Mary of Maillé's (d. 1414) vision of a wounded child elevated in the host. It could also be deeply loving: Agnes of Montepulciano (d. 1317) and Margaret of Faenza (d. 1330) were each so intoxicated with the baby they saw they refused to give it up, and Ida of Louvain played with the child revealed to her" (*Corpus Christi*, 344).

63. Of St. Catherine of Genoa it was said in the *Spiritual Dialogues*, "No priest or friar objected to this need, the daily reception of the Blessed Sacrament, for such was the will of God" (Catherine of Genoa, *Purgation and Purgatory, the Spiritual Dialogue*, trans. Serge Hughes [New York: Paulist Press, 1979],110).

64. *Hadewijch: The Complete Works*, trans. Columba Hart (New York: Paulist Press, 1980), 280-281. For a discussion of this passage, see Caroline Bynum, *Fragmentation and Redemption: Essays on the Human Body in Medieval Mysticism* (New York: Zone Books, 1991), 119-20.

65. Rubin, *Corpus Christi*, 169.

66. Peter Dinzelbacher, *Vision und Visionliteratur im Mittelalter* (Stuttgart: Anton Hiersemann: 1981) 226; see also 229 and Elizabeth A. Petroff's *Medieval Women's Visionary Literature* (New York: Oxford University Press, 1986), esp. 5-20.

67. Jean Leclercq, "It was, then, among the Béguines of the thirteenth century... that the first evidence of the Wesenmystik is found" (*The Spirituality of the Middle Ages*, trans. the Benedictines of Holmes Eden Abbey [1961. London, Burns and Oates, 1968], 377).

68. Leclercq, *Spirituality*, 357. These religious women also showed a contempt for the hierarchy and an indifference to the sacraments, as well as moral license.

69. Jacques Le Goff writes, "Purgatory made even more impressive headway with the populace than it did with theologians and clergy" (*The Birth of Purgatory*, trans. Arthur Goldhammer [Chicago: University of Chicago Press, 1984], 289).

70. Newman, *From Virile Woman to WomanChrist*, 109.

71. Margaret Ebner, *Major Works*, 87-88.

72. Julian, *Revelation*, 108.

73. Ibid., 109.

74. Gertrude, *Herald,* 66.

75. Ibid., 61.

76. Ibid., 69.

77. Catherine of Genoa, *Purgation and Purgatory*, 75.

78. Quoted by Friedrich von Hügel, *The Mystical Element in Religion as Studied in Catherine of Genoa and Her Friends*, Vol. 1 (London: M. Dents and Sons, 1927), 283.

79. Hans Urs von Balthasar, *Dare We Hope "That All Men Be Saved"?* with a *Short Discourse on Hell*, trans. David Kipp and Lothar Krauth (San Francisco: Ignatius, 1988).

80. Ibid., 97-113.

81. Ibid., 99.

82. Ibid., 111.

83. Moller, "Sex Composition" 146.

84. K. E. Schmöger, *The Life of Anne Catherine Emmerich*, Vol. 1 (Rockford, Il: Tan Books and Publishers, Inc., 1976), 195.

85. Ibid., 196.

86. Marina Warner, "Blood and Tears," *New Yorker* 72:7 (8 April 1996): 69. E. Michael Jones, editor of *Fidelity*, has made a career of exposing false revelations, or at least ones he has decided are false. Women figure prominently in them.

87. Ibid., 65.

88. Ong, *Fighting for Life*, 170.

89. Ibid., 170-171.

90. Ibid., 139.

91. Schindler, *Heart of the Church, Heart of the World: Communio Ecclesiology, Liberalism, and Liberation* (Grand Rapids, Michigan: William B. Eerdmans Publishing Company, 1996), 242. See also Hans Urs von Balthasar, *Theodramatik*, Vol. 4, *Das Endspiel* (Einsiedeln: Johannes Verlag, 1983), 80.

92. David Martin, *A Sociology of English Religion* (London: SCM Press Ltd, 1967), 127.

93. Terman and Miles, *Sex and Personality*, 117.

94. Paula D. Nesbitt, *Feminization of the Clergy in America: Occupational and Organizational Perspectives* (New York: Oxford University Press, 1997).

95. Ibid., 160. Nesbitt notes that "Conservative Protestant denominations have been less affected by a declining supply of young men." (ibid., 104).

96. In Hauke's critique of feminist theology in *God or Goddess*, it is clear that women are irked by the identification of women and obedience, and the consequent special duty of women to obey to avoid being "unnatural," that is, unfeminine. Feminists therefore often reject both obedience and the concept of a binding revelation.

97. Kaye Ashe, *The Feminization of the Church?* (Kansas City: Sheed and Ward, 1997), 25.

98. Ibid., 32.

99. Ibid., 37.

100. Ibid., 39.

101. Ibid., 40.

8 *Countercurrents*

1. Bernard of Clairvaux, *Treatises III: On Grace and Free Choice; In Praise of the New Knighthood*, trans. Daniel O'Donovan and Conrad Greenia (Kalamazoo: Cistercian Publications Inc., 1977).

2. Ibid., 134.

3. Ibid.

4. Ibid., 135.

5. Ibid.

6. Simone Roison writes: "C'est à la Vierge que va l'affection sensible des moines comme l'amour ardent des moniales tend vers le Christ eucharistique, l'Époux céleste" (It is to the Virgin that the devotion of the senses of the monks was directed as the ardent love of the nuns tended to the Eucharistic Christ, the heavenly Bridegroom) (Simone Roisin, *L'Hagiographie cistercienne dans le diocèse de Liège au XIIIe siècle.* [Louvain: Bibliothèque de l'Université, 1947], 115).

7. Caroline Walker Bynum, *Jesus as Mother: Studies in the Spirituality of the High Middle Ages* (Berkley: University of California Press, 1982).

8 Hilda Graef, *Mary: A History of Doctrine and Devotion.* Two volumes in one. (1963. Westminster, Maryland: Christian Classics, 1985), 241.

9. Ibid., 289.

10. Graef quotes Bernadine of Siena: "one Hebrew woman invaded the house of the eternal King; one girl, I do not know by what caresses, pledge or violence, seduced, deceived and, if I may say so, wounded and enraptured the divine heart and ensnared the Wisdom of God" (*Mary*, Vol. 1, 317).

11. Ibid., 295-296. See also Prudence Allen, *The Concept of Women: The Aristotelian Revolution 750 BC - AD 1250* (1985. Grand Rapids, Michigan: William B. Eerdmans Publishing Company, 1997), 376-383.

12. Ibid., 297.

13. Graef again quotes Bernadine of Siena that Mary "has added certain perfections to the Maker of the universe" (*Mary*, Vol. 1, 317).

14. Ibid., 41.

15. Quoted, Ibid., 117.

16. *The Documents of Vatican II* (New York: Herder and Herder, 1966) ed. Walter J. Abbott, 95.

17. Leo Steinberg, *The Sexuality of Christ in Renaissance Art and Modern Oblivion* (London: Faber and Faber Limited, 1984).

18. Robert Harvey, *Ignatius Loyola: A General in the Church Militant* (Milwaukee: Bruce Publishing Co. 1936), 182.

19. Heinrich Boehmer, *The Jesuits: An Historical Study*, trans. Paul Zeller Strodach, (Philadelphia: The Castle Press, 1928), 40.

20. Quoted by Harvey, *Ignatius*, 192.

21. Ignatius wrote of himself: "Up to the age of twenty-six, he was a man given to the vanities of the world; and what he enjoyed most was warlike sport, with a great and foolish desire to win fame" (*Autobiography*, in *Ignatius of Loyola: Spiritual Exercises and Selected Works*, ed. George E. Ganss [New York: Paulist Press, 1991], 68).

22. Ignatius, *Autobiography*, 77. Robert Harvey finds it natural to give his biography (above) chapter headings such as "The Setting for the First Struggle," "The Call to Arms," "The First Recruits," "The Manual of Discipline," "The Articles of War," "The Campaign Against Heresy," and with a modern touch, "The Baptism of Fire."

23. Ibid., 74.

24. Ignatius uses the image in such passages as "in Christ the Lord, the bridegroom, and in His spouse the Church" (*Exercises*, 160).

25. Ignatius, *Exercises*, 145. Ignatius also compares Satan to "a woman" because he "is a weakling before a show of strength, and a tyrant if he has his will" (*Exercises*, 145).

26. Ibid., 43.

27. Ibid., 44.

28. Ibid., 60.

29. Quoted by Harvey, *Ignatius*, 149.

30. Alice Corbin Henderson, *Brothers of Light: The Penitentes of the Southwest* (New York: Harcourt. Brace and Co., 1937), 105.

31. André Vauchez notes "the Crusades illustrate the birth of a new religious sensibility within Western Christianity: what is known as 'penitential' spirituality" (*The Laity in the Middle Ages: Religious Beliefs and Devotional Practices*, ed. Daniel E. Boorstein, trans. Margery J. Schneider [Notre Dame, University of Notre Dame Press, 1993], 49).

32. In a foreshadowing of later conflicts, "when the master-general of the Dominican Order imposed the *Regola dei fratelli e delle sorore della penitenzia di S. Dominico* on the confraternities affiliated with the Dominicans, thereby making the admission of members subject to the authorization of the Dominicans, the male members withdrew. And is it not the case that the only noteworthy members of these pious congregations in the fourteenth century were women, *mantellate* like St. Catherine of Siena and Maria of Venice?" (Vauchez, *Laity*, 115).

33. Vauchez, *Laity*, 123.

34. "Women were excluded from them for obvious reasons" (Ibid., 123).

35. Vauchez, *Laity*, 127.

36. Stanley Brandes, *Metaphors of Masculinity: Sex and Status in Andalusian Folklore* (University of Pennsylvania Press, 1980), 201.

37. Ibid., 201-202.

38. Ibid., 202.

39. Christopher J. Kauffman, *Faith and Fraternalism: The History of the Knights of Columbus 1882–1982* (New York: Harper and Row, 1982), 124.

40. Basil Pennington, "The Cistercians" in *Christian Spirituality: Origins to the Thirteenth Century*, ed. Bernard McGinn and John Meyendorff (Crossroad: New York: 1986), 216.

41. Christine E. Gudorf describes the situation of the Church at the beginning of Vatican II: "as the Church lost ground to liberalism in attempting to retain its former niche in the world, it shifted the grounds of religion's defense from the public political sphere to the private domestic sphere. This reinforced religion's feminine image by suggesting that there was indeed a special connection between religion and the feminine domestic sphere" ("Renewal or Repatriarchalization: Responses of the Roman Catholic Church to the Feminization of Religion," *Horizons* 10 [1982]: 234).

42. Ibid., 251.

43. Patrick M. Arnold, *Wildmen, Warriors, and Kings: Masculine Spirituality in the Bible* (Crossroad: New York, 1991), 77.

44. Richard Rohr, "Introduction," in David C. James, *What Are They Saying About Masculine Spirituality?* (New York: Paulist Press, 1996), 3.

45. Peter N. Stearns, *Be a Man! Males in Modern Society*, 2nd ed. (New York: Holmes and Meier, 1990), 39.

46. Paul Tillich, *Systematic Theology*, Vol. 3 (Chicago: University of Chicago Press, 1963), 313.

47. Marc Leinhard, "Luther and the Beginnings of the Reformation," in *Christian Spirituality: High Middle Ages and Reformation*, ed. Jill Raitt (New York: Crossroad, 1987), 293.

48. Heiko A. Oberman, *Luther: Man Between God and the Devil*, trans. Eileen Walliser-Schwarzbart (New Haven: Yale University Press, 1989), 104.

49. Merry Weisner, "Luther and Women: The Death of Two Marys" in *Disciplines of Faith: Studies in Religion, Politics, and Patriarchy*, ed. Jim Obelkevich, Lyndal Roper, and Raphael Samuell (London: Routledge and Kegan Paul, 1987), 103.

50. André Bieler, *L'homme et la femme dans la morale calviniste* (Geneva: Labor et Fides, 1963), 36, 48-49.

51. Gail Malmgreen, "Domestic Discords: Women and the Family in East Cheshire Methodism, 1750-1830" in *Disciplines of Faith*, 60.

52. Herbert Moller, "Sex Composition and Correlated Cultural Patterns of Colonial America," *William and Mary Quarterly*, 3rd series, 2 (1945): 152.

53. Winthrop S. Hudson, *American Protestantism* (Chicago: University of Chicago Press), 78.

54. David W. Kling, *A Field of Divine Wonders: The New Divinity and Village Revivals in Northwestern Connecticut 1792 - 1822* (University Park, Pennsylvania: Pennsylvania State University Press, 1993), 14.

55. Marc C. Carnes, *Secret Ritual and Manhood in Early America* (New Haven: Yale University Press, 1989), 72.

56. Gerald F. Moran, "Christian Revivalism in Early America" *Modern Christian Revivals*, ed. Edith L. Blumhofer and Randall Balmer (Urbana: University of Illinois Press, 1993), 52-53.

57. Ibid., 53. Terry D. Bilhartz observed that in the early nineteenth century "revivalistic Methodist and belatedly evangelistic Presbyterian congregations slowed the feminization process of Baltimore's religious institutions" (*Urban Religion and the Second Great Awakening: Church and Society in Early National Baltimore* [Rutherford, New Jersey: Fairleigh Dickinson University Press, 1986], 97).

58. Jonathan Edwards had delivered a sermon on the same theme in the earlier part of the century: "It is surprising and almost amazing to hear what a swift pass the nation has got to in the present day, and what a swift progress Deism and heresies have lately made in this nation. Those that deny all revealed religion, that deny Scripture to be the word of God, that deny all the gospel, deny that Christ was anything but

a mean cheat, and deny all that is said about the way of salvation by him, they are vastly multiplied as of late years, yea, even as to threaten to swallow up the nation, and to root the very name of Christianity out of it; they are become the very fashionable sort of men (quoted by Perry Miller, "Jonathan Edward's Sociology of the Great Awakening," *New England Quarterly* 21 (1948): 54–55.

59. Kling, *A Field of Divine Wonders*, 10.

60. Ibid., 170.

61. Kling writes: "The large percentage of married men converted and then admitted to Church membership, either simultaneously with their wives or following their wives' conversion, suggests that for many males, conversion came at the behest of their spouses" (*A Field of Divine Wonders*, 217).

62. *The Christian Advocate*, March 4, 1858, quoted by Richard Carwardine, *Transatlantic Revivalism* (Westport, Connecticut: Greenwood Press, 1978), 169.

63. Marion L. Bell, *Crusade in the City: Revivalism in Nineteenth Century Philadelphia* (Lewisburg: Bucknell University Press, 1978), 169.

64. Jay P. Dolan, *Catholic Revivalism: the American Expedience 1830 - 1900* (Notre Dame: University of Notre Dame Press, 1978), 121.

65. See Norman Vance, *The Sinews of the Spirit: The Ideal of Christian Manliness in Victorian Literature and Religious Thought* (Cambridge: Cambridge University Press, 1985).

66. Ibid., 16.

67. *Charles Kingsley: His Letters and His Age*, Vol. 1. (London: Henry S. King and Co., 1877), 204.

68. Ibid., 204.

69. David Rosen writes: "For Kingsley, the ideal of self-actualization, the fulfillment of manly potential, becomes a moral imperative" ("The volcano and the cathedral: muscular Christianity and the origins of primal manliness" in Donald E. Hall, ed., *Muscular Christianity: Embodying the Victorian Age* (Cambridge: Cambridge University Press, 1994), 35.

70. *Charles Kingsley: His Letters*, Vol. 1, 399.

71. Quoted by Laura Fasick, "Charles Kingsley's Scientific Treatment of Gender," in *Muscular Christianity*, 93.

72. Vance, *The Sinews*, 3.

73. Ibid., 17–26.

74. Gail Bederman, "'The Women Have Had Charge of the Church Work Long Enough': The Men and Religion Forward Movement of 1911 - 1912 and the Masculinization of Middle-Class Protestantism," *American Quarterly* 41 (1989): 444.

75. Bederman summarizes: "According to Census figures, in 1906 the Protestant churches, combined, had been 39.5 percent male. By 1926, the proportion had grown 6.3 percent to 41.8 percent male. Some denominations…has gained even more new men. For example, the proportion of men in Congregational churches grew by 10.9 percent. In the Northern Presbyterian (U. S. A.) churches, male membership was up by 11.2 percent. The proportion of Episcopalian men grew by a whopping 20.8 per-

cent" ("Men and Religion," 454). Indeed, reports in 1925 were that "male converts had nearly equaled female converts during the past several years" (ibid., 455) although the previous state of the church persisted: "Protestant churches still had more women than men." (ibid., 454).

76. Bruce Barton, *The Man Nobody Knows: A Discovery of the Real Jesus* (Indianapolis: Bobbs Merrill Co., 1925), 28.

77. Ibid., 69.

78. Ibid., 40-41.

79. Ibid., 42 43.

80. Ibid., 121.

81. Ibid., 179. Other writers have pointed to this dichotomy as a source of masculine discomfort with religion. Martin W. Pable writes: "Unfortunately, most Christian men I know don't think their job has anything to do with their spiritual life" and quotes Pope Paul VI: "'one of the greatest evils of out time is the separation of religion from the rest of life'" (*A Man and His God* [Notre Dame: Ave Maria Press, 1988], 59).

82. Ibid., 179.

83. Ibid., 180.

84. Harry Emerson Fosdick, *The Manhood of the Master* (New York: Association Press, 1913), 116.

85. Ibid., 41.

86. Ibid., 88.

87. Margaret Lamberts Bendroth, *Fundamentalism and Gender:1875 to the Present* (New Haven: Yale University Press, 1993), 64.

88. Bendroth notes that by the 1940s "the overrepresentation of women in the movement's rank and file visibly contradicted the claim that orthodoxy was a masculine reserve, setting off fears of feminization that had been part of the fundamentalist ethos since its earliest stages" (*Fundamentalism*, 90).

89. Bendroth, *Fundamentalism*, 19.

90. Goldwert, "Machismo and Christ: The New Formula" *Contemporary Review* 145 (1984): 185.

91. Ibid., 185.

92. Pope John Paul II likes the substance of Saint Louis Marie Grignon de Montfort's *Treatise of True Devotion to the Blessed Virgin*, but admits that the book "can be a bit disconcerting, given its rather florid and baroque style" (*Gift and Mystery: On the Fiftieth Anniversary of My Priestly Ordination* [New York: Doubleday, 1996], 29).

9 *Masculinity as Religion: Transcendence and Nihilism*

1. Gail Bederman writes of the influence of the popular press of Theodore Roosevelt's time: "middle-class constructions of male power would become firmly based on the violence and sexuality of his journalistic version of primitive masculinity" (*Man-*

liness and Civilization: A Cultural History of Gender and Race in the United States, 1880–1917 [Chicago: The University of Chicago Press, 1995],215). Sports became more violent at the end of the nineteenth and the beginning of the twentieth centuries.

2. Charles Pickstone, *The Divinity of Sex: The Search for Ecstasy in a Secular Age* (New York: St. Martin's Press, 1996), 175.

3. Ibid., 3, 175.

4. G. Stanley Hall, *Adolescence, Its Psychology and Its Relation to Physiology, Anthropology, Sociology, Sex, Crime, Religion, and Education*, vol. 2 (New York: D. Appleton and Company, 1911), 292-293.

5. Bederman, *Manliness and Civilization*, 104. George Albert Coe notes "a connection between adolescent conversions and the sexual instinct" (*The Psychology of Religion* [Chicago, University of Chicago Press: 1916],163).

6. Hall, *Adolescence*, vol. 2, 123.

7. For an analysis of Lawrence's sacralization of sexuality, see Pickstone, *Divinity of Sex*, 62-65.

8. Elliot J. Gorn writes: "Sports taught manliness in a violent world. All that was feminine, sentimental, or romantic - and many late nineteenth-century writers worried aloud that America had become "womanized' - was expunged on athletic fields of battle" (*The Manly Art: Bare-Knuckle Prize Fighting in America* [Ithaca: Cornell University Press, 1986], 189).

9. Donald J. Mrozek, *Sports and American Mentality 1880-1910* (Knoxville, University of Tennessee Press, 1983), 233.

10. John Carroll, "Sport: Virtue and Grace," Theory, *Culture, and Society* 3, no. 1 (1986): 93.

11. Ibid., 94.

12. Michael A. Messner, *Power at Play: Sports and the Problem of Masculinity* (Boston: Beacon Press, 1992), 87.

13. Quoted in J. A. Mangan, *Athleticism in the Victorian and Edwardian Public School: The Emergence and Consolidation of an Educational Ideology* (Cambridge: Cambridge University Press, 1981), 9.

14. Ibid., 196.

15. Carroll, "Sport," 97.

16. Ibid.

17. Michael Novak writes: "sports flow outward into action from a deep natural impulse that is radically religious: an impulse of freedom, respect for ritual limits, a zest for symbolic meaning, and a longing for perfection" (*The Joy of Sports: End Zones, Bases, Baskets, Balls, and the Consecration of the American Spirit* rev. ed. [1967. Lanham, Maryland: Madison Books, 1994], 19).

18. Charles S. Prebish, "Religion and Sport: Convergence or Identity?" *Religion and Sport: The Meeting of Sacred and Profane Religion and Sport* (Westport, Connecticut: Greenwood Press, 1993) ed. Charles S. Prebish, 63.

19. Ibid., 63.

20. Howard Slushler, "Sport and the Religious," in *Religion and Sport*, 178.

21. Michael Novak, *The Joy of Sports*, 5.

22. Willaim J. Morgan, "An Existential, Phenomenological Analysis of Sport as a Religious Experience" in *Religion and Sport*, 132.

23. Quoted Ibid., 131.

24. D. Stanley Eitzen and George H. Sage, "Sport and Religion" in *Religion and Sport*, 96.

25. Brian W. W. Anderson asked Christian athletes whether they had any psychological high or any sense of God's presence when they played, "And in every interview the answer was the same, a categorical 'no'; sports can be fun and a very significant part of their lives but it is more like work than religion" ("The Emergence of Born-Again Sport," in *Religion and Sport*, 209).

26. Alan M. Klein analyzes this reaction: "the weakness that lives at the core of so many bodybuilders, and the vulnerability they struggle to overcome, is responsible for the elaboration of a lifestyle that brooks no weakness or vulnerability" (*Little Big Men: Bodybuilding Subculture and Gender Construction* [Albany: State University of New York Press, 1993], 19).

27. Sam Fussell, *Muscle: Confessions of an Unlikely Bodybuilder* (1991. New York: Avon Books, 1992), 85.

28. Klein, *Little Big Men*, 40.

29. The resemblances between bodybuilding and fascism that Klein detects ("Body, Fascist Imagery, and Masculinity" in *Little Big Men*, 253-264) are the sense of powerlessness and victimization that leads to the pursuit of power and hardness as means of protection.

30. Ryszard Kapuski, *The Soccer War* (1977. Random House, Inc., Vintage International, 1986), 182.

31. Michael Banc, *Over the Edge: A Regular Guy's Odyssey in Extreme Sports* (New York: Macmillan, 1996), 187.

32. Ibid., 190.

33. Rob Schultheis, *Bone Games: Extreme Sports, Shamanism, Zen, and the Search for Transcendence* (New York: Breakaway Books, 1996).

34. Ibid., 12.

35. Ibid., 11.

36. Ibid., 13.

37. Ibid., 21.

38. Ibid., 25.

39. Ibid., 18-20.

40. Ibid., 54.

41. Ibid., 67.

42. Ibid., 175.

43. Ibid., 176.

44. Ibid.

45. Ibid., 178.

46. Serge Hutin notes: "on peut dire sans paradoxe que la Franc-Maçonnerie

moderne a repris et continué l'ésotérisme des Rose-Croix, reprenant leurs symboles hermétiques les plus typiques, comme la pélican, le phénix qui renait de ses cendres, l'aigle bicéphale, etc." (one can say without paradox that modern Freemasonry has picked up and continued the esotericism of the Rosicrucians, taking up its very typical hermetic symbols, such as the pelican, the phoenix which is reborn from its own ashes, the two-headed eagle, etc.)(*Les Sociétés secrètes* [Paris: Presses Universitaires de France, 1970], 56; for the involvement of the hermeticist Robert Fludd in the rise of Freemasonry, see ibid., 63).

47. J. N. Casavis claims in *The Greek Origins of Freemasonry* (New York: The Square Press, 1955) "Modern Masonry is historically based upon the Ancient Greek Mysteries" and that "Even at such a late date as the year 1583 A. D., Hermes was claimed as the founder of Freemasonry, for such he is taken and accepted in the Old Masonic manuscript No. One of the Grand Lodge of England, and in all the other old documents of the order" (*Greek Origins*, 34). A direct historical connection with antiquity is doubtful, but a strong influence through the revival of hermeticism in the Renaissance looks likely.

48. Paul Goodman, *Towards a Christian Republic: Antimasonry and the Great Transition in New England, 1826–1836* (New York: Oxford University Press, 1988) 167. Women were among the strongest antimasons, since the Lodges took men away from home and church; see Goodman, ibid., 80ff.

49. Mark C. Carnes writes: "The *Voice of Masonry* added that because churches were attended mostly by women, they should be given a greater share of church governance. Men, on the other hand, should rest content with their exclusive dominion over the religion of the lodge" (*Secret Ritual and Manhood in Early America* [New Haven: Yale University Press, 1989], 76).

50. Carnes: "In the early twentieth century, lodges outnumbered churches in all large cities" (*Secret Ritual* 89).

51. Carnes: "The founders of fraternal groups emphasized ritual from the outset and added other activities almost by chance" (*Secret Ritual*, 9).

52. See Carnes, *Secret Ritual*, 94-107.

53. Case tries to answer the question "Why do many men prefer the lodge to the church?" but ignores the ritual aspects, concentrating on the social advantages of mutual aid and recreation. See "Men and the Lodge" in *The Masculine in Religion*, 98-99.

54. Carnes, *Secret Ritual*, 57.

55. Ibid., 56-57.

56. Ibid., 72.

57. Michael Rosenthal claims: "For Scouting was from the very beginning conceived as a remedy to Britain's moral, physical, and military weakness - conditions that the Boer war seemed to announce - especially to Tory politicians, social imperialists, and military leaders - were threatening the Empire (*The Character Factory: Baden-Powell and the Origins of the Boy Scout Movement* [London: Collins, 1986], 3).

58. Norman E. Richardson and Ormond E. Lewis, *The Boy Scout Movement Applied by the Church* (New York, Charles Scribner's Sons, 1916), 19.

59. *Boy's Life*, December 1993, 19.

60. Gilmore, *Manhood in the Making*, 65–74.

61. "A True Story of Scouts in Action: Their House Caught on Fire!" *Boys' Life*, December 1997, 44.

62. Ted Brennan, "The Point of Reenacting Battles," *Washington Post*, 6 June 1996.

63. Klaus Theweleit, *Male Fantasies*, Vol. I. *Women Floods Bodies History*, trans. Stephen Conway (1977. Minneapolis: University of Minnesota Press, 1987), Vol. II. *Male Bodies: Psychoanalyzing the White Terror*, trans. Erica Carter and Chris Turner with Stephen Conway (Minneapolis: University of Minnesota Press, 1989).

64. Gibson, *Warrior Dreams: Paramilitary Culture in Post-Vietnam America* (New York: Hill and Wang, 1994) 41.

65. Ibid., 22.

66. Ibid., 37-38.

67. Gibson, "the highest form of friendship is the brotherhood of war" (*Warrior Dreams*, 138).

68. Ibid., 179.

69. Ibid., 178.

70. Ibid., 306.

71. Ibid., 308.

72. Gibson: "No matter how secular the New Age warrior may appear with his high-tech weapons and tremendous 'efficient' kills, he is essentially a religious figure" (*Warrior Dreams*, 102-103). An NRA official explained to a reporter, "You would get a far better understanding if you approached us as if you were approaching one of the great religions of the world" (*Warrior Dreams*, 252). *Soldier of Fortune* magazine provides men with "religious transcendence" (*Warrior Dreams*, 167). Paramilitarism seeks to transform men, to help them transcend the secular, ordinary world into a sacred realm above the merely natural.

73. David Jones, *In Parenthesis* (New York: Chilmark Books, 1961), 153.

74. Walter Ong examines the type of education based on intellectual, masculine combat in *Fighting for Life: Contest, Sexuality, and Consciousness.* (1981. Amherst: University of Massachusetts Press, 1989).

75. Quoted in Paul Booker, *The Faces of Fraternalism: Nazi German, Fascist Italy, and Imperial Japan* (New York: Oxford University Press, 1991) 62. Theodore Roosevelt puts it less elegantly: "The woman who, whether from cowardice, from selfishness, from having a false and vacuous ideal shirks her duty as wife and mother, earns the right to our contempt, just as does the man who, from any motive, fears to do his duty in battle when his country calls him" (quoted by Michael C. C. Adams, *The Great Adventure: Male Desire and the Coming of World War I* [Bloomington: Indiana University Press, 1990], 7).

76. William Broyles, Jr. *Brothers in Arms: A Journey from War to Peace* (New York: Knpof, 1986), 201. Roy Raphael quotes a Stan B.: " I now almost regret that I didn't serve overseas during the Vietnam War. I think that there must be some parallel that

war is to men what childbirth is to women. I've heard from buddies of mine who are veterans, that there's no intensity of human emotion greater than being under fire" (*The Men from the Boys: Rites of Passage in Male America* [Lincoln, Nebraska: University of Nebraska Press, 1988], 150).

77. Adrian Caesar feels this implication in Owen: "For he not only criticised warfare, he celebrated, even glorified it because it is the site of suffering and of love. In his work, war is seen as appalling, but it is this very quality which engenders the loving sacrifice of the men" (*Taking It Like a Man: Suffering, Sexuality, and the War Poets* [Manchester: Manchester University Press: 1993], 167).

78. Evelyn Waugh, *The End of the Battle* (Boston: Little, Brown and Company, 1961), 305.

79. Samuel Hynes points out that this is not a literary conceit: "there are moments in war when men become *different* men, who can do things that in their peacetime lives they would call monstrous and inhuman. We don't like to believe this – that men can change their essential nature—but it must be true, or there would be no atrocities. But there *are* atrocities, in every age, in every war" (*The Soldiers' Tale: Bearing Witness to Modern War* [New York: Viking Penguin, 1997], 10).

80. Jünger, *Storm of Steel* (1929. New York: Howard Fertig, 1975), 254-55.

81. Ibid., 255.

82. Ibid.

83. Ibid., 317.

84. Ibid., 220.

85. Ibid., 118.

86. Ibid., 109.

87. It was designed by Fritz Erler for the German War Loan of 1917. It is reproduced in George L. Mosse, *Fallen Soldiers: Reshaping the Memory of the World Wars* (New York: Oxford University Press, 1990), 134.

88. "The Great Sacrifice," reproduced in Joanna Bourke, *Dismembering the Male: Men's Bodies, Britain and the Great War* (London: Reaktion Books, 1996), 213.

89. George L. Mosse, *Fallen Soldiers*, 35.

90. See Gavin White, "The Martyr Cult of the First World War" in Diana Wood, ed. *Martyrs and Martyrologies: Papers Read at the 1992 Summer Meeting and the 1993 Winter Meeting of the Ecclesiastical History Society* (Oxford: Blackwell Publishers, for the Ecclesiastical History Society, 1993), 383-388. Georges Duhamel wrote *The New Book of Martyrs* (trans. Florence Simmonds [New York: George H. Doran Company, 1918]) about "the sacrificial victims of the race" (ibid. 221) who crawl "up the slopes of a Cavalry" (ibid., 78).

91. Henri Barbusse, *Under Fire: The Story of a Squad*, trans. Fitzwater Wray (1917. New York: E. P. Dutton and Co., Inc., Everyman's Library, 1928), 282.

92. Ibid., 357.

93. J. Glenn Gray, *The Warriors: Reflections on Men in Battle* (New York: Harper and Row, 1966), 46-47.

94. The danger and excitement of sports can also break down the barriers be-

tween men. Arnold R. Beisser observes "Perhaps some mitigation is to be found in sports and athletics. A football player who is a linebacker can encouragingly pat his lineman on the behind in full view of a hundred thousand people. Baseball players hug each other and may even kiss each other (*The Madness in Sports: Psychosocial Observations on Sports* [New York: Appleton-Century Crofts, 1967], 196). Michael Novak also sees this happening: "Sports brings out in every ideal team a form of gentleness and tenderness so intense that it is no misnomer to call it love; and coaches generally speak to their supposed macho males like golden-tongued preachers of love, brotherhood, comradeship. Tears, burning throats, and raw love of male for male are not unknown among athletes in the heat of preparation…and in the solemn battle" (*The Joy of Sports*, 46).

95. Paul Fussell, "Soldier Boys" in *The Great War and Modern Memory* (New York: Oxford University Press, 1975), 270-309.

96 J. R. R. Tolkien, *The Lord of the Rings*. Part 3, *The Return of the King* (1965. Boston, Houghton Mifflin Company, Collector's Edition, n.d.), 186.

97. Leo Steinberg, in *The Sexuality of Christ in Renaissance Art and Modern Oblivion* (London: Faber and Faber Limited, 1984) examines the portrayals of the sexuality of Christ. The genitals are often the central point of a Madonna and Child, and even in the Crucifixion the blood, contrary to gravity, ran down from the side to the genitals to emphasize the connection between maleness and sacrifice.

98. I believe that it is this feeling that military men refer to when they talk about *group cohesiveness* and why they say that homosexuals in a combat unit ruin it.

99. F. L. Carsten, *The Rise of Fascism*, 2nd ed. (Berkeley: University of California Press, 1980), 14.

100. Quoted in Caroline Tisdall and Angelo Bozzolla, *Futurism* (New York: Oxford University Press, 1978), 153.

101. Mosse, *Fallen Soldiers*, 55.

102. Mussolini, although he preferred Futurism, turned against it and made Social Realism the official art of the state, because it was accessible to the masses. Similar processes of work in other totalitarian regimes strangled the avant-garde. See Igor Golomstock's *Totalitarian Art in the Soviet Union, the Third Reich, Fascist Italy and the People's Republic of China*, trans. Robert Chandler (IconEditions. New York: HarperCollins Publishers, 1990).

103. Curzio Malaperte, *Kaputt*, trans. Cesare Foligno (Marlboro, Vermont: The Marlboro Press, 1982), 169.

104. Otto Weininger sees the formlessness of women and Jews as their common characteristic. Both lack transcendence. Weininger writes: "Die Kongruenz zwischen Judentum und Weiblichkeit scheint ein völlige zu werden, sobald auf der unendliche Veränderungsfähigkeit des Juden zu reflektieren gegonnen wird…. Der Jude…hat keinen Teil am höheren, ewigen Leben" (*Geschlect und Charakter* [Munich: Matthew und Seitz Verlag], 429).

105. Barbara Ehrenreich,, "Forward" to Klaus Theweleit's *Male Fantasies* Vol. One, *Women Floods Bodies History*, xiii.

106. Ibid.

107. Raphael: "The frustrations of unfulfilled masculinity are, I fear, potentially dangerous. What if our male anxiety gets projected onto the political arena, where an overcompensation for personal inadequacy can easily get transformed into militaristic jingoism? In the wake of World War I, the severe emasculation of German males - militaristically, economically, socially—provided fertile ground for pathological politics" (*The Men from The Boys*, 187).

108. Alfred Bäumler at the beginning of the Nazi era wrote: "Mann steht daneben Mann, Säule neben Säule, das is die Schlachtreibe, das is der Tempel, das ist das Heiligtum, das is der Staat" (*Männerbund und Wissenschaft* [Berlin: Junker und Dünnhaupt Verlag, 1934], 39). This Männerbund with its male eros (which sometimes became openly homosexual) was the model for the SA (destroyed in the Röhm purge), and was suppressed by the Nazis in favor of a mass political movement (see Mosse, *Crisis of German Ideology: Intellectual Origins of the Third Reich* [New York: Schocken Books, 1981], 309). However, anxiety about masculinity contributed to the rise of Naziism. Elisabeth Badinter says: "the anxiety of German and Austrian men over their identity was not unrelated to the rise of Naziism and more generally to European fascism. Hitler's accession to power resonated unconsciously with the promise that manliness would be restored" (*XY: On Masculine Identity*, trans. Lydia Davis [New York: Columbia University Press, 1995], 17).

109. Quoted by Lionel Tiger, *Men in Groups* (New York, Random House, 1969) 69.

110. This was the warning that Pope John Paul II addressed in his encyclical *Veritatis Splendor* to moral theologians who were undermining the absolute, objective nature of moral obligations. The Pope had personally experienced the results of such relativism in the Nazi occupation of Poland.

111. Hermann Rauschning was an associate of Hitler who turned against him and fled to the United States and wrote *The Revolution of Nihilism: Warning to the West* (New York: Longmans, Green and Co., 1939). He warned that the Nazis espoused "the utter destruction of all traditional spiritual standards, utter nihilism" (*Revolution*, xii), that even its racist philosophy was but a front for the adoration of pure power and activity without any purpose except further activity.

10   *The Future of Men in the Church*

1. See Thomas C. Reeves, *The Empty Church, The Suicide of Liberal Christianity* (New York: Free Press, 1996), 146-151.

2. James E. Ditties, *Driven by Hope: Men and Meaning* (Louisville, Kentucky: Westminster John Knox Press, 1996), 142.

3. Gordon Dalbey, *Healing the Masculine Soul: An Affirming Message for Men and the Women Who Love Them* (Waco, Texas: Word Books, 1988), 55-58.

4. Ditties, *Driven by Hope*, 9.

5. Ibid., 67.

6. Ibid., 69.

7. Ceslaus Spicq discusses this passage: "Touché de cette ferveur, le Maitre repond alors le mot même de Pierre, (v. 17). Vraiment? Tu m'aimes encore? Je puis croire que tu es un ami véritable? Je puis avoir confiance en ta parole et en ton cœur?" (Touched by such fervor, the Master replies with the same word of Peter, 'Do you love (philesi) me?' Truly? You still love me? Can I believe that you are a true friend? Can I have confidence in your word and in your heart?)(*Agape dans le nouveau testament: Analyse des textes* [Paris: Librairie Lecoffre, 1959], 234). Many commentators see Jesus' use of "friends" to be simply synonymous with people or neighbors, and some explicitly place the bridal relationship higher. Spicq points out that in John friendship is the most intimate type of love between the Father and the Son. The Son does what he sees the Father doing, "Il n'a pas de secret pour son Fils, qui est initié à ses pensées et ses intentions les plus cachées. L'amour de Dieu est ici un amour d'intimité, il rend compte de la confiance et des confidances du Père envers son Fils incarné qu'il traite en ami" (There is no secret from the Son, who is initiated into the most secret thoughts and intentions. The love of God is here a love of closeness, it takes account of the trust and the confidence of the Father toward the incarnate Son, whom he treats as a friend) (ibid, 220). Spicq points that that this is exactly what *philos* is, "non un amour religieux et réflechi de supérieur à inférieur, mais un abandon spontané entre deux êtres unis par une dilection réciproque qui les met à niveau" (Not a religious love and reflected from the superior to the inferior, but a spontaneous abandon between two beings united by a reciprocal affection (ibid., 220). Aquinas along the same line defines charity as the friendship of man for God (*Summa Theologica*, IIa-IIae, Q. 23, Art. 1).

8. Thomas More is perhaps the most accessible, but his sanctity consisted in a response to crisis. Martyrdom is a clear choice, but at present, in the West anyway, outright martyrdom is rarely a possibility. The modern religious martyrs of the West whose sanctity has been recognized either officially or unofficially displayed great masculine virtues, but they were all clerics: Maximilian Kolbe, Titus Brandesma, and the priest whose deeds are the subject of the heartbreaking *Au Revoir Les Enfants*.

Bibliography

Abrams, Mark, David Gerard and Noel Timms. *Values and Social Change in Britain*. London, Macmillan, 1985.

Adams, Michael C. C. *The Great Adventure: Male Desire and the Coming of World War I*. Bloomington: Indiana University Press, 1990.

Aiken, Rian W. W. "The Emergence of Born-Again Sport" In *Religion and Sport: The Meeting of Sacred and Profane*, ed. Charles S. Prebish. Westport, Connecticut: Greenwood Press, 1993.

Alacoque, Margaret Mary. *The Autobiography of Saint Margaret Mary Alacoque*. Translated by the Sisters of the Visitation. Rockford, Illinois: Tan Books and Publishers, 1986.

Alberione, James. *Woman: Her Influence and Zeal as an Aid to the Priesthood*. Translated by the Daughters of St. Paul. Boston: St. Paul Editions, 1964.

Allen, Prudence. *The Concept of Women: The Aristotelian Revolution 750 BC - AD 1250*. 1985. Grand Rapids, Michigan: William B. Eerdmans Publishing Company, 1997.

Alphonsus de Ligouri. *The True Spouse of Jesus Christ*. Translated and edited by Eugene Grimm. 1929. Rockford, IL; Tan Books, n.d.

Argyle, Michael. *Religious Behaviour*. London: Routledge and Kegan Paul, 1958.

———, and Beit-Hallahmi, Benjamin. *The Social Psychology of Religion*. London: Routledge and Kegan Paul, 1975.

Arintero, Juan González, *The Song of Songs: A Mystical Exposition*, with a preface by Alberto Colunga. Translated by James Valender and José L. Morales. 1974. Rockford IL: Tan Books, 1992.

Aristotle. *The Complete World of Aristotle*. 2 vols. Edited by Jonathan Barnes. Princeton: Princeton University Press, 1984.

Arnold, F. X. *Woman and Man: Their Nature and Mission*. New York: Herder and Herder, 1963.

Arnold, Patrick M. *Wildmen, Warriors, and Kings: Masculine Spirituality in the Bible*. New York: Crossroad, 1990.

Ashe, Kaye. *The Feminization of the Church?* Kansas City: Sheed and Ward, 1997.

Astell, Anne. W. *The Song of Songs in the Middle Ages*. Ithaca: Cornell University Press, 1990.

Athanasius. *Apologia ad Constantinum*, in *Historical Tracts of S. Athanasius*. Translated by John Henry Parker. London: J. G. F. and J. Rivington, 1853.

———. *The Life of Antony and the Letter to Marcellus*. Translated by Robert C. Gregg. New York: Paulist Press, 1980.

Badinter, Elisabeth. *XY: On Masculine Identity*. Translated by Lydia Davis. 1992. New York: Columbia University Press, 1995.

Bakan, David. *The Duality of Human Existence: Isolation and Communion in Western Man*. Boston: Beacon Press, 1966.

Baker, Paul M. and Kathy S. Chopik, "Abandoning the Great Dichotomy: Sex vs. Masculinity-Femininity as Predictors of Delinquency." *Sociological Inquiry* 52 (1982): 349-357.

Baker, Derek, ed. *Medieval Women*. Oxford: Blackwell, 1978.

Bane, Michael. *Over the Edge: A Regular Guy's Odyssey in Extreme Sports*. New York Macmillan, 1996.

Barbusse, Henri. *Under Fire: The Story of a Squad*. Translated by Fitzwater Wray. 1917. New York: Everyman's Library, E. P. Dutton and Co., Inc., 1928

Barker, Pat. *The Ghost Road*. New York: Penguin Books USA, Dutton, 1995.

Barna, George. "The Battle for the Hearts of Men" *New Man* 4, no. 1 (January-February 1997): 43.

———. *Index of Leading Spiritual Indicators*. Dallas: Word Publishing, 1996.

Barth, Karl. *Church Dogmatics*, Vol. 3, 2, *The Doctrine of Creation*. Translated by Harold Knight et al. Edinburgh: T. & T. Clark, 1960.

Barton, Bruce. *The Man Nobody Knows: A Discovery of the Real Jesus*. Indianapolis: Bobbs Merrill Publishing Co., 1925.

Basher, Brenda E. *Godly Women: Fundamentalism and Female Power*, New Brunswick, New Jersey: Rutgers University Press, 1998.

Batson, C. Daniel, and W. Larry Ventis. *The Religious Experience: A Social Psychological Perspective*. New York: Oxford University Press, 1982.

Bäumler, Alfred. *Männerbund und Wissenschaft*. Berlin: Junker und Dünnhaupt Verlag, 1934.

Baym, Nina. "Onward Christian Women: Sarah J. Hale's History of the World." *New England Quarterly* 63 (1990): 249-270.

Bederman, Gail. *Manliness and Civilization: A Cultural History of Gender and Race in the United States, 1880-1917*. Chicago: The University of Chicago Press, 1995.

————. "'The Women Have Had Charge of the Church Work Long Enough': The Men and Religion Forward Movement of 1911-1912 and the Masculinization of Middle-Class Protestantism." *American Quarterly* 41 (1981): 432-65.

Beisser, Arnold R. *The Madness in Sports: Psychosocial Observations on Sports*. New York: Appleton-Cenutury Crofts, 1967.

Bell, Marion L. *Crusade in the City: Revivalism in Nineteenth Century Philadelphia*. Lewisburg: Bucknell University Press, 1978.

Bendroth, Margaret Lamberts. *Fundamentalism and Gender, 1875 to the Present*. New Haven: Yale University Press, 1993.

Benedict. *The Rule of St. Benedict: the Abingdon Copy*. Edited by John Chamberlain. Toronto: Pontifical Institute of Medieval Studies, 1982.

Benson, Peter L., and Carolyn H. Elkin. *Effective Christian Education: A National Study of Protestant Congregations, A Summary Report on Faith, Loyalty, and Congregational Life*. Minneapolis, Minn.: Search Institute, 1990.

Beowulf. Edited and translated by Michael Swanton. 1978. Manchester: Manchester University Press, 1997.

Bernard of Clairvaux. *On The Song of Songs*, Vol. 1. Translated by Kilian Walsh. Spencer, Mass: Cistercian Publications, 1971.

————. *Treatises III: On Grace and Free Choice; In Praise of the New Knighthood*. Translated by Daniel O'Donovan and Conrad Greenia. Kalamazoo: Cistercian Publications Inc., 1977.

Berthold von Regensburg. *Predigten*. Vol. 1 and 2. Edited by Franz Pfeiffer. Vienna: Wilhelm Braumüller, 1962.

Bettelheim, Bruno. *Symbolic Wounds: Puberty Rites and the Envious Male.* London: Thames and Hudson, 1955.

Biéler, André. *L'homme et la femme dans la morale calviniste.* Geneva: Labor et Fides, 1963.

Bilhartz, Terry. *Urban Religion and the Second Great Awakening: Church and Society in Early National Baltimore.* Rutherford, New Jersey: Farleigh Dickinson University Press, 1986.

Birgitta of Sweden. Life and Selected Revelations. Ed. by Marguerite Tjader Harris, trans. by Albert Ryle Kezel. New York: Paulist Press, 1990.

Blumhofer, Edith L. and Randall Balmer, eds. *Modern Christian Revivals.* Urbana: University of Illinois Press, 1993.

Boehmer, Heinrich. *The Jesuits: An Historical Study.* Translated by Paul Zeller Strodach. Philadelphia: The Castle Press, 1928.

Boff, Leonardo. *The Maternal Face of God: the Feminine and Its Religious Expressions.* Translated by Robert R. Barr and John W. Diercksmeier. 1979. San Francisco: Harper and Row, Publishers, 1987.

Bolton, Brenda M. "Vitae *Matrum*: A Further Aspect of the *Frauenfrage*." In *Medieval Women*, edited by Derek Baker. Oxford: Blackwell, 1978.

Booker, Paul. *The Faces of Fraternalism: Nazi German, Fascist Italy, and Imperial Japan.* New York: Oxford University Press, 1991.

Boulard, Fernand. *Matériaux pour l'histoire religieuse du peuple français XIXᵉ-XXᵉ siècles.* Paris: Editions de L'Ecole des Hautes Etudes en Sciences Sociales, 1982.

Bourke, Joanna. *Dismembering the Male: Men's Bodies, Britain and the Great War.* London: Reaktion Books, 1996.

Bouyer, Louis. *Woman in the Church.* Translated by Marilyn Teichert. 1976. San Francisco: Ignatius Press, 1979.

Boyd, Stephen, W. Merle Longwood, and Mark Muesse editors. *Redeeming Men; Religion and Masculinities.* Kentucky: Westminster John Knox Press, 1996.

Brandes, Stanley. *Metaphors of Masculinity: Sex and Status in Andalusian Folklore.* University of Pennsylvania Press, 1980.

Bridgman, Howard Allen. "Have We a Religion for Men?" *Andover Review* (1890): 388-96.

Brierley, Peter. *"Christian" England: What the 1989 Church Census reveals* (London: MARC Europe, 1991.

Brod, Harry, ed. *The Making of Masculinities: the New Men's Studies.* Boston, Allen and Unwin, 1987.

Brown, Peter. *The Body and Society: Men, Women and Sexual Renunciation in Early Christianity*. New York: Columbia University Press, 1988.

Broyles Jr., William. *Brothers in Arms: A Journey from war to Peace*. New York: Knopf, 1986.

Bugge, John. *Virginitas: An Essay in the History of a Medieval Idea*. The Hague: Martinus Nijhoff, 1975.

Butler, Cuthbert. *Benedictine Monachism: Studies in Benedictine Life and Rule*. London, 1919.

Bynum, Caroline Walker. "And Woman His Humanity," In *Gender and Religion: On the Complexity of Symbol*, ed. Caroline Walker Bynum, Steven Harrell, Paula Richman. Boston: Beacon Press, 1986.

————. *Fragmentation and Redemption: Essays on the Human Body in Medieval Mysticism*. New York: Zone Books, 1991.

————. Harrell, Steven, and Richman, Paula, editors. *Gender and Religion: On the Complexity of Symbols*. Boston: Beacon Press, 1986.

————. *Holy Feasts and Holy Fasts: The Religious Significance of Food to Medieval Women*. Berkeley: University of California Press, 1987

————. *Jesus as Mother: Studies in the Spirituality of the High Middle Ages*. Berkeley: University of California Press, 1982.

Carnes, Mark C. *Secret Ritual and Manhood in Early America*. New Haven: Yale University Press, 1989.

Carroll, John. "Sport: Virtue and Grace." *Theory Culture, and Society* 1 (1986).

Carsten, F. L. *The Rise of Fascism*. 2nd ed. Berkley: University of California Press, 1980.

Carter, Paul. *Another Part of the Twenties*. New York: Columbia University Press, 1977.

Carwardine, Richardine. *Translatlantic Revivalism*. Westport, Connecticut: Greenwood Press, 1978.

Casavis, J. N. *The Greek Origins of Freemasonry*. New York: The Square Press, 1955.

Case, Carl Delos. *The Masculine in Religion*. Philadelphia: American Baptist Publication Society, 1906.

Castelli, Jim, and Joseph Gremillion. *The Emerging Parish: The Notre Dame Study of Catholic Life Since Vatican II*. San Francisco: Harper and Row, 1987.

Catherine of Genoa. *Purgation and Purgatory, The Spiritual Dialogue*. Translated by Serge Hughes. New York: Paulist Press, 1979.

Catherine of Siena. *The Dialogue*. Translated by Suzanne Nofftke. New York: Paulist Press, 1980.

Cesar, Adrian. *Taking It Like a Man: Suffering, Sexuality, and the War Poets.* Manchester: Manchester University Press, 1993.

Chevasse, Claude. *The Bride of Christ: An Inquiry into the Nuptial Element in Early Christianity.* London, Faber and Faber, 1940.

Chodorow, Nancy. *The Reproduction of Mothering: Psychoanalysis and the Sociology of Gender.* Berkeley: University of California Press, 1978.

Cholvy, Gerard and Yves-Marie Hilaire. *Histoire religieuse de la France contemporaine.*, Vol. III. Toulouse: Bibliothecque histoire privat, 1985.

Christen, Yves. *Sex Differences: Modern Biology and the Unisex Fallacy.* Translated by Nicholas Davidson. 1987. New Brunswick, New Jersey: Transaction Publishers, 1981.

Christian, William A. Jr. *Person and God in a Spanish Valley.* New York and London: Seminar Press, 1972.

Clark, Stephen B. *Man and Woman in Christ: An Examination of the Roles of Men and Women in the Light of Scripture and the Social Sciences.* Ann Arbor, Michigan: Servant Books, 1986.

Clarke, Howard W. *The Art of the Odyssey.* Englewood Cliffs, New Jersey: Prentice, 1967.

Coackley, John. "Friars, Sanctity, and Gender: Mendicant Encounters with Saints, 1250-1325." In *Medieval Masculinities: Regarding Men in the Middle Ages,* edited by Clare A. Lees. Minneapolis: University of Minnesota Press, 1994.

Coe, George Albert. *The Psychology of Religion.* Chicago: University of Chicago Press, 1916.

Colgrave, Bertram, ed. and trans. *Two Lives of Saint Cuthbert: A Life by an Anonymous Monk of Lindisfarne and Bede's Prose Life.* 1940. Cambridge: Cambridge University Press, 1985.

Collinson, Patrick: *Godly People: Essays on English Protestantism and Puritanism.* London: Hambledon Press, 1983.

Craig, Leon Harold. *The War Lover: A Study of Plato's Republic.* 1994. Toronto; University of Toronto Press, 1996.

Crook, Eugene J. "Pagan Gold in *Beowulf,*" *American Benedictine Review* 25 (1974): 218-234.

Cross, Whitney R. *The Burned-Over District: The Social and Intellectual History of Enthusiastic Religion in Western New York, 1800-1850.* Ithaca: Cornell University Press, 1950. New York: Harper and Row. Harper Torchbooks, 1965.

Crump, C. G. and E. F. Jacob. *The Legacy of the Middle Ages.* Oxford: Clarendon, 1926.

Cumont, Franz. *The Mysteries of Mithras.* Translated by Thomas J. McCormick. 1903. New York: Dover Publications, Inc., 1956,

Dalbey, Gordon. *Healing the Masculine Soul: An Affirming Message for Men and for the Women Who Love Them.* Waco, Texas: Word Books, 1988.

Davidson, Nicholas. *The Failure of Feminism.* Buffalo: Prometheus Books, 1988.

Davie, Grace. *Religion in Britain since 1945: Believing without Belonging.* Oxford: Blackwell, 1994.

Davies, Douglas, Charles Watkins, Michael Winter. Caroline Pack, Susanne Seymour, and Christopher Smart. *Church and Religion in Rural England.* Edinburgh: T and T Clark, 1991

De Beauvoir, Simone. *The Second Sex.* Translated and edited by H. M. Parshley. 1953. New York: Alfred E. Knopf. Everyman's Library, 1993.

De Ganck, Roger. *Beatrice of Nazareth in Her Context.* Kalamazoo: Cistercian Publications, 1991.

De Vaus, David, and Ian McAllister. "Gender Differences in Religion: A Test of the Structural Location Theory." *American Sociological Review* 52 (1987): 472-481.

De Vinck, José. *Revelations of Women Mystics from the Middle Ages to Modern Times.* New York: Alba House, 1985.

De Vries, Jan. *Heroic Song and Heroic Legend.* Translated by B.J. Timmer. London: 1963.

Dictionnaire de Spiritualité, Ascetique, et Mystique, Doctrine et Histoire, Paris: G. Beauchesne et ses fils, 1937-1995.

Dimock Jr., George E. "The Name of Odysseus." In *Homer: A Collection of Critical Essays,* edited by George Steiner and Robert Fagles. Englewood Cliffs, New Jersey: Prentice, 1962.

Dinzelbacher, Peter. *Vision und Visionnliteratur im Mittelalter.* Stuttgart: Anton Hiersemann, 1981.

Ditties, James E. *Driven by Hope: Men and Meaning.* Louisville, Kentucky: Westminster John Knox Press, 1996.

The Documents of Vatican II. Edited by Walter J. Abbott. New York: Herder and Herder, 1966.

Dolan, Jay P. *Catholic Revivalism: the American Experience 1830 - 1900.* Notre Dame: University of Notre Dame Press, 1978.

Douglas, Ann. *The Feminization of American Culture.* New York: Alfred E. Knopf, 1977.

Dow, Janet H. "Beowulf and the 'Walkers in Darkness'" *Connecticut Review* 4 (1970): 42-48.

Dragland, S. L. "Monster Man in Beowulf." *Neophilologus* 61 (1977): pp. 606-618.

Duhamel, Georges. *The New Book of Martyrs*. Translated by Florence Simmonds. New York: George H. Doran Company, 1918.

Dunn, Mary Marples. "Saints and Sinners: Congregational and Quaker Women in the Early Colonial Period" *American Quarterly* pp. 582-601.

Edsman, Carl-Martin. *Le Baptême de feu*. Leipzig, Alfred F. Lorenz, 1940.

Eitzen, D. Stanley and George H. Sage. "Sport and Religion." In *Religion and Sport*, edited by Charles S. Prebish. Westport. Connecticut: Greenwood Press, 1993.

Elder, E. Rozanne. *The Spirituality of Western Christendom*, Vol. 2, *The Roots of the Western Tradition*. Kalamazoo: Cistercian Publications, Inc., 1984.

Eliade, Mircea. "L'initiation et le monde moderne." In *Initiation: Contributions to the Theme of the Study-Conference of the International Association of the History of Religions Held at Strasbourg, September 17th to 22nd, 1964*, edited by C. J. Bleeker. Leiden, J. Brill, 1965.

———. *Rites and Symbols of Initiation: The Mysteries of Birth and Rebirth*, Translated by Williard R. Trask. 1958. New York: Harper Torchbooks, 1965.

Epstein, Barbara Leslie. *The Politics of Domesticity: Women, Evangelism, and Temperance in Nineteenth-Century America*. Middletown, Connecticut: Wesleyan University Press, 1981.

Evdokimov, Paul. *Woman and the Salvation of the World: A Christian Anthropology on the Charisms of Women*. Translated by Anthony P. Gythiel. Crestwood, New York: St. Vladimor's Seminary Press, 1994.

Everson, William O. (Brother Antoninus). *The Crooked Lines of God*. Detroit: University of Detroit Press, 1962.

Farrell, Warren. *The Myth of Male Power: Why Men Are the Disposable Sex*. New York: Simon and Schuster, 1993.

Fasick, Laura. "Charles Kingsley's Scientific Treatment of Gender," in *Muscular Christianity: Embodying the Victorian Age*, edited by Donald E. Hall. Cambridge University Press 1994.

Fast, Irene. *Gender Identity: A Differentiation Model*. Hillsdale, New Jersey: The Analytic Press, 1984.

Fichter, Joseph H. *Social Relations in the Urban Parish*. Chicago: University of Chicago Press, 1954.

———. "Why Aren't Males So Holy?" *Integrity* 9 (May 1955): 3-11.

Ford, David C. *Women and Men in the Early Church: The Full Views of St.*

John Chrysostom. South Canaan, Pennsylvania: St. Tikhon's Seminary Press, 1996.

Forrest, Tom. "Is the Church Attractive to Men?" *Origins* 17, no. 21 (November 5, 1987)

Fosdick, Harry Emerson. *The Manhood of the Master*. New York: Association Press, 1913.

Fussell, Paul. *The Great War and Modern Memory*. New York: Oxford University Press, 1975.

Fussell, Sam. *Muscle: Confessions of an Unlikely Bodybuilder*. 1991. New York: Avon Books, 1992

Gallup, George Jr., and Jim Castelli. *The People's Religion: American Faith in the 90's*. New York, Macmillan, 1989.

Gerard, David. "Religious Attitides and Values" in *Values and Social Change in Britain*. Edited by Mark Abrams, David Gerard and Noel Timms. London: Macmillan, 1985.

Gertrude of Helfta. *The Herald of Divine Love*. Translated and edited by Margaret Winckworth. New York: Paulist Press, 1993.

Gibson, James William. *Warrior Dreams: Paramilitary Culture in Post-Vietnam America*. New York: Hill and Wang, 1994.

Gilkes, C. T. "Together and in Harness: Women's Traditions in the Sanctified Churches." *Signs: Journal of Women in Culture and Society* 10 (1985): 678-699.

Gillam, Doreen M . E. "The use of the term 'æglæca' in Beowulf at Lines 893 and 2592." *Neophilologus* 61 (1977): 600-618

Gilmore. David D. *Manhood in the Making: Cultural Concepts of Masculinity*. New Haven: Yale University Press, 1990.

Godbeer, Richard. "'Love Raptures': Marital, Romantic, and Erotic Images of Jesus Christ in Puritan New England, 1670-1730." *New England Quarterly* 68 (1990): 355-84.

Goldberg, Herb. *The Hazards of Being Male: Surviving the Myth of Male Privilege*. 1976. New York: Signet, 1987.

Goldwert, Marvin. "Machismo and Christ: The New Formula." *Contemporary Review* 145 (1984): 184-185.

Golomstock, Igor. *Totalitarian Art in the Soviet Union, the Third Reich, Fascist Italy and the People's Republic of China*. Icon Editions. New York: HarperCollins Publishers, 1990.

Goodman, Paul. *Towards a Christian Republic: Antimasonry and the Great Transition in New England, 1826-1836*. New York: Oxford University Press, 1988.

Gorn, Elliot J. *The Manly Art: Bare-Knuckle Prize Fighting in America.* Ithaca: Cornell University Press, 1986.

Graef, Hilda. *Mary: A History of Doctrine and Devotion.* 1963. Westminster, Maryland: Christian Classics, 1985.

Graham, Ruth. "Women versus Clergy, Women pro Clergy." In *French Women and the Age of the Enlightenment,* edited by Samia I. Spencer. Bloomington: Indiana University Press, 1984.

Gray, J. Glenn. *The Warriors: Reflections on Men in Battle.* New York: Harper and Row, 1966.

Greenson, Ralph R. "Dis-Identifying from Mother: Its Special Importance for the Boy" *International Journal of Psychoanalysis.* 49 (1968): 370-74.

Grundmann, Herbert. *Religiöse Bewegungen im Mittelalter: Untersuchungen uber die geschichtlichen Zusammenhänge zwischen der Ketzerie, den Bettelorden und der religiösen Grundlagen der deutschen Mystik,* 2nd rev. ed. with supplement, "Neue Beiträge..." Hildesheim: Georg Olms Verlagsbuchhandlung, 1961.

———. *Religious Movements in the Middle Ages.* Translated by Steven Rowan. Notre Dame: University of Notre Dame Press, 1995.

Gudorf, Christine E. "Renewal or Repatiarchalization." *Horizons* 10 (1982): 231-51.

Guentert, Kenneth. "Kids Need to Learn Their Faith From Men, Too." *U. S. Catholic,* February 1990, 14-16.

Hadewijch: The Complete Works. Translated by Columba Hart. New York: Paulist Press, 1980.

Hale, Sarah J. *Women's Record: or Sketches of Distinguished Women.* New York, Harper and Brothers, 1860.

Hall, Donald E., ed. *Muscular Christianity: Embodying the Victorian Age* (Cambridge: Cambridge University Press 1994.

Hall, G. Stanley. *Adolescence, Its Psychology and Its Relation to Physiology, Anthropology, Sociology, Sex, Crime, Religion, and Education.* 2 vols. New York: D. Appleton and Company, 1911.

Hansen, Ron. *Mariette in Ecstasy.* HarperCollins Publishers, Harper Perennial, 1991.

Hardenbrook, Weldon M. *Missing from Action: Vanishing Manhood in America.* Nashville, Tn.: Thomas Nelson, 1987.

Harrison, James. "Warning: the Male Sex Role May Be Dangerous to Your Health" *Journal of Social Issues* 34, no. 1 (1978): 65-86.

Hartman, Mary S. and Lois Banner, eds. *Clio's Consciousness Raised: New*

Perspectives in the History of Women. New York: Harper and Row, 1974.

Harvey, Robert. *Ignatius Loyola: A General in the Church Militant.* Milwaukee: Bruce Publishing Co., 1937.

Hauke, Manfred. *God or Goddess? Feminist Theology: What Is It? Where Does It Lead?* Translated David Kipp. San Francisco: Ignatius Press, 1995.

————. *Women in the Priesthood: A Systematic Analysis in the Light of the Order of Creation and Redemption.* Translated by David Kipp. 1986. San Francisco: Ignatius Press, 1988.

Heine, Susanne. *Women and Early Christianity: A Reappraisal.* Translated by John Bowden. 1987. Minneapolis: Augsburg Publishing House, 1988.

The Heliand: The Saxon Christ. Translated by G. Ronald Murphy. New York: Oxford University Press, 1992.

Henderson, Alice Corbin. *Brothers of Light: The Penitentes of the Southwest.* New York: Harcourt, Brace, and Co., 1937.

Henry, P. L. "Furor Heroicus" *Studia Germania Gandensis* 3 (1961): 235-242.

Herdt, Gilbert A. *Guardians of the Flutes: Idioms of Masculinity.* New York: McGraw Hill Book Company, 1981.

Herik, Judith van. *Freud on Femininity and Faith.* Berkeley: University of California Press, 1982.

Herlihy, Davis. "Life Expectancies for Women in Medieval Society" in *The Role of Women in the Middle Ages,* edited by Rosemary Morewedge. Albany: State University of New York, 1975.

Hewitt, W. E. "Basic Christian Communities of the Middle – Classes in the Archdiocese of Sãp Paolo" *Sociological Analysis* 48 (1987): 158-66.

Hildegard of Bingen, *Symphonia: A Critical Edition of the Symphonia armonie celestium revelationum [Symphony of the Harmony of Celestial Revelations].* Translated and edited by Barbara Newman. Ithaca: Cornell University Press, 1988.

Hilliard, David. "UnEnglish and Unmanly: Anglo-Catholicism and Homosexuality." *Victorian Studies* 25 (1982): 181-210.

Hitchcock, Helen Hull. *The Politics of Prayer: Feminist Language and the Worship of God.* San Francisco: Ignatius Press, 1992.

Hoge, Dean R., and David A. Roozen. "Research on Factors Influencing Church Commitment." In *Understanding Church Growth and Decline, 1950-1978.* Edited by Dean R. Hoge and David A. Roozen. New York: Pilgrim Press, 1979.

Homer. *The Odyssey of Homer.* Translated Richard Lattimore. 1965, New York: Perennial Library, Harper 1975.

Hood, William. *Fra Angelico at San Marco.* New Haven: Yale University Press, 1993.

Horney, Karen. "The Dread of Women." *International Journal of Psycho-Analysis* 13 (1932): 348-360.

Horowitz, Helen Lefkowitz. *Alma Mater: Desire and Experience in the Women's Colleges from Their Nineteenth Century Beginnings to the 1930's.* New York: Alfred A. Knopf, 1985.

Howe, Elizabeth Teresa. *Mystical Imagery: Santa Teresa de Jesús and San Juan de la Cruz.* New York: Peter Lang, 1987.

Howitt, Alfred W. *The Native Tribes of South-East Australia.* London: Macmillan, 1904.

Hudson, Liam and Bernadine Jacot. *The Way Men Think: Intellect, Intimacy, and the Erotic Imagination.* New Haven: Yale University Press, 1991.

Hudson, Winthrop S. *American Protestantism.* Chicago: University of Chicago Press, 1961.

Hughes, Thomas. *Tom Brown's Schooldays.* New York: Puffin Books, 1983.

Hutin, Serge. *Les Sociétés secrèts.* Paris: Presses Universitaires de France, 1970.

Hynes, Samuel. *The Soldiers' Tale: Bearing Witness to Modern War.* New York: Viking Penguin, 1997.

Ignatius of Loyola: Spiritual Exercises and Selected Works. Translated and edited by George E. Ganss. New York: Paulist Press, 1991.

Jacobs, Eric and Robert Worcester. *We British: Britain under the MORIscope.* London: Weidenfield and Nicholson, 1990.

James, David C. *What Are They Saying About Masculine Spirituality?* New York: Paulist Press, 1996.

James, John Angell. *Female Piety.* 1860. Pittsburgh: Soli Deo Gloria Publications, 1994.

Jantzen, Grace M. *Power, Gender and Christian Mysticism.* Cambridge: Cambridge University Press.

Jarrett, Bede. *Social Theories of the Middle Ages, 1200- 1500.* New York: F. Ungar, 1966.

John Paul II. *On the Dignity and Vocation of Women (Mulieris Dignitatem).* Vatican translation. Boston: St. Paul Books and Media, n. d.

———. *Gift and Mystery. On the Fiftieth Anniversary of My Priestly Ordination.* New York: Doubleday, 1996.

Johnson, Curtis D. *Island of Holiness: Rural Religion in Upstate New York 1790-1860*. Ithca: Cornell University Press, 1985.

Johnson, Paul. *A Shopkeeper's Millennium: Society and Revivals in Rochester, New York 1815-1837*. New York: Hill and Wang, 1978.

Johnson, Paul. "Anglicanism, Organic Sin, and the Church of Sodom" *The Spectator* 277 (Nov. 22, 1996): p. 30.

Jones, David. *In Parenthesis*. New York: Chilmark Books, 1961.

Julian of Norwich. *The Revelation of Divine Love in Sixteen Showings*. Translated by M. L. del Mastro. Ligouri, Missouri: Ligouri Publications, Triumph Books, 1994.

Jünger, Ernst. *Storm of Steel*. 1929. New York: Howard Fertig, 1975.

Kaspar, Walter. "Church as *communio*" *Communio* vol. 13, no. 2 (Summer 1986): 100-17

Kauffman, Christopher J. *Faith and Fraternalism: The History of the Knights of Columbus 1882-1982*. New York: Harper and Row, 1982.

Kett, Joseph *Rites of Passage: Adolescence in America 1790 to the Present*. New York: Basic Books, 1977.

King, Catherine Callen. *Achilles: Paradigms of the War Hero from Homer to the Middles Ages*. Berkeley: University of California Press, 1987.

Kingsley, Charles. *Charles Kingsley: His Letters and His Age*. 2 vols. London: Henry S. King and Co., 1877.

Kirkley, Evelyn A. "Is It Manly To Be Christian? The Debate in Victorian and Modern America" In *Redeeming Men; Religion and Masculinities*, edited by Stephen B. Boyd, W. Merle Longwood, and Mark Muesse. Louisville, Kentucky: Westminster John Knox Press, 1996.

Klein, Alan M. *Little Big Men: Bodybuilding Subculture and Gender Construction*. Albany: State University of New York Press, 1993.

Kling, David W. *A Field of Divine Wonders: The New Divinity and Village Revivals in Northwestern Connecticut 1792 -1822*. University Park, Pennsylvania: Pennsylvania State University Press, 1993.

Knox, Ronald A. *Enthusiasm: A Chapter in the History of Religion*. 1950. Westminster, Md.: Christian Classics, 1983

Kosmin, Barry A., and Seymour P. Lachman. *One Nation Under God: Religion in Contemporary American Society*. Harmony Books, New York. 1993.

Kristeva, Julia *In the Beginning Was Love: Psychoanalysis and Love*. Translated by Arthur Goldhammer. 1985. New York: Columbia University Press, 1987.

Langlois, Claude. "Féminisation du catholicisme." In *Histoire de la France religieuse*. Vol 3, *Du rois Très Chrétien à la laicité républicaine*, edited by Jacques Le Goff. Paris: Editions du Seuil, 1991.

Le Bras, Gabriel. *Etudes de sociologie religieuse*. 2 vols. Paris: Presses Universitaire de France, 1955.

Le Goff, Jacques. *The Birth of Purgatory*. Translated by Arthur Goldhammer. 1981. Chicago: University of Chicago Press, 1984.

———. *Histoire de la France religieuse*. Vol. 3, *Du rois Très Chrétien à la laicité républicaine*. Paris: Enditions du Seuil, 1991

Leclercq, Jean. *Monks and Love in Twelfth Century France: Pyscho-Historical Essays*. Oxford: at the Clarendon Press, 1979.

———, François Vandenbroucke and Louis Bouyer. The *Spirituality of the Middle Ages*. Translated by the Benedictines of Holmes Eden Abbey. 1961. London, Burns and Oates, 1968.

Lees, Clare A., ed. *Medieval Masculinities: Regarding Men in the Middle Ages*. Minneapolis: University of Minnesota Press, 1994.

Leinhard, Marc. "Luther and the Beginnings of the Reformation." In *Christian Spirituality*, edited by Jill Raitt.

Lenski, Gerhard E. "Social Correlates of Religious Interest." *American Sociological Review* 18 (1953): 533-44.

Levant, Ronald F. and William S. Pollack, editors. *A New Psychology of Men*. New York: Basic Books, 1995.

Levant, Ronald F. "Toward a Reconstruction of Masculinity." In *A New Psychology of Men*, edited by Ronald F. Levant and William S. Pollack.

Levin, Michael. *Feminism and Freedom*. New Brunswick: Transaction Books, 1987.

Lewis, Gilbert. "Payback and Ritual in War in New Guinea." In *War: A Cruel Necessity? The Bases of Institutionalized Violence*, ed. Robert A. Hinde and Helen E. Watson London.

The Life of Beatrice of Nazareth. Edited and translated by Roger De Ganck with the assistance of John Baptist Housbrouck. Kalamazoo, Michigan: Cistercian Publications, 1991

Lison-Tolosana, Carmela. *Belmonte de los Cabelleros: A Sociological Study of a Spanish Town*. 1966. Princeton: Princeton University Press, 1983.

Maccoby, Eleanor Emmons and Carol Nagy Jacklin. *The Psychology of Sex Differences*. Stanford: Stanford University Press, 1974.

Macleod, David I. *Building Character in the American Boy: The Boy Scouts, YMCA, and Their Forerunners, 1870-1920*. Madison: University of Wisconsin Press, 1983.

Mahon, Leo T. "Machismo and Christianity." *Catholic Mind* 63 (February 1965): 4-11.

Miao, Eugene S. *St. John of the Cross: The Imagery of Eros.* Madrid: Playor, 1973.

Malaperte, Curzio. *Kaputt.* Translated by Cesare Foligno. 1946. Marlboro, Vermont: The Marlboro Press, 1982.

Malmgreen, Gail. "Domestic Discords: Women and the Family in East Cheshire Methodism, 1750 - 1830." In *Disciplines of Faith: Studies in Religion, Patriarchy, and Politics,* edited by Jim Obelkevich, Lyndal Roper, and Raphael Samuel. London: Routledge and Kegan Paul, 1987.

Malone, Edward C. *The Monk and the Martyr: The Monk as the Successor of the Martyr.* Washington, DC: Catholic University of America Press, 1950.

Malperte, Curzio. *Kaputt.* 1946. Marlboro, Vermont: The Marlboro Press, 1982.

Mangan, J. A. *Athleticism in the Victorian and Edwardian Public Schools: The Emergence and Consolidation of an Educational Ideology.* Cambridge: Cambridge University Press, 1981.

Marcilhacy, Christianne. *Le Diocèse d'Orléans sous le épiscopat de Msgr. Dupanloup.* Paris: Librarie Plon, 1962.

Margaret Ebner. *Major Works.* Translated and edited by Leonard P. Hindsley. New York: Paulist Press, 1993.

Martin David A. *A Sociology of English Religion.* London: SCM Press Ltd, 1967.

Martin, Francis. *The Feminist Question: Feminist Theology in the Light of the Christian Tradition.* Grand Rapids: William B. Eerdmans Company, 1994.

———. "Feminist Theology: A Proposal." *Communio* 20 (1993): 334-76.

Matarasso, Pauline, ed. and trans. *The Cistercian World : Monastic Writings of the Twelfth Century,* New York: Penguin Books, 1993.

Mather, Cotton. *Ornaments for the Daughter of Sion.* Boston, 1648.

———. *A Glorious Espousal.* Boston, 1719.

Mathews, Donald G. *Religion in the Old South.* Chicago: University of Chicago Press, 1977.

McCartney, Bill. "God is Calling Us to a Higher Love," in *Go the Distance: The Making of a Promise Keeper,* ed. John Trent. Colorado Springs, Colorado: Focusonteh Family Publishing, 1996.

McDannell, Colleen. *The Christian Home in Victorian America, 1840-1900.*

Bloomington and Indianapolis: Indiana University Press, 1986; Midland Book Edition, 1994.

McDannell, Colleen. "'True Men as We Need Them': Catholicism and the Irish-American Male." *American Studies* 27 (1986): 19-36.

McDonnell, Ernest W. *The Beguines and Beghards in Medieval Culture with Special Emphasis on the Belgian Scene.* New Brunswick: Rutgers University Press, 1954.

McGinn, Bernard and John Meyendorff, eds. *Christian Spirituality: Origins to the thirteen Century.* New York: Crossroad, 1986.

McLeod, Hugh. *Piety and Poverty: Working-Class Religion in Berlin, London, and New York.* New York: Holmes and Meier, 1996.

McLeod, Hugh. *Religion and Society in England, 1850-1914.* New York: St. Martin's Press, 1966.

Mead, Margaret. *Male and Female: A Study of the Sexes in a Changing World.* 1944. Westport, Connecticut: Greenwood Press, 1977.

Messner, Michael A. *Power at Play: Sports and the Problem of Masculinity.* Boston: Beacon Press, 1992.

Michelet, Jules. *Du Prêtre, de la femme, de la famille.* 4th Edition. Paris: Hachette, 1845.

Miles, Rosalind. *The Rites of Man: Love, Sex and Death in the Making of the Male.* London: Grafton Books, 1991.

Miller, John W. *Biblical Faith and Fathering: Why We Call God "Father."* Mahwah, New Jersey: Paulist Press, 1989.

Miller, Perry. "Jonathan Edward's Sociology of the Great Awakening." *New England Quarterly* 21 (1948): pp. 50-77.

Moberg, David O. *The Church as Social Institution: The Sociology of American Religion.* Englewood Cliffs, NJ: Prentice Hall, Inc., 1962.

Moller, Herbert. "Sex Composition and Correlated Culture Patterns of Colonial America." *William and Mary Quarterly*, 2 (1945): 113-53.

Montague, George T. *Our Father, Our Mother: Mary and the Faces of God.* Steubenville, Ohio: Franciscan University Press, 1990.

Moore, Harold G. and Joseph L. Galloway. *We Were Soldiers Once...and Young: Ia Drang - The Battle That Changed the War in Vietnam.* New York: Random House, 1992.

Moore, James R. *Religion in Victorian Britain.* Vol. 3, *Sources*, Manchester: Manchester University Press, 1988.

Moore, Robert, and Douglas Gillette. *King Warrior Magician Lover: Rediscovering the Archetypes of the Mature Masculine.* New York: HarperSanFrancisco, 1990.

Moran, Gerald F. "Christian Revivalism in Early America." In Blumhofer and Balmer, eds. *Modern Christian Revivalism,* edited Edith L. Blumhofer and Randall Balmer.

Moran, Gerald F. and Maris A. Vinovskis. *Religion, Family, and the Life Course: Explorations in the Social History of Early America.* Ann Arbor: University of Michigan Press, 1992.

Morewedge, Rosemarie, ed. *The Role of Women in the Middle Ages.* Albany: State University of New York, 1975.

Morgan, William J. "An Existential, Phenomenological Analysis of Sport as a Religious Experience." In Charles S. Prebish, editor, *Religion and Spot: The Meeting of Sacred and Profane.*

Mosse, George L. *The Crisis of German Ideology.* 1964. New York: Schocken Books, 1981.

————. *Fallen Soldiers: Reshaping the Memory of the World Wars.* New York: Oxford University Press, 1990.

Mrozek, Donald J. *Sports and American Mentality 1880-1910.* Knoxville, University of Tennessee Press, 1983.

Mudie-Smith, Richard. *The Religious Life of London.* London: Hodder and Saughton, 1904.

Myers, Carol. *Discovering Eve: Ancient Israelite Women in Context.* New York: Oxford University Press, 1988.

Myers, Cortland. *Why Men Do Not Go to Church.* New York: Funk and Wagnalls Co., 1899.

Nelson, Claudia. "Sex and the Single Boy: Ideals of Manliness and Sexuality in Victorian Literature." *Victorian Studies* 32 (1989): 525-55.

Nelson, James B. *The Intimate Connection: Male Sexuality, Male Spirituality.* Philadelphia, The Westminster Press, 1988.

Nesbitt, Paula D. *Feminization of the Clergy in America: Occupational and Organizational Perspectives.* New York: Oxford University Press, 1997.

Newman, Barbara. *From Virile Woman to WomanChrist: Studies in Medieval Religion and Literature.* Philadephia: University of Pennyslvania Press, 1995.

Nietzsche, Friedrich. *Basic Writings of Nietzsche.* Translated and edited by Walter Kaufman. New York: Modern Library, 1968.

Novak, Michael. *The Joy of Sports: End Zones, Bases, Baskets, Balls, and the Consecration of the American Spirit* rev. ed. 1967. Lanham, Maryland: Madison Books, 1994.

Obelkevich, Jim, Lyndal Roper, and Raphael Samuel. *Disciplines of Faith: Studies in Religion, Politics and Patriarchy.* London: Routledge and Kegan Paul, 1987.

Oberman, Heiko A. Luther: *Man Between God and the Devil.* Translated by Eileen Walliser-Schwartzbart. 1982. New Haven: Yale University Press, 1989.

Oddie, William. "My Time at Homoerotic College" *The Spectator* 277 (7 December 1996): 26.

———. *What Will Happen to God? Feminism and the Reconstruction of Christian Belief.* 1984. San Francisco: Ignatius. 1988.

Ong, Walter. *Fighting for Life: Contest, Sexuality, and Consciousness.* 1981. Amherst: University of Massachusetts Press, 1989

Origen. *Contra Celsum* 3.45, in *Ante-Nicene Fathers*, Vol. 4. Edited by Alexander Roberts and James Donaldson. 1885. Henrickson Publishers, Inc., 1995.

———. *The Song of Songs: Commentary and Homilies.* Translated by R. P. Lawson. Westminster, Maryland: The Newman Press, 1957.

Otto, Rudolf. *The Idea of the Holy.* 1923. Oxford University Press, 1958.

Ownby, Ted. *Subduing Satan: Religion, Recreation, and Manhood in the Rural South 1965-1920.* Chapel Hill: University of North Carolina Press, 1990.

Pable, Martin W. *A Man and His God.* Notre Dame: Ave Maria Press, 1988.

Pearse, Edward. *The Best Match: or the Souls Espousal to Christ, opened and approved.* London, 1673.

Pennington, Basil. "The Cistercians." In *Christian Spirituality: Origins to the Thirteenth Century*, edited by Bernard McGinn and John Meyendorff. New York: Crossroad, 1986.

Petroff, Elizabeth Alvida. *Medieval Women's Visionary Literature.* New York: Oxford University Press, 1986.

Pickstone, Charles. *The Divinity of Sex: The Search for Ecstasy in a Secular Age.* New York St. Martin's Press, 1996.

Pike, Nelson. *Mystic Union: An Essay in the Phenomenology of Mysticism.* Ithaca: Cornell University Press, 1992.

Pittman, III, Frank S. *Man Enough: Fathers, Sons and the Search for Masculinity.* New York: G. P. Putnams; Sons, 1993.

Pope, Robert G. *The Half-Way Covenant: Church Membership in Puritan New England.* Princeton: Princeton University Press, 1969.

Porterfield, Amanda. *Female Piety in Puritan New England: The Emergence of Religious Humanism.* New York: Oxford University Press, 1992.

———. *Feminine Spirituality in America: From Sarah Edwards to Martha Graham.* Philadelphia: Temple University Press, 1980.

Prebish, Charles S. "Religion and Sport. Convergence or Identity?" In *Religion and Sport: The Meeting of Sacred and Profane*, ed. Charles S. Prebish. Westport, Connecticut: Greenwood Press, 1993.

Rahner, Hugo. *Greek Myths and Christian Mystery.* 1957. London: Burns and Oats, 1963.

Raitt, Jill ed. *Christian Spirituality: High Middle Ages and the Reformation.* New York: Crossroad, 1987.

Randall, Robert. Return of the Pleiades. *Natural History* 96 (June 1987): 43-52.

Raphael, Roy. *The Men from the Boys: Rites of Passage in Male America.* Lincoln, Nebraska: University of Nebraska Press, 1988.

Rauschenbusch, Walter. *Christianity and the Social Gospel.* 1970. Louisville, Kentucky: Westminster / John Knox Press, 1991.

Rauschning, Hermann. *The Revolution of Nihilism: Warning to the West.* New York: Longmans, Green and Co., 1939.

Reed, John Shelton. "A Female Movement: The Feminization of Nineteenth Century Anglo-Catholicism." *Anglican and Episcopal History* 57 (1988): 199-238.

Reed, John Shelton. "'Giddy Young Men' A Counter-Cultural Aspect of Victorian Anglo-Catholicism." *Comparative Social Research* 11 (1989): 209-226.

Reed, John Shelton. *Glorious Battle: The Cultural Politics of Victorian Anglo-Catholicism.* Nashville: Vanderbilt University Press, 1996.

Reeves, Thomas C. *The Empty Church, The Suicide of Liberal Christianity.* New York: Free Press, 1996.

Renzetti, Claire M., and Daniel J. Curran. *Women, Men, and Society: The Sociology of Gender.* Boston: Allyn and Bacon, 1989.

Reuther, Rosemary Radford. "Christianity and Women in the Modern World." In *Today's Women in World Religions*, ed. Arvind Sharma. Albany: State University of New York Press, 1994.

Reuther, Rosemary Radford and Rosemary Skinner Keller. *Women and Realign in America.* Vol 1, *The Nineteenth Century.* San Francisco: Harper and Row, 1981.

Richardson, Norman E. and Ormond E. Lewis. *The Boy Scout Movement Applied by the Church.* New York, Charles Scribner's Sons, 1916.

Roblack, Ulinka. "Female Spirituality and the Infant Jesus in Late Medieval Dominican Convents." *Gender and History* 6 (1994): 37-57.

Roisin, Simone. *L'Hagiographie cistercienne dans le diocèse de Liège au XIIIe siècle.* Louvain: Bibliothèque de l'Université, 1947.

Rose, Susan D. "Women Warriors: The Negotiation of Gender in a Charismatic Community." *Sociological Analysis* 48 (1987): 245-58.

Rosen, David. "The volcano and the cathedral: muscular Christianity and the origins of primal manliness." In *Muscular Christianity: Embodying the Victorian Age*, edited by Donald E. Hall.

Rosenthal, Michael. *The Character Factory: Baden-Powell and the Origins of the Boy Scout Movement.* London: Collins, 1986.

Rubin, Miri. *Corpus Christi: The Eucharist in Late Medieval Culture.* Cambridge: Cambridge University Press, 1993.

Ryan, Mary. *Cradle of the Middle Class: The Family in Oneida County, New York.* Cambridge: Cambridge University Press, 1981.

Sapp, Stephen. *Sexuality, the Bible, and Science.* Philadelphia: Fortress Press, 19xx.

Schaller, Lyle E. *It's a Different World: the Challenge for Today's Pastor.* Nashville: Abingdon Press, 1987.

Schindler, David L. *Heart of the Church, Heart of the World: Communio Ecclesiology, Liberalism, and Liberation.* Grand Rapids, Michigan: William B. Eerdmans Publishing Company, 1996.

Schmöger, Carl E. 1885. *The Life of Anne Catherine Emmerich.* Rockford, Ill.: Tan Books and Publishers, Inc. 1976.

Schneider-Böklen and Dorothea Vorländer. *Feminismus und Glaube.* Mainz: Matthia-Grünewald-Verlag, 1991.

Schultheis, Rob. *Bone Games: Extreme Sports, Shamanism, Zen, and the Search for Transcendence.* 1984. New York: Breakaway Books, 1996.

Sexton, Patricia Cayo. *The Feminized Male: Classrooms, White Collars, and the Decline of Manliness.* New York: Vintage, 1969.

Sharma, Arvin, ed. *Today's Women in World Religions.* Albany, State University of New York Press, 1994.

Sheilds, Richard D. "The Feminization of American Congregationalism 1730-1835." *American Quarterly* 33 (Spring 1981), 46-62.

Slushler, Howard. "Sport and the Religious." In *Religion and Sport: The Meeting of Sacred and Profane*, edited by Charles S. Prebish. Westport, Connecticut: Greenwood Press, 1993.

Southern, R. W. *Western Society and Church in the Middle Ages.* Harmondworth: Penguin Books, 1970.

Spencer, Samia I., ed. *French Women and the Age of the Enlightenment.* Bloomington: Indiana University Press, 1984.

Spicq, Ceslaus. *Agape dans le nouveau testament: Analyse des textes.* Paris: Librairie Lecoffre, 1959.

Stark, Rodney. *The Rise of Christianity: A Sociologist Reconsiders History.*

Princeton: Princeton University Press, 1996.

Starr, Ann Lee. *The Bible Status of Women*. New York: F. H. Revell Co., 1926. New York: Garland Publishing, Inc., 1987.

Stearns, Peter N. *Be a Man! Males in Modern Society*. 2nd ed. New York: Holmes and Meier, 1990.

Steinberg, Leo. *The Sexuality of Christ in Renaissance Art and Modern Oblivion*. London: Faber and Faber Limited, 1984.

Stoller, Robert J. *Presentations of Gender*. New Haven: Yale University Press, 1985.

Strauss, Leo. "On the Interpretation of Genesis." *L'homme* 21 (1981): 5-20.

Straw, Carole. *Gregory the Great: Perfection in Imperfection*. Berkeley and Los Angeles: University of California Press, 1988.

Suso, Henry. *The Exemplar: Life and Writings of Blessed Henry Suso*. 2 vol. Edited by Nicholas Heller and translated by Sister M. Ann Edward. Dubuque, Iowa: The Priory Press, 1962.

Tanner, J. M. *Fetus Into Man: Physical Growth from Conception to Maturity*. Cambridge, Mass.: Harvard University Press, 1978.

Taylor, Edward. *The Poems of Edward Taylor*. Edited by Donald E. Stanford. New Haven: Yale University Press, 1960.

Terman, Lewis M. and Catherine Cox Miles, assisted by Jack W. Dunlop and others. *Sex and Personality: Studies an Masculinity and Femininity*. 1936. New York: Russell and Russell, 1968.

Theweleit, Klaus. *Male Fantasies*. Vol. 1, *Women Floods Bodies History*. Translated by Stephen Conway. 1977. Minneapolis: University of Minnesota Press, 1987. Vol. 2, *Male Bodies: Psychoanalyzing the White Terror*. Translated by Erica Carter and Chris Turner in collaboration with Stephen Conway. 1978. Minneapolis: University of Minnesota Press, 1989.

Thomas Aquinas, *Basic Writings of Saint Thomas Aquinas*, 2 vols. Edited by Anton C. Pegis. New York: Random House, 1945.

Thomas, David. *Not Guilty: In Defense of Men*. New York: William Murrow and Company, Inc.

Thompson, Jr., Edward H. "Beneath the Status Characteristic: Gender Variations in Religiousness." *Journal for the Scientific Study of Religion* 30 (1991): 381-394.

Thompson, Sally. "The Problem of the Cistercian Nuns in the Twelfth and Early Thirteenth Century." In *Medieval Women*, edited by Derek Baker. Oxford: Blackwell, 1978.

Tiger, Lionel. *Men in Groups*. New York, Random House, 1969.

Tillich, Paul. *Systematic Theology*. 3 vols. Chicago: University of Chicago Press, 1951-1963.

Tisdall, Caroline and Angelo Bozzolla, *Futurism*. New York: Oxford University Press, 1978.

Tolkien, J. R. R. *The Lord of the Rings*. 1965. Boston, Houghton Mifflin Company, Collector's Edition, n.d.

Toon, Peter. *Let Women Be Women: Equality, Ministry, and Ordination*. Gracewing. Leominster: Fowler Wright Books, 1990.

Treadwell, Perry. "Biological Influences on Masculinity." In *The Making of Masculinities: the New Men's Studies*, edited by Harry Brod.

Trent, John, ed. *Go the Distance; The Making of a Promise Keeper*. Colorado Springs, Colorado: Focus on the Family Publishing, 1996.

Trollope, Frances. *Domestic Manners of the Americans*. 2 vols. New York: Dodd, Meade, and Company, 1894.

Turner, Denys. *Eros and Allegory: Medieval Exegesis of the Song of Songs*. Kalamazoo, MI: Cistercian Publications, 1995.

Turner, Victor. "Betwixt and Between: The Liminal Period in Rites of Passage." In *Betwixt and Between: Patterns of Masculine and Feminine Initiation*, edited by Louise Carus Mahdi, Steven Foster, and Meredith Little. LaSalle, Illinois: Open Court, 1987.

Van Gennep, Arnold. *The Rites of Passage*. Translated by Monika K. Vizedom and Gabrielle L. Caffee. 1909. London: Routledge and Kegan Paul, 1960.

Vance, Norman. *The Sinews of the Spirit: The Ideal of Christian Manliness in Victorian Literature and Religious Thought*. Cambridge: Cambridge University Press, 1985.

Vauchez, André. *The Laity in the Middle Ages: Religious Beliefs and Devotional Practices*. Edited by Daniel E. Boorstein and translated by Margery J. Schneider. Notre Dame, University of Notre Dame Press, 1993.

Vauchez, André. *La Sainteté en Occident aux derniers siècles du moyen age*. Rome: École Française de Rome, 1981.

Vizedom, Monika. *Rites and Relationships: Rites of Passage and Contemporary Anthropology*. Sage Research Papers in the Social Sciences: Cross Cultural Studies Series, No. 90-027, vol. 4. 1976.

Von Balthasar, Hans Urs. *Dare we Hope "That All Men Be Saved"* with A Short Discourse on Hell. Translated by David Kripp and Lothar Krauth. San Francisco: Ignatius Press, 1988

———. *New Elucidations*. Translated by Mary Theresilde Skerry. San Francisco: Ignatius Press, 1986.

———. *Theodramatik*, Vol 4. *Das Endspiel*. Einsedeln: Johannes Verlag, 1983.

Von Hügel, Friedrich. *The Mystical Element in Religion as Studied in Catherine of Genoa and Her Friends*. 2 vols. London: M. Dents and Sons, 1927.

Von le Fort, Gertrud. *Eternal Woman: The Woman in the Timeless Woman* Translated by Placid Jordan. Milwaukee: Bruce Publishing Co., 1961.

Von Rad, Gerhard. *Old Testament Theology*. Translated by I. D. M. G. Stalker. New York: 1962.

Walter, Tony. "Why Are Most Churchgoers Women?" *Vox Evangelica* 20 (1990): 73-90.

Warner, Marina. "Blood and Tears." *New Yorker* 72, no. 7. (April 8, 1996): pp. 63-69.

Warren, Anna K. *Anchorites and Their Patrons in Medieval England*. Berkeley: University of California Press, 1985.

Waugh, Evelyn. *Brideshead Revisited*. 1945. Boston: Little, Brown, and Co., 1978.

———. *The End of the Battle*. Boston: Little, Brown and Company, 1961.

———. *When the Going Was Good*. Boston: Little, Brown, and Co., 1984.

Weinandy, Thomas G. *The Father's Spirit of Sonship: Reconceiving the Trinity*. Edinburgh: T and T Clark, 1995.

Weinginer, Otto. *Geschlect und Charakter*. 1906. Munich: Matthew und Seitz Verlag, 1980.

Weinstein, Donald and Bell, Rudolph M. *Saints and Society: Christendom, 1000 - 1700*. Chicago: University of Chicago Press, 1977.

Weisner. Merry? "Luther and Women: The Death of Two Marys." In *Disciplines of Faith*, edited by Jim Obelkevich, Lyndal Roper, and Raphael Samuel.

Welter, Barbara. "The Feminization of American Religion: 1800-1860." In *Clio's Consciousness Raised: New Perspectives in the History of Women*, edited by Mary S. Hartman and Lois Banner. New York: Harper and Row, 1974.

Wessley, Stephen E. "The Thirteenth-Century Guglielmites: Salvation Through Women." In *Medieval Women*, edited by Derek Baker.

White, Gavin. "The Martyr Cult of the First World War." In *Martyrs and Martyrologies: Papers Read at the 1992 Summer Meeting and the 1993 Winter Meeting of the Ecclesiastical History Society*, edited by Diana Wood. Oxford: Blackwell Publishers, 1993.

White, John K. "Men and the Church: A Case Study of Ministry to Men in a Medium Size Congregation" D.M. Thesis, Trinity Evangelical Divinity School, Deerfield, Illinois, 1990.

Wilcock, Ed. "How We Lost Our Manliness." *Integrity* ? (May 1955): 12.

Wiley, Juli Loesch. "In Defense of God the Father." In *The Politics of Prayer: Feminist Language and the Worship of God*, ed. Helen Hull Hitchcock. San Francisco: Ignatius Press, 1992.

Willoughby, Harold W. *Pagan Regeneration: A Study of Mystery Initiations in the Greco-Roman World*. Chicago, University of Chicago Press, 1929. Midway Reprint, 1974.

Wolff, Hope Nash. *A Study in the Narrative Structure of Three Epic Poems: Gilgamesh, The Odyssey, Beowulf*. New York: Garland Publishing, Inc., 1987.

Wood, Diana, editor. *Martyrs and Martyrologies: Papers Read at the 1992 Summer Meeting and the 1993 Winter Meeting of the Ecclesiastical History Society*. Oxford: Blackwell Publishers, 1993.

Woodward, Kenneth. "Gender and Religion: Who's Really Running the Show." *Commonweal* 120:6: 9-14.

Index

A Note on the Author

Leon J. Podles earned his bachelor's degree at Providence College and his doctorate in English at the University of Virginia. He later studied Old Icelandic at the University of Iceland. He has worked as a teacher and federal investigator and has written for numerous journals, including *America*, the *American Spectator*, *Crisis*, and the *American Enterprise*. He is a contributing editor of *Touchstone*. Dr. Podles and his wife have six children and live in Naples, Florida, and Baltimore.

This book was designed and set into type
by Mitchell S. Muncy,
with cover art by Stephen J. Ott,
and printed and bound
by Thomson-Shore, Inc.,
Dexter, Michigan.

The text face is Caslon,
designed by Carol Twombly
and issued in digital form by Adobe Systems,
Mountain View, California, in 1989.

The paper is acid-free and is of archival quality.

13